COLLECTOR'S VALUE GUIDE™

The BOYDS COLLECTION LTD.

Boyds Plush Animals

SIXTH EDITION

Secondary Market Price Guide & Collector Handbook

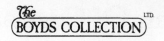

The BOYDS COLLECTION LTD.

EDITORIAL

Managing Editor: Jeff Mahony
Associate Editors: Melissa A. Bennett
Jan Cronan
Gia C. Manalio
Mike Micciulla
Paula Stuckart
Assistant Editors: Heather N. Carreiro
Jennifer Renk
Joan C. Wheal
Editorial Assistants: Timothy R. Affleck
Beth Hackett
Christina M. Sette
Steven Shinkaruk

WEB (CollectorsQuest.com)

Web Graphic Designer: Ryan Falis

PRODUCTION

Production Manager: Scott Sierakowski

ART

Creative Director: Joe T. Nguyen
Assistant Art Director: Lance Doyle
Senior Graphic Designers: Marla B. Gladstone
Susannah C. Judd
David S. Maloney
Carole Mattia-Slater
David Ten Eyck
Graphic Designers: Jennifer J. Bennett
Sean-Ryan Dudley
Kimberly Eastman
Melani Gonzalez
Jim MacLeod
Jeremy Maendel
Chery-Ann Poudrier

R&D

Product Development Manager: Paul Rasid
R&D Specialist: Priscilla Berthiaume

ISBN 1-58598-143-5

CheckerBee PUBLISHING

306 Industrial Park Road
Middletown, CT 06457

CollectorsQuest.com

Table Of Contents

Introducing The Collector's Value Guide™

Have you ever wondered who that crazy guy on QVC is who keeps showing up in weird costumes? Maybe you're curious as to how much your Boyds plush animals are worth. The Collector's Value Guide™ is the source to answer those questions and more!

You'll read all about "Yer Old Uncle Bean" Gary Lowenthal, the man who turned his creative talent into a magnificent menagerie of cuddly plush creations. Discover the up-to-date value of these furry critters and, if you're wondering why your version of "Helmut" the moose has a green sweater instead of a red one, you can read all about the wild world of variations.

The Collector's Value Guide™ will be your guide through the wild and wooly world of Boyds. You'll be able to navigate your way through the herds of animals, ornaments, puppets and other wild but cute creatures who populate your collection – and a few that you may not have seen yet!

Look Inside For:

- All the latest information on soon-to-be-retired pieces and new items for 2001
- The story of Gary's memorable antics on QVC
- The inside scoop on Boyds' generous work for the Starlight Children's Foundation
- A firsthand account of the creation of a Boyds piece
- A look at the uncanny resemblance of Boyds plush pieces to some other recognizable characters
- And more!

The Boyds Are Back In Town: An Overview

In the world of collectible plush, there's your run-of-the mill plush – and then there's Boyds. For 15 years, The Boyds Collection Ltd. has delighted collectors with its ever-growing line of adorable and quirky bears, hares, cows, moose and other critters (would you believe even camels?). Now the Boyds gang are among the most recognizable collectibles around.

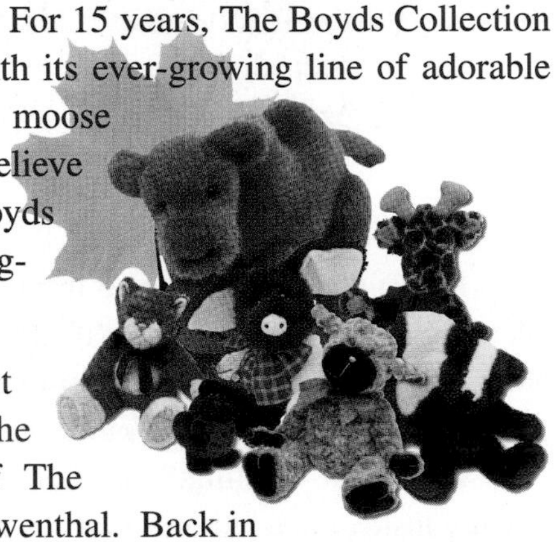

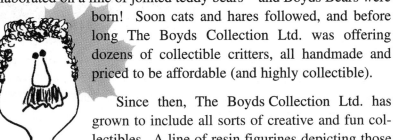

But plush animals weren't the first creative effort by the founder and "Head Bean" of The Boyds Collection Ltd., Gary Lowenthal. Back in 1979, Gary left a successful designing career at New York City's famous department store, Bloomingdales, and instead set up shop in Boyds, Maryland – an antique shop, to be exact. There, he and his partner and wife Justina sold hand carved duck decoys and other charming but affordable antique reproductions.

After dabbling in wool teddy bears, Gary designed a handful of fuzzy plush animals in various poses and colors in 1987. Soon after, he was set on the road to plush glory when he and artist Gae Sharp collaborated on a line of jointed teddy bears – and Boyds Bears were born! Soon cats and hares followed, and before long The Boyds Collection Ltd. was offering dozens of collectible critters, all handmade and priced to be affordable (and highly collectible).

Since then, The Boyds Collection Ltd. has grown to include all sorts of creative and fun collectibles. A line of resin figurines depicting those lovable characters, The Bearstone Collection®, made its debut in late 1993 and was an instant hit. Three other resin lines, The Folkstone Collection®,

Yesterday's Child – The Dollstone Collection™ and The Shoe Box Bears™ followed. In 1996, the company really branched out with a line of porcelain dolls called Yesterday's Child . . . ™ The Doll Collection. Boyds' latest offerings include The Purrstone Collection™ (take a guess!) and a line of resin houses called Boyds Town.™

Bears and Hares Of Their Own

Whether you're new to collecting Boyds Bears or if you're a "grizzled" veteran, you have a lot to look forward to. Since 1987, an astounding approximately 1,600 different Boyds plush critters have hit the shelves, and The Boyds Collection Ltd. shows no signs of slowing down.

What's more incredible is that each Boyds plush is hand crafted, from eyebrows down to footpads, making every critter a true original with its very own personality. This personal attention has helped make Boyds plush the immensely popular collectible line it is today. And don't forget those patented names, like "Felicia Fuzzbuns," "Tallulah Baahead," and "Goober Padoodle" – as if you could!

The Boyds Collection Ltd. groups its immense collection of plush into different series, each with its own unique style or theme. If you like your bears to have a little fashion sense, then the dapper dandys of *T.J.'s Best Dressed* or *The Uptown Bears* might be for you. The jointed critters of *J.B. Bean & Associates* are fully poseable, while *The Artisan Series* features classic-style bears designed by a host of talented artists.

More recent series have only added to the fun, including the toddler-friendly *Huggle-Fluffs*, two different puppet series and the *Raggedymuffs* series of 19" rag dolls. In 2000, The Boyds Collection introduced its first seasonal and holiday-themed groupings, such as

The Big Egg Day (Easter) and *Boogedy Boos* (Halloween). These grouping include plush and resin figurines, and sometimes ornaments and other items.

Limited And Loving It

The bedrock of the collection is the Bailey & Friends series of annual limited editions. "Bailey," a fashionable bear, is named for Gary's daughter and was the first limited edition to be released (1992). Since then, she's been joined by "Edmund" the bear and "Emily Babbit" the rabbit. All three are released two times a year, in the spring and the fall, and each time with a new themed outfit. Two other limited editions, "Matthew" the bear (named after Gary's son) and "Indy" the dog (you guessed it, the Lowenthal family pooch) are typically only released in the fall. In addition to being the most popular characters in the plush collection, these limited editions tend to be among the most valuable on the secondary market.

Catch Me If You Can

In addition to the plush critters available to all Boyds retailers, the Head Bean frequently designs special plush that are available only through selected stores and other retail outlets. These exclusives usually have a very low production quantities and are gone for good once they sell out (which they tend to do very quickly!). QVC, the television home shopping network, has been a favorite outlet for exclusive Boyds plush and resin for several years. As exciting as the QVC exclusives are, Gary's QVC antics are an absolute must-see!

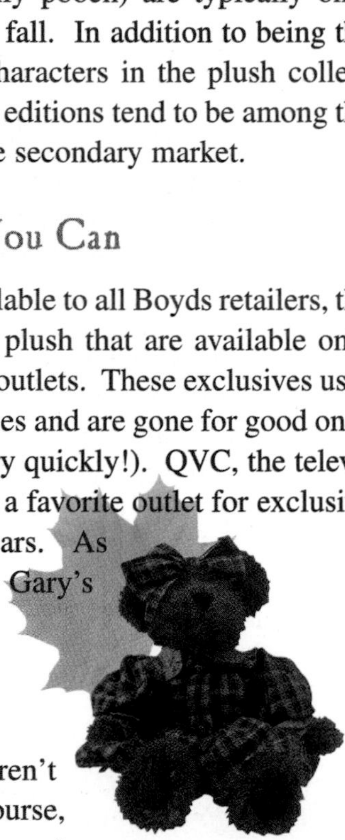

The Art Of Accessorizing

It's not that Boyds plush critters aren't cute enough on their own (and of course, they need some things to keep them from getting bored), but The Boyds Collection Ltd. has kindly created a whole host of accessories that will make your Boyds plush come alive. Choose from different styles of glasses for your plush critters, garden accessories, baskets, books, beds, rocking chairs, tables, quilts, dressers – even sleds and skis!

The Furriest Club Around

In June 1996, Boyds Bears fans all over the country were rewarded with their very own official collector's club, The Loyal Order of Friends of Boyds (F.o.B.). In addition to keeping members informed (and amused!) with a year's subscription to the *F.o.B Bear Inquirer*, the club offers both resin and plush membership gifts as well as exclusive pieces available only to club members. (See the club brochure at the back of the book for details on how you can become a loyal F.o.B.)

And The Winner Is . . .

Of course, loyal Boyds fans aren't the only ones who recognize Gary Lowenthal's talent and creativity. In 1997, the National Association of Limited Edition Dealers (NALED) recognized Gary as "Artist of the Year" and The Boyds Collection Ltd. has racked up three Teddy Bear of the Year (TOBY) Public's Choice Awards as well as two other NALED awards ("Plush Collectible of the Year" and "Doll Of The Year"). In 2000, the plush bear "Patches B. Beariluved" added another TOBY award to the Boyds coffee table, and we can only wait to see how The Head Bean wins them over this year!

A Very Special Bear

While The Boyds Collection Ltd. has earned its share of honors, it also has taken time to honor others as well. Take the case of devoted Boyds Bears collector Burke Derr, a young Pennsylvania man who

was seriously ill with cystic fibrosis. Young Burke received a letter from Gary Lowenthal in the spring of 1997 and told him that a plush bear was being created in his honor. Burke's courageous battle inspired Lowenthal to deliver the prototype of the special bear to Burke at his hospital bed only a week before the boy passed away on June 17, 1997.

Since then, "Burke P. Bear" has inspired others all around the world. Proceeds from the sale of the special bear have raised over $100,000 for Pennsylvania Cystic Fibrosis, Inc. If you're interested in joining "Burke P. Bear" in fighting cystic fibrosis, contact Pennsylvania Cystic Fibrosis Inc. (PACFI) at 1-800-900-2790, or check their web site at *www.pacfi.org*.

What More Can He Do?

Who would have thought that a man who started out making wooden duck decoys would one day be the toast of the collectibles world? For The Boyds Collection Ltd., the winning combination was a bunch of cuddly stuffed animals, an even bigger bunch of loyal fans and a very creative and fun-loving guy named Gary. And the best part is, there's even more to come in 2001!

If you really want to keep up-to-date on all the late-breaking Boyds Bears news and information, check out the official web site of The Boyds Collection Ltd. at *www.boydsstuff.com.* There, you'll find everything from new releases and retirements to lists of exclusive pieces and F.o.B. club information. You can also sign up to receive a free Boyds e-mail newsletter. For another great source for news on Boyds Bears and other collectibles, visit CheckerBee's own *www.collectorsquest.com.*

Spotlight On Boyds Resin

With the success of his line of plush critters tucked in his back pocket, Gary Lowenthal turned to other creative ways of depicting the entire plush gang. Loyal Boyds collectors will remember 1993 as the year of the resin explosion!

The Bearstone Collection®

At the head of the Boyds resin table are the bears, hares and other crazy critters of The Bearstone Collection. Their quirky Boyds humor has made the over 400 Bearstones a huge hit with collectors. Some are grouped in fun series, such as *Noah's Pageant Series, Holiday Pageant Series* and *Classic Beary Tales Series.* The Bearstone Collection includes figurines, ornaments, musicals, frames, votive holders – even wearable pins!

The Folkstone Collection®

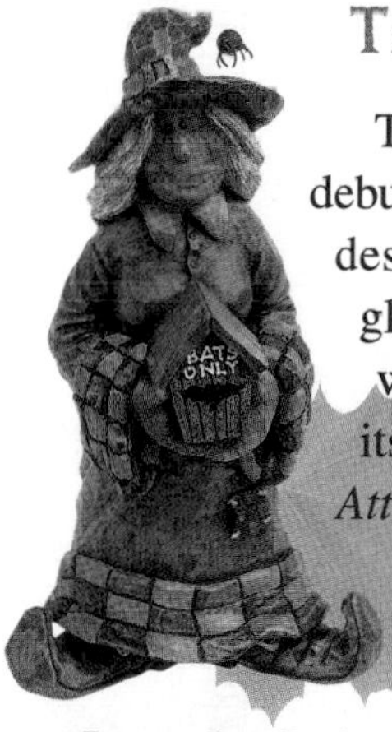

This collection of folk-art, pencil-style figurines debuted in 1994 and has grown to include over 300 designs, including figurines, ornaments, water globes and frames. *The Wee Folkstones*, a series within the collection, has a few spin-off series of its own, including *Ribbit & Co., Squeaks In The Attic, The Moose Troop* and *Snow Dooodes.*

Yesterday's Child . . . The Dollstone Collection

Instead of the rough textures of Boyds' resin critters, the adorable, bright-eyed children of The Dollstone Collection have smooth complexions and heartwarming expressions that are amazingly lifelike. First introduced in 1995, the collection now includes over 100 figurines, ornaments, musicals and votive holders.

The Shoe Box Bears™

Gary Lowenthal's follow-up to The Dollstones gave collectors more of that signature Boyds' whimsy with a twist! The upright, but fun-loving, Shoe Box Bears have jointed arms and legs to keep them active. First introduced in 1996, The Shoe Box Bears have grown to include over two dozen figurines.

Yesterday's Child™ . . . The Doll Collection

As if The Dollstone Collection wasn't adorable enough, Boyds introduced a collection of porcelain dolls in 1997. These stylish little darlings come in 16" limited editions and 12" open editions. There are now over 50 dolls in the collection, including 11 new ones for spring 2001.

DeskAnimals™

This collection of resin animals is like none you've ever seen! Each was a two or three-piece set, designed to look as if it were swimming on your coffee table, computer monitor or wherever you put them! The DeskAnimals were introduced in 1998 and none have been issued since 1999.

The Purrstone Collection™

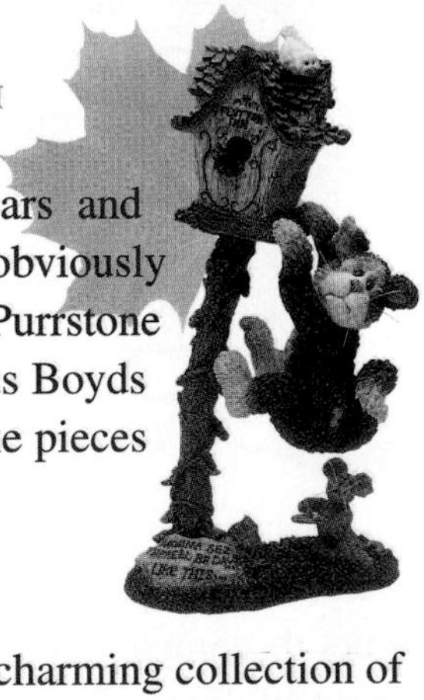

After Boyds cornered the market on bears and hares, could cats have been far behind? Well, obviously the answer is no. Introduced in 1999, The Purrstone Collection features frisky tabbies in that famous Boyds resin style. There have been about 20 Purrstone pieces to date, including two frames.

Boyds Town™

The newest resin offering from Boyds is a charming collection of resin houses. Each piece is intricately detailed and has a removable roof so if you look underneath, you can find a special surprise inside!

The village has grown to include nearly 20 houses and several accessory sets to make your own "bearly-built" village come alive!

The Crumpletons™

Among Boyds' latest innovations is this series of 12" figurines that debuted on QVC in 2000. The Crumpletons are made from resin and – believe it or not – a bit of papier-mache. There are three figurines in the series to date.

Uncle Bean's Treasure Boxes™

This new series of finely-sculpted resin boxes "belongs" to the McNibble family, a group of cute little mice who have hidden themselves in yarn baskets, planters and trunks. Each hinged box has a removable inset with a tiny critter tucked inside!

Dream Bubbles™

Another unique offering is this series of minature waterglobes (at 2-1/2" tall, we mean miniature!) depicting adorable resin characters on whimsical bases such as a pumpkin, a ball of yarn and a tea cup.

What's New For Boyds Plush Animals

Once again, The Head Bean has introduced a plethora of plush for the new season. Also new for 2001 are the Uncle Bean's *Huggle-Fluffs* – a series of cuddly plush designed especially for the young, but also perfect for the young-at-heart.

Bears

Adeline LaBearsley – Adeline wears a big straw hat to keep the sun from bleaching her fur.

Alfred Q. Rothsbury – Alfred's old-fashioned style will transport you back to the good old days of yesteryear!

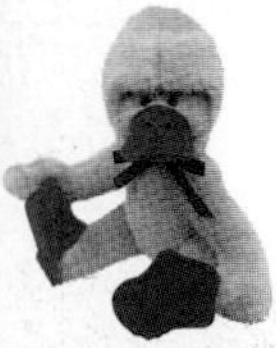

Alouysius Quackenwaddle – It seems Alouysius has been having an identity crisis.

Antoinette DeBearvoire – There's nothing like a stylish velvet hat for a stroll along the Champs d'Élysée!

Arlington B. Beanster – Arlington's snowy fur is as creamy white as his favorite vanilla ice cream!

Ashlyn Bloomengrows – Ashlyn is ready for the year's classiest garden party!

Ashlyn LaBearsley – Ashlyn is fashionably prepared to join Adeline for an outing in the country!

B.A. Scholar – B.A. is all dressed and ready to hightail it to the beach – right after graduation, of course!

B.Y. Lotsaluck – B.Y.'s lucky shamrock just might be an extra bit of good fortune that you are looking for!

Bailey (Spring 2001) – Bailey should have no trouble finding a handsome prince – or is that what the frog is for?

Bashful T. Bearhugs – Not even that snug sweater is as warm and toasty as Bashful's big heart!

Bernadette DeBearvoire – Bernadette's hat has a wire brim, so you can shape it to your liking.

Buddy – A bear this soft and cuddly would be a perfect buddy for little arms to hug and love!

Buster McRind – Buster's sweater keeps him warm through the winter months.

Buttercup Pufflefluff – Buttercup will always feel safe and secure with his blanket.

Cal Doubleplay – Cal invokes instant nostalgia for the ballpark, hot dogs and Cracker Jacks!

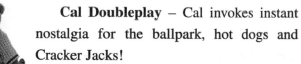

Clem Claddiddlebear – It's those specially-shaped arms that make Clem the ideal bear for hugging!

Cooper T. Wishkabibble – Cooper is extremely pleased and proud of his prize-winning porcine pal.

Daisy Bloomengrows – A colorful ribbon and lovely pink sweater sure give Daisy, and you, something to smile about!

Dawson B. Bearsworth – Did Dawson have help tying that big, elaborate knot in his big cheery bow? It must be tough without any fingers!

Edmund (Spring 2001) – Has Edmund really turned into a dragon or is he just breathing fire?

Egbert Q. Bearsford – Egbert has assumed the role of a giant Easter egg that is hatching out all over!

F.E.B.B. First Ever Bean Bear – This dignified fellow commemorates Boyd's first bean-filled bear!

Flora B. Flutterby – Flora always dreamed of flitting from flower to flower!

G.P. Hugabunch – G.P. put her heart and soul into making that wonderful quilt just for her grandma.

Ginnie Witebred – What a flirt! Ginnie loves to curtsey and show off her tan pantaloons.

Gloria Bearsevelt – No one can match the regal Gloria for her combination of patriotism and fashion sense!

Griffin W. Bearsley – Do I hear bells? Why yes, they are around Griffin's neck, I see!

H.B. Bearwish – It doesn't matter when your birthday is – H.B. is ready to celebrate your special day by your side!

Herbie Bearlove – Through a lovesick haze, Herbie spent all night working on that Valentine's Day gift. Wonder who for.

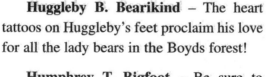

Hucklebeary B. Bear – You just can't have the American flag without blue. And Hucklebeary finishes out the Grand Ol' Flag bears with his sapphire fur!

Huggleby B. Bearikind – The heart tattoos on Huggleby's feet proclaim his love for all the lady bears in the Boyds forest!

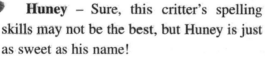

Humphrey T. Bigfoot – Be sure to make plenty of room for Humphrey and his 18" size!

Huney – Sure, this critter's spelling skills may not be the best, but Huney is just as sweet as his name!

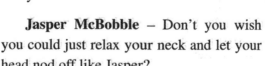

Ido Loveya – The key that Ido carries around just might unlock the heart of the one you love.

Jasper McBobble – Don't you wish you could just relax your neck and let your head nod off like Jasper?

Jocelyn Bloomengrows – The garden parties that Jocelyn gives are famous.

Leiselle Bloomengrows – Even though she'd rather be romping through the mud, Leiselle can enjoy a good garden party too!

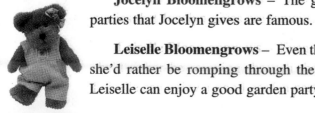

Little Bearpeep and Friends – No honorable wolf would ever attack this dedicated shepherdess who takes the trouble to carry her sheep around!

Macy Sunbeary – It looks like Macy has a new duck friend who shares her exquisite taste in clothes.

Mae B. Bearlove – There's no maybe about it, you will love Mae B. Bearlove.

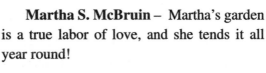

Martha S. McBruin – Martha's garden is a true labor of love, and she tends it all year round!

McKinley Bearington – With an ornate hat, McKinley pays homage to the splendid Victorian days of old!

Melanie McRind – It's too bad Melanie's lovely dress won't be clean for long – you know how messy eating watermelon can be!

Merci Bearcoo – There's no bear more grateful than Merci. Every day, she gives thanks for her good fortune.

Meridian Wishkabibble – You'd better hope your pie meets with Meridian's approval – she's quite the picky judge!

Miss Macintosh – Thank a teacher if you can read the letters and numbers on the knowledgeable Miss Macintosh's jacket.

Momma McNew With Hugsley – There's no better way to express motherhood than with a warm, loving hug!

Mr. Everlove – It seems that Mr. Everlove has finally overcome his lifelong bachelorhood.

Mr. McSnickers – Step right up and see the sights! Mr. McSnickers is all set to sell you a ticket to a world of circus wonders!

Mrs. Everlove – It's a special day for Mrs. Everlove. Her vows this day will live on in the Boyds history of love!

Nana Bearhug – This "overstuffed" bear is an enormous 40" tall.

O. Howie Luvsya – With a heart as beautiful as Howie's velvet one, how can any warm-hearted lady bear – or collector – resist him?

Patrick Bearsevelt – The Clan Bearsevelt is known for its proud patriotism, and Patrick takes it up a notch with an embroidered star on his foot!

Peter Potter – Peter has just a little bit of stomach showing. Better lay off the honey, Peter!

Pipley McRind – Pipley's talent for watermelon seed-target spitting is legendary in the Boyds village!

Putnam P. Bearsley – At a petite 6", Putnam is cuddly proof that great things come in small packages!

Rudy McRind – After a long, hard season of tending to his watermelon crop, Rudy is all set for the harvest – and the crazy feast to follow!

Ruskin K. Woodruff – His poseable stature makes Ruskin a true work of art.

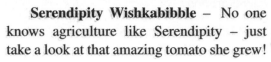

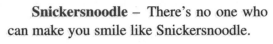

Serendipity Wishkabibble – No one knows agriculture like Serendipity – just take a look at that amazing tomato she grew!

Snickersnoodle – There's no one who can make you smile like Snickersnoodle.

Sturbridge Q. Patriot – No one can question Sturbridge's strong loyalty to his native land!

Sugar McRind – Sugar is as sweet as the watermelon she grows.

Timothy & Tiny Jodibear – When the Boyds circus comes to town, it's Timothy and Tiny who lead the majestic parade!

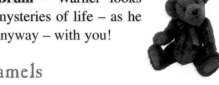

Uncle Sam – With his reversible tie (navy or red with white spots) Uncle Sam wants YOU – for an owner, that is!

Warner Von Bruin – Warner looks ready to share the mysteries of life – as he understands them, anyway – with you!

Camels

Sir Humpsley – If you ever find yourself stranded in the great desert, Sir Humpsley and his canteen would be a most welcome sight!

Cats

Amy Z. Sassycat – With a hat that's fully poseable, Amy breaks ground as the first Boyds' cat to wear a hat!

Auden S. Penworthy – If you go down to your local coffeehouse, you might hear Auden reciting his latest epic poems.

Claudette Prissypuss – Cats do love to strut. And Claudette will attract plenty of attention in a spiffy hat like this!

Dreyfus Q. Wordsworth – Famed for his dramatic oratory skill, Dreyfus is never at a loss for words!

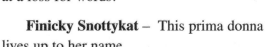

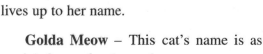

Finicky Snottykat – This prima donna lives up to her name.

Golda Meow – This cat's name is as straightforward as her attire.

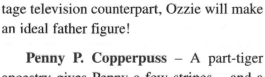

Ozzie N. Harrycat – Just like his vintage television counterpart, Ozzie will make an ideal father figure!

Penny P. Copperpuss – A part-tiger ancestry gives Penny a few stripes – and a lot of stylish flair!

Rowena Prissypuss – All set for her first stroll on the town, Rowena is sure to turn a head or two.

Sly Alleyruckus – Sly is indeed a cat of mystery – perhaps the one who starts all those crazy cat parties in the alley?

Vanessa V. Fluffypaws – It looks like Vanessa lost a fight in the dye factory. But that rainbow ribbon will brighten up even the rainiest day!

Cows

Butch Hoofenutter – In his red bandanna, this cow demands attention on the farm!

Corabelle Hoofenutter – Most cows use their tails to ward off flies, but Corabelle's poseable one is also good for decoration.

Fernando Uttermost – This bovine is an utterly classy cow.

Florabelle Uttermost – Florabelle will bring uttermost joy to your heart.

Dogs

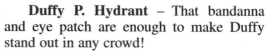

Duffy P. Hydrant – That bandanna and eye patch are enough to make Duffy stand out in any crowd!

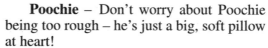

Poochie – Don't worry about Poochie being too rough – he's just a big, soft pillow at heart!

Ducks

Quackie – Just when you think Gary has run out of animals to immortalize in plush, he comes up with something new!

Elephants

Hannibel Trunkster – Since the circus left town, Hannibel has been searching for another gig. Why not hire him?

Isadora T. Lightfoot – You've got to be pretty confident to cross a high wire in a pink tutu – especially if you're an elephant!

Frogs

Paddies – Living in the local pond just wasn't enough for Paddies who now wants to hop into your collection!

Giraffes

Wilt Stiltwalker – Wilt is quite proud of his majestic species and holds his head up high to show it!

Hares

Dabney P. Powderfoot – You'll need a good fence around Dabney whose big feet make it easy for him to leap off the shelf!

Delanie D. Hopplebuns – No one in the rabbit hutch knows how to coordinate fashion as well as Delanie.

Emily Babbit (Spring 2001) – Emily adds to her tribe's splendor in a classic medieval dress!

Flopsie – With those crazy ears and soft "hugability," Flopsie's cuteness is impossible to resist!

Fluff Pufflepoof – If you need something to cuddle, you can't go wrong with a bunny like Fluff and his blanket!

Graham Quackers – Graham wants to see what it's like to be a duck and swim instead of hop!

Hattie Hopsalot – Hattie just can't wait for the garden party! Where else can a rabbit get unlimited lettuce?

Higgins D. Nibbleby – What dignity! What poise! Higgins just loves to stand tall and proud.

Keefer P. Lightfoot – Be careful not to take this cutie too lightly!

Key Lime Thumpster – With a bow and paw pads in a charming green pattern, Key Lime embodies the springtime!

Lula Mae Loppenhop – Since she has naturally springy ears, Lula Mae certainly has a lot to smile about – and she'll never stop (and neither will you)!

Mazie Q. Lightfoot – Mazie looks a bit like a chocolate bunny – almost good enough to eat!

Miracle Gardenglow – It seems that Miracle has found the very best carrot of the season! Doesn't it look delicious?

Rosalie Bloomengrows – After a long, hard day of harvesting, Rosalie has found herself a great lunch!

Tangerine Thumpster – The faded red pattern of Tangerine's paw pads and bow give this critter a relaxed and rustic look!

Tatters T. Hareloom – He may have a few patches here and there, but that just means Tatters is well-loved!

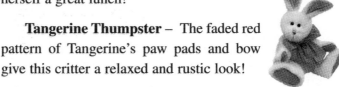

Tessie T. Nibblenose – The carrot patch on her overalls gives Tessie an air of authority around the garden.

Tina Marie Hopgood – this lovely hare will be sure to jump right into your heart.

Twigley Hopsalot – After years of leaping and jumping, Twigley wants to bend his flexible knees and jump into your home.

Vanna Hopkins – Vanna is dressed and ready to dance the night away!

Webster Hopplebuns – In his hand-knit sweater, Webster looks quite ducky.

Kangaroos

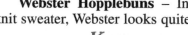

Adelaide and Joey Downunder – With her baby safe in her pouch, Adelaide is Boyds' first kangaroo!

Lambs

Flossie – With all that soft fleece, who wouldn't want to cuddle up with Flossie?

Liza Fuzzyfleece – It's a whole new world for Boyds lambs this year. Liza's has a whole different kind of coat!

Lucibelle Fuzzyfleece – Lucibelle is only the "black sheep" of the family because Gary made her that way!

Mice

Swiss C. Mouski – Swiss asks the question we all sometimes ask – "Got Cheez?"

Monkeys

Simianne Z. Jodibear – This monkey looks all set to bang those cymbals together in celebration of this old-fashioned look!

Pandas

Domino – With a most unusual face, this thoughtful panda shows great wisdom behind those black eyes!

Pigs

Farley O'Pigg – Ah, the life of a pig. Farley plans to try his hardest at eating, loafing, eating, loafing and eating some more!

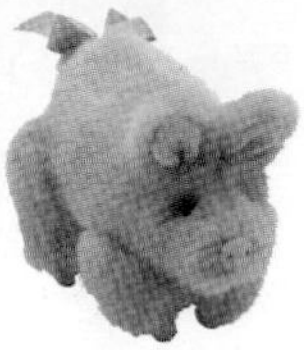

Hamlet – According to legend, the design for Hamlet is based on an antique pig that someone sent to "Yer Old Uncle Bean."

Ivy Bloomengrows – Ivy sure has a preference for colorful sweaters!

Pinkie – Pinkie may have a reputation for being lazy, but if you're an infant's snuggly toy, that's just what you should be!

Raggedymuffs

Kissimmee – The simple folkish charm of Kissimmee honors antique rag dolls.

Skunks

Oda Perfume – If Boyds' first skunk gets a bit gamy, have no fear, she comes with a clothes pin, suitable for your nose!

Squirrels

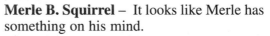

Merle B. Squirrel – It looks like Merle has something on his mind.

Ornaments

You can literally hang up your love for Boyds with this great new assortment of nine ornaments, with everything from ladybugs to ducks to of course those bears and hares we have all come to love!

Pins

That's no regular fuzz on your lapel, that's a piece of the new collection of Wuzzie pins. With three new styles to choose from you can hop right into fashion.

Puppets

You'll be waving your hands high with Boyds on them. With three new critters to choose from, let your hands do the talking with these fabulous puppets.

Collector's Club News

In the new century, it's time to follow that crazy parade of bears, hares and friends, because the "Greatest F.o.B. on Earth" circus is in town and the fun is all under the bigtop! When you join The Loyal Order of Friends of Boyds, you will have the best seat in the house for the festivities as this year's F.o.B. members are entitled to the best three-ring show in town, complete with all you've come to expect from those wild and crazy Boyds critters!

The First Act

When you take your seat by the first ring, you'll be treated to the clowning of "Gadget." He may look like a silent clown at first, but don't let that quiet 6" demeanor fool you! Before you know it, his wry antics will drag you into the act and have you laughing your head off!

The second ring is more daring. Ever seen a bear on a bike? Well, "Gizmoe" is no regular bear – check him out juggling while balancing on a unicycle and trying not to smudge his colorful resin attire with all that clown makeup. This is not an easy stunt – don't try it at home!

That's not all you'll find under the tent. You'll also find the "Greatest F.o.B. 2001 Bearwear Pin," bearing the timeless image of "Gizmoe" doing his best to juggle all those objects at once. You can even pick up a big window cling (you know, one of those stickers that stick without glue) to spice up the view through any pane of glass!

Then read all about it with The Boyds *F.o.B. Inquirer*, where you can catch up on all the latest gossip about the company activities and the animals, and enjoy The Head Bean's unique writing

style! If the newsletter were just a little bit smaller, you could store it on "Noah's Book Shelf," a resin piece available for purchase only to club members.

The Second Act

But that's just the first part of the show – with more excitement and exclusive pieces to buy for a small fee. "Gizmoe's Big Top with Giggle McNibble" reveals a world of pleasant little surprises. What kind of surprises, you ask? Well, if we told you that, they wouldn't be surprises now would they?

And no Boyds circus is complete without "Melvin Sortalion" showing off his musical talent. You do have to convince him to play, however, but that's easy: all you have to do is wind him up.

Every circus has to have a tightrope walker, and "Gussie . . . Life is a Balancing Act" foots the bill with her brave-hearted wire stroll, separated from the ground by . . . well, by centimeters, anyway! We never said it was a high wire act!

Get Yer Tickets Here!

Admission to this carnival is only $34.50 which gets you into the first act of clowning and juggling, but this wild and crazy circus will only be in town until December 31, 2001. So you'd better saddle up to the ticket counter at:

> **The Boyds Collection LTD**
> **PO Box 4386 F.o.B. Department**
> **Gettysburg, PA 17325-4386**

Future Retirements

Boyds animals are always looking forward to the next chapter in life and every year, some get the chance at a whole new world of golf, fishing and general laziness. That's right, folks, we're talking about RETIREMENT! Boyds usually schedules the pieces to retire at a certain time, but others get a "sudden death" retirement – in other words, the piece is retired immediately, and collectors have until the warehouses run out of it to get their paws on it. Here's a list of pieces set to be retired by December 31, 2001, along with their issue year.

Retiring In 2001

BEARS

- ❑ Abercrombie B. Beanster (1999)
- ❑ Amanda K. Huntington (1999)
- ❑ Andrew Huntington (1999)
- ❑ Archibald McBearlie (1998)
- ❑ Ashley Huntington (1999)
- ❑ Aunt Fanny Fremont (1999)
- ❑ Aunt Yvonne Dubeary (1998)
- ❑ Auntie Lavonne Higgenthorpe (2000)
- ❑ Bailey (Fall 2000)
- ❑ Bailey (Spring 2001)
- ❑ Bailey & Matthew (w/resin ornaments, Fall 2000)
- ❑ Bashful T. Bearhugs (2001)
- ❑ Bethany Bearington (2000)
- ❑ Bethany Thistlebeary (1999)
- ❑ Betsie B. Jodibear (2000)
- ❑ Biff Grizzwood (2000)
- ❑ Billy Bob Bruin With Froggie (2000)
- ❑ Bixby Trufflebeary (1999)
- ❑ Boris Berriman (1998)
- ❑ Braxton B. Bear (1998)
- ❑ Burlington P. Beanster (1999)
- ❑ Caledonia (1997)
- ❑ Clementine (1998)
- ❑ Cleveland G. Bearington (2000)
- ❑ Clover L. Buzzoff (1999)
- ❑ Cori Beariburg (2000)
- ❑ Craxton B. Bean (1998)
- ❑ Denton P. Jodibear (1999)
- ❑ Devin Fallsbeary (1999)

BEARS, cont.

- ❑ Doolittle Buckshot (1999)
- ❑ Dwight D. Bearington (2000)
- ❑ Edmund (Fall 2000)
- ❑ Edmund (Spring 2001)
- ❑ Egbert Q. Bearsford (2001)
- ❑ Elmer O. Bearroad (2000)
- ❑ Forrest B. Bearsley (1999)
- ❑ Gary M. Bearenthal (1999)
- ❑ General P.D.Q. Pattington (2000)
- ❑ Ginnie Higgenthorpe (2000)
- ❑ Hampton T. Bearington (2000)
- ❑ Hayden T. Bearsford (2000)
- ❑ Hazelnut B. Bean (2000)
- ❑ Hemingway K. Grizzman (1999)
- ❑ Henley Fitzhampton (1999)
- ❑ Herbert Henry Jodibear (1999)
- ❑ Herbie Bearlove (2001)
- ❑ Huggleby B. Bearikind (2001)
- ❑ Humboldt (1996)
- ❑ Huney B. Keeper (2000)
- ❑ Jaxton D. Bear (2000)
- ❑ Katie B. Berrijam (1999)
- ❑ Kayla Mulbeary (1999)
- ❑ Klaus Von Fuzzner (1998)
- ❑ Kyle L. Berriman (2000)
- ❑ Lillian K. Bearsley (1998)
- ❑ Lisa T. Bearringer (1998)
- ❑ Liza J. Berrijam (1999)
- ❑ Madeline Willoughby (1999)
- ❑ Mae B. Bearlove (2001)
- ❑ Magarita (1998)
- ❑ Maris G. Pattington (2000)

BEARS, cont.

- ❑ Maximillian (2000)
- ❑ Maya Berriman (1999)
- ❑ McKenzie (1997)
- ❑ McKinley Bearington (2001)
- ❑ Mercedes Fitzbruin (1998)
- ❑ Mitchell Bearsdale (1999)
- ❑ Mr. Noah And Friends (2000)
- ❑ Mr. Trumbull (1998)
- ❑ Mrs. Mertz (1999)
- ❑ Nadia Berriman (1999)
- ❑ Naomi Bearlove (2000)
- ❑ Natasha Berriman (1998)
- ❑ O. Howie Luvsya (2001)
- ❑ Paxton P. Bean (1998)
- ❑ Percy (1994)
- ❑ Radcliffe Fitzbruin (2000)
- ❑ Rockwell B. Bruin (2000)
- ❑ Ross G. Jodibear (2000)
- ❑ Sarah Beth Jodibear (1999)
- ❑ Skylar Thistlebeary (1999)
- ❑ Snookie Snicklefritz (2000)
- ❑ Tami P. Rally (2000)
- ❑ Thayer (1997)
- ❑ Tilly F. Wuzzie (1999)
- ❑ Tipton F. Wuzzie (1999)
- ❑ Webber Vanguard (2000)
- ❑ Wilcox J. Beansford (1999)
- ❑ Winnie II (1998)
- ❑ Woodruff K. Bearsford (1999)
- ❑ Wookie Snicklefritz (2000)

CATS

- ❑ Catherine Q. Fuzzberg (1997)
- ❑ Cookie Grimilkin (1991)
- ❑ Dorchester Catsworth With Artie (2000)
- ❑ Kattelina Purrsley (1999)
- ❑ Lola Ninelives (1999)
- ❑ Marissa P. Pussyfoot (1999)
- ❑ Momma McFuzz And Missy (2000)
- ❑ Robyn Purrsmore (2000)
- ❑ Taylor Purrski (2000)
- ❑ Walter Q. Fuzzberg (1997)
- ❑ Zachariah Alleyruckus (1999)

DOGS

- ❑ Checkers P. Hydrant (2000)
- ❑ Indy (Fall 2000)
- ❑ Philo Puddlemaker (1999)
- ❑ Snuffy B. Barker (2000)

FROGS

- ❑ G. Kelly Ribbit (1999)

HARES

- ❑ Anastasia (1998)
- ❑ Edith Q. Harington (2000)
- ❑ Emily Babbit (Fall 2000)
- ❑ Emily Babbit (Spring 2001)
- ❑ Graham Quackers (2001)
- ❑ Kerry Q. Hopgood (1999)
- ❑ Roscoe P. Bumpercrop (1999)
- ❑ Roslyn Hiphop (2000)
- ❑ Stellina Hopswell (2000)
- ❑ Sterling Hopswell (2000)
- ❑ Tami F. Wuzzie (1999)
- ❑ Tina Marie Hopgood (2001)

LAMBS

- ❑ Embraceable Ewe (2000)

MICE

- ❑ Monterey Mouski (1999)
- ❑ Sharp McNibble (1999)

MONKEYS

- ❑ Dalton Monkbury (1998)
- ❑ Darwin Monkbury (1998)

MOOSE

- ❑ Martin V. Moosington (2000)
- ❑ Montana Mooski (1999)

PANDAS

- ❑ Bamboo Bearington (2000)
- ❑ Hsing-Hsing Wongbruin (1999)
- ❑ Yolanda Panda (1998)

PENGUINS

- ❑ Tuxie Waddlewalk (1999)

PIGS

- ❑ Kaitlin McSwine III (1998)

RAGGEDYMUFFS

- ❑ Delray (2000)
- ❑ Sanibel (2000)

ORNAMENTS

- ❑ Angelina II (1998)
- ❑ Cappuccino Frenzy (1999)
- ❑ Chillin' Sockley (2000)
- ❑ Espresso Frisky (1999)
- ❑ Flip Hopsey (2001)
- ❑ Lilly R. Ribbit (2000)
- ❑ Meltin' Sockley (2000)
- ❑ Mocha Mooseby (1999)
- ❑ Molasses (2000)
- ❑ Sassafrass (2000)
- ❑ Skip Hopsey (2001)
- ❑ Truelove F. Wuzzie (2001)

Plush Top Five

As with all collectible items, Boyds plush creations start to rise in value when they retire . . . and some of them reach impressive levels of worth! To show you what we mean, we've put together a list of the five most valuable plush pieces. (Please note that this list does not include Boyds plush exclusives.)

Bailey (Fall 1992)
Issued 1992 – Retired 1993
Original Price: N/A
Secondary Market Value: **$770**

Eleanor Bear (set/3)
Issued 1990 – Retired 1990
Original Price: N/A
Secondary Market Value: **$575**

Nana
Issued 1991 – Retired 1992
Original Price: $27
Secondary Market Value: **$525**

Rudolf
Issued 1992 – Retired 1992
Original Price: N/A
Secondary Market Value: **$510**

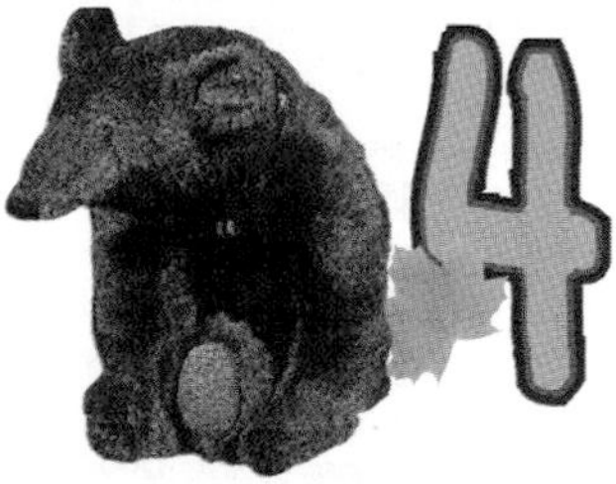

Beatrice
Issued 1991 – Retired 1991
Original Price: $63
Secondary Market Value: **$475**

How To Use Your Value Guide

1. **FIND** your piece in the Value Guide section. The section is broken down by animal type and all the animals are in alphabetical order: bears, camels, cats, cows, crows, dogs, donkeys, ducks, elephants, foxes, frogs, giraffes, gorillas, hares, kangaroos, lambs, lions, mice, monkeys, moose, pandas, penguins, pigs, raccoons, Raggedymuffs, skunks, squirrels, ornaments, pins, puppets, tree toppers, collector's club pieces and exclusives. Each piece is listed alphabetically within its animal type. A guide to the plush series abbreviations appears below.

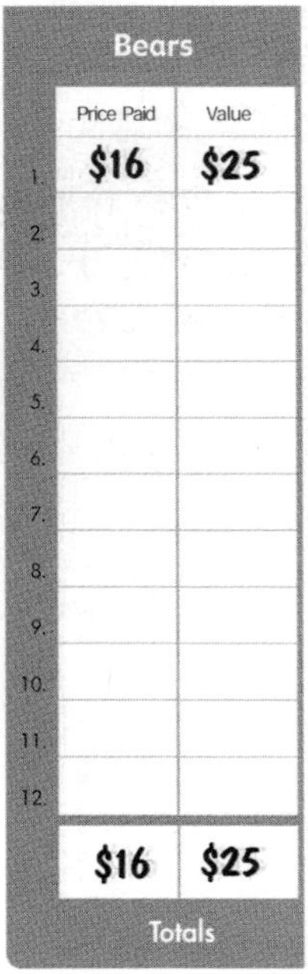

Bears
Price Paid
Value
1. $16 $25
2.
3.
4.
5.
6.
7.
8.
9.
10.
11.
12.
$16 $25
Totals

2. **RECORD** the price you paid for the piece in its corresponding box in the "Price Paid" box in the corner of the page. Also record the secondary market value in the "Value" box. Any piece for which no value has been established will be listed as "N/E." Current pieces will each have their 2001 suggested retail price next to their value.

3. **ADD** up all the boxes in each column and record the total in the "Totals" boxes at the bottom. Be sure to use a pencil so you can change the totals as your collection grows!

4. **TRANSFER** the totals of each page to the "Total Value Of My Collection" worksheets at the end of the Value Guide section.

5. **ADD** the totals to determine the total value of your collection.

AM Animal Menagerie	**DB** Doodle Bears	**IF** ImagineBeary Friends	**RM** Raggedymuffs
AR The Artisan Series	**FH** From The Heart	**JB** J.B. Bean & Associates	**SA** Stringalongs
AS The Archive Series	**FL** The Flatties	**JJ** Jolly Jinglers	**SB** Snow Bears
BA Bears In The Attic	**FM** Fuzzmits	**LS** Lovestruck	**SQ** Squeekies
BB The Bubba Bears	**GB** Grizzly Bears	**MB** The Mohair Bear	**TF** T.F. Wuzzies
BB Boogedy Boos	**HD** Himalayan Dancing Bears	**NL** Northern Lights	**TJ** T.J.'s Best Dressed
BY BabyBoyds	**HF** Huggle-Fluffs	**OR** Ornaments	**UB** Uptown Bears
CB The Choir Bears	**HQ** Hugs 'N Quacks	**PM** Prime Minister's Cabinet	**WB** Wool Boyds Series
CC Clintons Cabinet	**HT** Hares In Toyland		**WW** Wearable Wuzzies
CH The Choir Hares			

Boyds Plush Animals

Since Boyds first turned up, collectors have been able to build entire zoos of cuddly plush animals. Their expressive faces and adorable manner have made them quite the coveted items. With almost 100 brand new pieces in the zoo this season, Gary Lowenthal's fans will surely encourage him to send that number even higher in the years to come!

Bears

1

A.J. Blixen
8" • #917307 • TJ
Issued: 2000 • Retired: 2000
Orig. Price: $16 • **Value: $25**

2

Abercrombie B. Beanster
16" • #510400-05 • JB
Issued: 1999 • To Be Retired: 2001
Orig. Price: $26 • **Value: $26**

3

Abigail Bramblebeary
6" • #913963 • TJ
Issued: 2000 • Current
Orig. Price: $13 • **Value: $13**

4

Ace Bruin
10" • #5122 • JB
Issued: Pre-1990 • Retired: 1996
Orig. Price: $14 • **Value: $43**

5

Ace Q. Dooright
12" • #900203 • UB
Issued: 1999 • Retired: 2000
Orig. Price: $95 • **Value: N/E**

6

Adaline Bearett
6" • #918437 • TJ
Issued: 2000 • Current
Orig. Price: $10 • **Value: $10**

7

Adams F. Bearington
6" • #590080-03 • MB
Issued: 1998 • Retired: 1998
Orig. Price: $18 • **Value: $42**

8

Addington
12" • #5701-05 • AS
Issued: 1993 • Retired: 199[illegible]
Orig. Price: $20 • **Value: $55**

9
New

Adeline LaBearsley
12" • #912657 • TJ
Issued: 2001 • Current
Orig. Price: $[illegible] • **Value: $27**

Bears

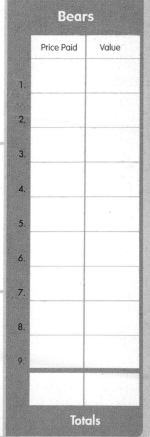

	Price Paid	Value
1.		
2.		
3.		
4.		
5.		
6.		
7.		
8.		
9.		
Totals		

1

Agatha Snoopstein
8" • #91870 • TJ
Issued: 2000 • Current
Orig. Price: $17 • **Value: $17**

2

Aissa Witebred
12" • #912070 • TJ
Issued: 2000 • Current
Orig. Price: $27 • **Value: $27**

3

Alabaster B. Bigfoot
18" • #51110-01 • JB
Issued: 2000 • Current
Orig. Price: $39 • **Value: $39**

4

Alastair
5.5" • #5725-08 • AS
Issued: 1996 • Retired: 1997
Orig. Price: $7 • **Value: $25**

5

Alastair & Camilla (set/2, bear and hare)
N/A • #98042 • TJ
Issued: 1996 • Retired: 1996
Orig. Price: N/A • **Value: $44**

6

Albert B. Bean
14" • #5123-03 • JB
Issued: 1993 • Retired: 1997
Orig. Price: $20 • **Value: $40**

7

Alec (also known as "Alex")
5.5" • #5711 • AS
Issued: 1990 • Retired: 1991
Orig. Price: $7 • **Value: $93**

8

Aletha . . . The Bearmaker (LE-500)
N/A • #9217 • N/A
Issued: 1994 • Retired: 1994
Orig. Price: $74 • **Value: $260**

9

Alex Berriman With Nikita
16" & 6" • #900202 • UB
Issued: 1999 • Retired: 2000
Orig. Price: $73 • **Value: N/E**

10

Alexis Berriman
16" • #912022 • TJ
Issued: 1998 • Retired: 2000
Orig. Price: $61 • **Value: $75**

11
New

Alfred Q. Rothsbury
12" • #57004-11 • AS
Issued: 2001 • Current
Orig. Price: $19 • **Value: $19**

12

Alice
11" • #1101-08 • CC
Issued: 1995 • Retired: 1995
Orig. Price: $12 • **Value: $25**

Bears

	Price Paid	Value
1.		
2.		
3.		
4.		
5.		
6.		
7.		
8.		
9.		
10.		
11.		
12.		
Totals		

1

Alice II
11" • #1101-08 • CC
Issued: 1996 • Retired: 1998
Orig. Price: $12 • **Value: $23**

2

Alissa Angelhope
12" • #83004 • AS
Issued: 2000 • Retired: 2000
Orig. Price: $21 • **Value: N/E**

3

Alouetta de Grizetta
6" • #91842 • TJ
Issued: 1996 • Retired: 1999
Orig. Price: $9 • **Value: $21**

4
New

Alouysius Quackenwaddle
10" • #91860 • TJ
Issued: 2001• Current
Orig. Price: $21 • **Value: $21**

5

Alvis Q. Bearnap With Snoozy T. Puddlemaker
14" • #900208 • UB
Issued: 1999 • Retired: 2000
Orig. Price: $39 • **Value: $50**

6

Amanda K. Huntington
16" • #912025 • TJ
Issued: 1999 • To Be Retired: 2001
Orig. Price: $59 • **Value: $59**

7

Amos
12" • #5700-03 • AS
Issued: 1995 • Retired: 1995
Orig. Price: $20 • **Value: $225**

8

Andrei Berriman
5.5" • #917300-06 • TJ
Issued: 1998 • Retired: 2000
Orig. Price: $13 • **Value: $22**

9

Andrew Huntington
6" • #918053 • TJ
Issued: 1999 • To Be Retired: 2001
Orig. Price: $12 • **Value: $12**

10

Anissa Whittlebear
12" • #912650 • TJ
Issued: 1999 • Current
Orig. Price: $26 • **Value: $26**

11

Ansel
6" • #91271 • TJ
Issued: 1996 • Retired: 1999
Orig. Price: $13 • **Value: $20**

12
New

Antoinette DeBearvoire
6" • #918440 • TJ
Issued: 2001 • Current
Orig. Price: $13 • **Value: $13**

Bears

	Price Paid	Value
1.		
2.		
3.		
4.		
5.		
6.		
7.		
8.		
9.		
10.		
11.		
12.		
Totals		

1

Anya Frostfire
16" • #912023 • TJ
Issued: 1999 • Retired: 2000
Orig. Price: $59 • **Value: $65**

2

Archibald McBearlie
6" • #91393 • TJ
Issued: 1998 • To Be Retired: 2001
Orig. Price: $13 • **Value: $13**

3

Photo Unavailable

Arctic Bear
info unavailable
Orig. Price: N/A • **Value: N/E**

4
New

Arlington B. Beanster
16" • #510400-03 • JB
Issued: 2001 • Current
Orig. Price: $26 • **Value: $26**

5

Arlo
8" • #9141 • TJ
Issued: 1994 • Retired: 1996
Orig. Price: $12 • **Value: $50**

6

Arlo
8 • #98040 • TJ
Issued: 1996 • Retired: 1997
Orig. Price: $12 • **Value: $50**

7

Artemus
8" • #1003-08 • CC
Issued: 1997 • Retired: 1999
Orig. Price: $7 • **Value: $16**

8

Arthur
16" • #5712 • AS
Issued: 1991 • Retired: 1992
Orig. Price: $32 • **Value: $185**

9

Arthur C. Bearington
9" • #590060-03 • MB
Issued: 1999 • Retired: 2000
Orig. Price: $29 • **Value: $32**

10

Ashley
14" • #5109 • JB
Issued: 1991 • Retired: 1992
Orig. Price: $20 • **Value: $200**

11

Ashley Huntington
6" • #918054 • TJ
Issued: 1999 • To Be Retired: 2001
Orig. Price: $12 • **Value: $12**

Bears

	Price Paid	Value
1.		
2.		
3.		
4.		
5.		
6.		
7.		
8.		
9.		
10.		
11.		
Totals		

1
New

Ashlyn Bloomengrows
12" • #912653 • TJ
Issued: 2001 • Current
Orig. Price: $27 • **Value: $27**

2
New

Ashlyn LaBearsley
8" • #918352 • TJ
Issued: 2001 • Current
Orig. Price: $20 • **Value: $20**

3

Asquith
8" • #5705-05 • AS
Issued: 1993 • Retired: 1995
Orig. Price: $13 • **Value: $40**

4

Astrid
9" • #9137 • TJ
Issued: 1994 • Retired: 1996
Orig. Price: $20 • **Value: $48**

5

Attlee
8" • #5705B • AS
Issued: 1992 • Retired: 1993
Orig. Price: N/A • **Value: $95**

6

Aubrey Tippeetoes
12" • #912054 • TJ
Issued: 2000 • Current
Orig. Price: $28 • **Value: $28**

7

Auggie Bruin
16" • #5125 • JB
Issued: 1992 • Retired: 1996
Orig. Price: $27 • **Value: $65**

8

Augusta
14" • #91010 • TJ
Issued: 1998 • Retired: 1998
Orig. Price: $36 • **Value: $58**

9

Aunt Becky Bearchild
12" • #912052 • TJ
Issued: 1998 • Retired: 2000
Orig. Price: $29 • **Value: $43**

10

Aunt Bessie Skidoo
9" • #91931 • TJ
Issued: 1998 • Current
Orig. Price: $30 • **Value: $30**

11

Aunt Fanny Fremont
8" • #918350 • TJ
Issued: 1999 • To Be Retired: 2001
Orig. Price: $23 • **Value: $23**

12

Aunt Mamie Bearington
4.5" • #590104 • MB
Issued: 2000 • Retired: 2000
Orig. Price: $11 • **Value: N/E**

Bears

	Price Paid	Value
1.		
2.		
3.		
4.		
5.		
6.		
7.		
8.		
9.		
10.		
11.		
12.		
Totals		

Value Guide — Boyds Plush Animals

1

Aunt Yvonne Dubeary
11" • #918450 • TJ
Issued: 1998 • To Be Retired: 2001
Orig. Price: $25 • **Value: $25**

2

Auntie Aleena de Bearvoire
10" • #918451 • TJ
Issued: 1999 • Retired: 2000
Orig. Price: $23 • **Value: $27**

3

Auntie Alice
10" • #9183 • TJ
Issued: 1993 • Retired: 1996
Orig. Price: $21 • **Value: $48**

4

Photo Unavailable

Auntie Bearburg
info unavailable
Orig. Price: N/A • **Value: N/E**

5

Auntie Erma
10" • #91832 • TJ
Issued: 1996 • Retired: 1997
Orig. Price: $21 • **Value: $48**

6

Auntie Iola
10" • #91612 • TJ
Issued: 1995 • Retired: 1997
Orig. Price: $30 • **Value: $60**

7

Auntie Lavonne Higgenthorpe
12" • #918452 • TJ
Issued: 2000 • To Be Retired: 2001
Orig. Price: $25 • **Value: $25**

8

Autumn Fallsbeary
10" • #91745 • TJ
Issued: 2000 • Current
Orig. Price: $20 • **Value: $20**

9

Avery B. Bean
14" • #5101 • JB
Issued: pre-1990 • Retired: 1990
Orig. Price: N/A • **Value: $190**

10

B.A. Blackbelt
10" • #917361 • TJ
Issued: 2000 • Current
Orig. Price: $21 • **Value: $21**

11
New

B.A. Scholar
10" • #917369 • TJ
Issued: 2001 • Current
Orig. Price: $26 • **Value: $26**

12
New

B.Y. Lotsaluck
10" • #917370 • TJ
Issued: 2001 • Current
Orig. Price: $15 • **Value: $15**

Bears

	Price Paid	Value
1.		
2.		
3.		
4.		
5.		
6.		
7.		
8.		
9.		
10.		
11.		
12.		
Totals		

1

Baaah'b
8" • #9131 • TJ
Issued: 1995 • Retired: 1997
Orig. Price: $17 • **Value: $42**

2

Baby
10" • #6105B • TJ
Issued: 1990 • Retired: 1991
Orig. Price: N/A • **Value: $300**

3

Bailey (Fall 1992)
8" • #9199 • TJ
Issued: 1992 • Retired: 1993
Orig. Price: N/A • **Value: $770**

4

Bailey (Spring 1993)
8" • N/A • TJ
Issued: 1993 • Retired: 1994
Orig. Price: N/A • **Value: $370**

5

Bailey (Fall 1993)
8" • #9170 • TJ
Issued: 1993 • Retired: 1994
Orig. Price: N/A • **Value: $420**

6

Bailey (Spring 1994)
8" • #9199-01 • TJ
Issued: 1994 • Retired: 1995
Orig. Price: $26 • **Value: $200**

7

Bailey (Fall 1994)
8" • #9199-02 • TJ
Issued: 1994 • Retired: 1995
Orig. Price: $26 • **Value: $68**

8

Bailey (Spring 1995)
8" • #9199-03 • TJ
Issued: 1995 • Retired: 1996
Orig. Price: $26 • **Value: $57**

9

Bailey (Fall 1995)
8" • #9199-04 • TJ
Issued: 1995 • Retired: 1996
Orig. Price: $24 • **Value: $52**

10

Bailey (Spring 1996)
8" • #9199-05 • TJ
Issued: 1996 • Retired: 1997
Orig. Price: $26 • **Value: $52**

11

Bailey (Fall 1996)
8" • #9199-06 • TJ
Issued: 1996 • Retired: 1997
Orig. Price: $26 • **Value: $46**

12

Bailey (Spring 1997)
8" • #9199-07 • TJ
Issued: 1997 • Retired: 1998
Orig. Price: $27 • **Value: $45**

Bears

	Price Paid	Value
1.		
2.		
3.		
4.		
5.		
6.		
7.		
8.		
9.		
10.		
11.		
12.		
Totals		

1

Bailey (Fall 1997)
8" • #9199-08 • TJ
Issued: 1997 • Retired: 1998
Orig. Price: $27 • **Value: $38**

2

Bailey (Spring 1998)
8" • #9199-09 • TJ
Issued: 1998 • Retired: 1999
Orig. Price: $27 • **Value: $38**

3

Bailey (Fall 1998)
8" • #9199-10 • TJ
Issued: 1998 • Retired: 1999
Orig. Price: $27 • **Value: $35**

4

Bailey (Spring 1999)
8" • #9199-11 • TJ
Issued: 1999 • Retired: 1999
Orig. Price: $27 • **Value: $35**

5

Bailey With Dottie (Fall 1999)
8" • #9199-12 • TJ
Issued: 1999 • Retired: 1999
Orig. Price: $30 • **Value: N/E**

6

Bailey (Spring 2000)
8" • #9199-14 • TJ
Issued: 2000 • Retired: 2000
Orig. Price: $27 • **Value: $33**

Bears

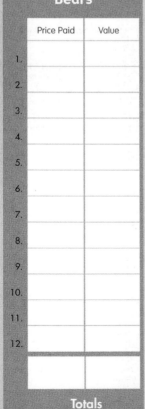

	Price Paid	Value
1.		
2.		
3.		
4.		
5.		
6.		
7.		
8.		
9.		
10.		
11.		
12.		
Totals		

7

Bailey (Fall 2000)
8" • #9199-15 • TJ
Issued: 2000 • To Be Retired: 2001
Orig. Price: $30 • **Value: $30**

8
New

Bailey (Spring 2001)
8" • #9199-16 • TJ
Issued: 2001 • To Be Retired: 2001
Orig. Price: $30 • **Value: $30**

9

Bailey & Matthew (w/resin ornaments, Fall 1996)
8" & 8" • #9224 • TJ
Issued: 1996 • Retired: 1996
Orig. Price: $70 • **Value: $85**

10

Bailey & Matthew (w/resin ornaments, Fall 1997)
8" & 8" • #9225 • TJ
Issued: 1997 • Retired: 1997
Orig. Price: $70 • **Value: $92**

11

Bailey & Matthew (w/resin ornaments, Fall 1998)
8" & 8" • #9227 • TJ
Issued: 1998 • Retired: 1998
Orig. Price: $71 • **Value: $85**

12

Bailey & Matthew (w/resin ornaments, Fall 1999)
8" & 8" • #9228 • TJ
Issued: 1999 • Retired: 1999
Orig. Price: $70 • **Value: $74**

1

Bailey & Matthew (w/resin ornaments, Fall 2000)
8" & 8" • #9229 • TJ
Issued: 2000 • To Be Retired: 2001
Orig. Price: $67 • **Value: $67**

2

Baldwin
5.5" • #5718 • AS
Issued: 1992 • Retired: 1999
Orig. Price: $7 • **Value: $25**

3

Barnaby B. Bean
10" • #5150-03 • JB
Issued: 1994 • Retired: 1999
Orig. Price: $16 • **Value: $30**

4

Bartholemew B. Bean
10" • #5103 • JB
Issued: 1992 • Retired: 1998
Orig. Price: $14 • **Value: $33**

5
New

Bashful T. Bearhugs
10" • #82004 • LS
Issued: 2001 • To Be Retired: 2001
Orig. Price: $19 • **Value: $19**

6

Baxter B. Bean
8" • #5151-05 • JB
Issued: 1994 • Retired: 1999
Orig. Price: $12 • **Value: $22**

7

Bea Bear
info unavailable
Orig. Price: N/A • **Value: N/E**

8

Bear-Among-Bears
16" • #5050 • N/A
Issued: pre-1990 • Retired: N/A
Orig. Price: N/A • **Value: $430**

9

Bear-Among-Bears
16" • #5051 • N/A
Issued: pre-1990 • Retired: N/A
Orig. Price: N/A • **Value: N/E**

10

Photo Unavailable

Bear-Among-Bears
info unavailable
Orig. Price: N/A • **Value: N/E**

11

Bear-Let
8" • #5020 • WB
Issued: pre-1990 • Retired: 1992
Orig. Price: $9 • **Value: $140**

12

Bear-Let
8" • #5021 • N/A
Issued: pre-1990 • Retired: N/A
Orig. Price: N/A • **Value: N/E**

Bears

	Price Paid	Value
1.		
2.		
3.		
4.		
5.		
6.		
7.		
8.		
9.		
10.		
11.		
12.		
Totals		

Value Guide — Boyds Plush Animals

1

Bearly-A-Bear
10" • #5030 • WB
Issued: pre-1990 • Retired: 1992
Orig. Price: $13 • **Value: $185**

2

Bearly-A-Bear
10" • #5031 • WB
Issued: pre-1990 • Retired: 1991
Orig. Price: $13 • **Value: $140**

3

Bears' Bear
12" • #5040 • WB
Issued: pre-1990 • Retired: 1992
Orig. Price: $18 • **Value: $285**

4

Bears' Bear
12" • #5041 • WB
Issued: pre-1990 • Retired: 1992
Orig. Price: $18 • **Value: $275**

5

Beatrice
14" • #6168 • TJ
Issued: 1991 • Retired: 1991
Orig. Price: $63 • **Value: $475**

6

Becky
6" • #91395 • TJ
Issued: 1995 • Retired: 1999
Orig. Price: $11 • **Value: $22**

7

Becky
6" • #91395-01 • TJ
Issued: 1996 • Retired: 1999
Orig. Price: $11 • **Value: $24**

8

Bedford B. Bean
10" • #5121-08 • JB
Issued: 1996 • Retired: 1996
Orig. Price: $14 • **Value: $65**

9

Photo Unavailable

Benjamin
10" • #9159 • TJ
Issued: 1993 • Retired: 1994
Orig. Price: $20 • **Value: $50**

10

Bennington W. Bruin
16" • #510400-08 • JB
Issued: 2000 • Current
Orig. Price: $26 • **Value: $26**

11
New

Bernadette DeBearvoire
6" • #918443 • TJ
Issued: 2001 • Current
Orig. Price: $13 • **Value: $13**

12

Berrybear
14" • #5762 • HD
Issued: 1992 • Retired: 1994
Orig. Price: $27 • **Value: $250**

Bears

	Price Paid	Value
1.		
2.		
3.		
4.		
5.		
6.		
7.		
8.		
9.		
10.		
11.		
12.		
Totals		

1

Bess W. Pattington
14" • #92001-02 • AR
Issued: 1999 • Retired: 1999
Orig. Price: $40 • **Value: $48**

2

Bethany Bearington
8" • #590053-01 • MB
Issued: 2000 • To Be Retired: 2001
Orig. Price: $27 • **Value: $27**

3

Bethany Thistlebeary
6" • #913955 • TJ
Issued: 1999 • To Be Retired: 2001
Orig. Price: $13 • **Value: $13**

4

Betsey
6" • #913952 • TJ
Issued: 1997 • Retired: 2000
Orig. Price: $13 • **Value: $22**

5

Betsie B. Jodibear
9" • #92000-07 • AR
Issued: 2000 • To Be Retired: 2001
Orig. Price: $21 • **Value: $21**

6

Bianca T. Witebred
8" • #912076 • TJ
Issued: 1998 • Retired: 1999
Orig. Price: $19 • **Value: $28**

7

Biff Grizzwood
14" • #912617 • TJ
Issued: 2000 • To Be Retired: 2001
Orig. Price: $30 • **Value: $30**

8

Big Ben Bearhugs
40" • #500050-05 • JB
Issued: 2000 • Retired: 2000
Orig. Price: $209 • **Value: N/E**

9

Big Boy
5.5" • #9108 • TJ
Issued: 1995 • Retired: 1997
Orig. Price: $12 • **Value: $50**

10

Billy Bob Bruin With Froggie
14" • #912622 • TJ
Issued: 2000 • To Be Retired: 2001
Orig. Price: $31 • **Value: $31**

11

Billy Ray
9" • #5850 • BB
Issued: 1992 • Retired: 1997
Orig. Price: $14 • **Value: $46**

12

Billy Ray Beanster With Petey Poker
16" • #900207 • UB
Issued: 1999 • Retired: 2000
Orig. Price: $51 • **Value: $56**

Bears

	Price Paid	Value
1.		
2.		
3.		
4.		
5.		
6.		
7.		
8.		
9.		
10.		
11.		
12.		
Totals		

1

Binkie B. Bear
16" • #5115 • JB
Issued: pre-1990 • Retired: 1993
Orig. Price: $27 • **Value: $110**

2

Binkie B. Bear II
16" • #5115 • JB
Issued: 1994 • Retired: 1996
Orig. Price: $27 • **Value: $80**

3

Bixby Trufflebeary
12" • #56390-10 • BA
Issued: 1999 • To Be Retired: 2001
Orig. Price: $16 • **Value: $16**

4

BJ Bearricane
12" • #83003 • JJ
Issued: 2000 • Retired: 2000
Orig. Price: $23 • **Value: $30**

5

Blackstone
6" • #5840-07 • GB
Issued: 1997 • Retired: 1999
Orig. Price: $9 • **Value: $26**

6

Blanche de Bearvoire
6" • #91841 • TJ
Issued: 1996 • Retired: 1999
Orig. Price: $9 • **Value: $24**

Bears

	Price Paid	Value
1.		
2.		
3.		
4.		
5.		
6.		
7.		
8.		
9.		
10.		
11.		
Totals		

7

Blinkin
18" • #5807 • SB
Issued: 1991 • Retired: 1992
Orig. Price: $32 • **Value: $210**

8

Bluebeary
8" • #56421-06 • BA
Issued: 1998 • Retired: 2000
Orig. Price: $11 • **Value: $24**

9

Bobbie Jo
12" • #5853 • BB
Issued: 1992 • Retired: 1997
Orig. Price: $20 • **Value: $55**

10

Bonnie
6" • #913951 • TJ
Issued: 1997 • Retired: 2000
Orig. Price: $13 • **Value: $23**

11

Boris Berriman
6" • #918021 • TJ
Issued: 1998 • To Be Retired: 2001
Orig. Price: $12 • **Value: $12**

1

Bosley
8.5" • #91561 • TJ
Issued: 1997 • Retired: 1999
Orig. Price: $12 • **Value: $24**

2

Bradley Boobear
8" • #919610 • TJ
Issued: 1998 • Retired: 1999
Orig. Price: $13 • **Value: $22**

3

Bradshaw P. Beansford
14" • #51091-08 • JB
Issued: 1999 • Retired: 1999
Orig. Price: $20 • **Value: $25**

4

Brady Bearimore
10" • #918321 • TJ
Issued: 2000 • Current
Orig. Price: $28 • **Value: $28**

5

Braxton B. Bear
14" • #51081-08 • JB
Issued: 1998 • To Be Retired: 2001
Orig. Price: $20 • **Value: $20**

6

Breezy T. Frostman
8" • #91522 • TJ
Issued: 1999 • Retired: 2000
Orig. Price: $13 • **Value: N/E**

7

Breven B. Bearski With Willie Waddlewalk
14" • #900206 • UB
Issued: 1999 • Retired: 2000
Orig. Price: $49 • **Value: N/E**

8

Brewin
10" • #5802 • SB
Issued: 1992 • Retired: 1995
Orig. Price: $20 • **Value: $80**

9

Brewin
10" • #5806 • SB
Issued: 1991 • Retired: 1991
Orig. Price: N/A • **Value: $80**

10

Brewster T. Bear
14" • #912627 • TJ
Issued: 2000 • Current
Orig. Price: $25 • **Value: $25**

11

Brianna Tippeetoes
6" • #913959 • TJ
Issued: 2000 • Current
Orig. Price: $13 • **Value: $13**

12

Bristol B. Windsor
8" • #57052-03 • AS
Issued: 2000 • Current
Orig. Price: $13 • **Value: $13**

Bears

	Price Paid	Value
1.		
2.		
3.		
4.		
5.		
6.		
7.		
8.		
9.		
10.		
11.		
12.		
Totals		

1

Bromley Q. Bear
8" • #5151-03 • JB
Issued: 1998 • Retired: 1999
Orig. Price: $13 • **Value: $24**

2

Brooke B. Bearsley
10" • #917400 • TJ
Issued: 2000 • Current
Orig. Price: $20 • **Value: $20**

3

Bruce
8" • #1000-08 • CC
Issued: 1993 • Retired: 1999
Orig. Price: $6 • **Value: $23**

4

Bruce
8" • #9157-08 • TJ
Issued: 1993 • Retired: 1994
Orig. Price: $14 • **Value: $68**

5

Bruce
8" • #98038 • TJ
Issued: 1996 • Retired: 1997
Orig. Price: $13 • **Value: $36**

6

Bruinhilda Von Bruin
6" • #5010-03 • WB
Issued: 1994 • Retired: 1995
Orig. Price: $12 • **Value: $56**

7

Bubba
16" • #5856 • BB
Issued: 1992 • Retired: 1997
Orig. Price: $27 • **Value: $60**

8

Buckingham
21" • #57221 • AS
Issued: 1997 • Retired: 1999
Orig. Price: $55 • **Value: N/E**

9

Buckley
8" • #9104 • TJ
Issued: 1995 • Retired: 1996
Orig. Price: $16 • **Value: $56**

10
New

Buddy
12" • #600000 • HF
Issued: 2001 • Current
Orig. Price: $19 • **Value: $19**

11

Buffington Fitzbruin
10" • #912031 • TJ
Issued: 1997 • Retired: 1998
Orig. Price: $20 • **Value: $39**

Bears

	Price Paid	Value
1.		
2.		
3.		
4.		
5.		
6.		
7.		
8.		
9.		
10.		
11.		
Totals		

1

Buffy
12" • #5639-10 • BA
Issued: 1995 • Retired: 1996
Orig. Price: $16 • **Value: $55**

2

Bumbershoot B. Jodibear
8" • #92000-03 • AR
Issued: 1999 • Retired: 2000
Orig. Price: $20 • **Value: $26**

3

Bumble B. Buzzoff
8" • #91773 • TJ
Issued: 2000 • Current
Orig. Price: $17 • **Value: $17**

4

Bundles B. Joy & Blankie
12" • #56391-04 • BA
Issued: 2000 • Current
Orig. Price: $23 • **Value: $23**

5

Burke P. Bear
14" • #5109-05 • JB
Issued: 1997 • Current
Orig. Price: $20 • **Value: $20**

6

Burl
10" • #91761 • TJ
Issued: 1996 • Retired: 1998
Orig. Price: $20 • **Value: $38**

7

Burlington P. Beanster
16" • #510400-07 • JB
Issued: 1999 • To Be Retired: 2001
Orig. Price: $26 • **Value: $26**

8
New

Buster McRind
8" • #915503 • TJ
Issued: 2001 • Current
Orig. Price: $15 • **Value: $15**

9

Buttercup C. Snicklefritz
9" • #51760-12 • BY
Issued: 1999 • Retired: 1999
Orig. Price: $12 • **Value: $18**

10
New

Buttercup Pufflefluff
14" • #56398-12 • BA
Issued: 2001 • Current
Orig. Price: $26 • **Value: $26**

11

Buzz B. Bean
10" • #5120 • JB
Issued: pre-1990 • Retired: 1990
Orig. Price: N/A • **Value: $200**

12

Buzzby
8" • #9143 • TJ
Issued: 1994 • Retired: 1995
Orig. Price: $18 • **Value: $69**

Bears

	Price Paid	Value
1.		
2.		
3.		
4.		
5.		
6.		
7.		
8.		
9.		
10.		
11.		
12.		
Totals		

1

C.Z. Comet
8" • #917308 • TJ
Issued: 2000 • Retired: 2000
Orig. Price: $16 • **Value: $22**

2

Photo Unavailable

Cabin Bear
info unavailable
Orig. Price: N/A • **Value: N/E**

3

Cagney
8" • #9189-01 • TJ
Issued: 1994 • Retired: 1996
Orig. Price: $20 • **Value: $66**

4
New

Cal Doubleplay
9" • #917710 • TJ
Issued: 2001 • Current
Orig. Price: $24 • **Value: $24**

5

Caledonia
6" • #5840-01 • GB
Issued: 1997 • To Be Retired: 2001
Orig. Price: $9 • **Value: $9**

6

Callaghan
8" • #5704 • AS
Issued: 1990 • Retired: 1996
Orig. Price: $12 • **Value: $60**

7

Calvin Ellis
8" • #91223 • TJ
Issued: 1996 • Retired: 1997
Orig. Price: $18 • **Value: $35**

8

Cambridge Q. Bearrister
12" • #57003-08 • AS
Issued: 2000 • Retired: 2000
Orig. Price: $20 • **Value: N/E**

9

Camille du Bear
6" • #91804 • TJ
Issued: 1996 • Retired: 1999
Orig. Price: $9 • **Value: $32**

10

Canute
6" • #9136 • TJ
Issued: 1994 • Retired: 1996
Orig. Price: $12 • **Value: $50**

11

Carmella de Bearvoire
6" • #918401 • TJ
Issued: 1999 • Current
Orig. Price: $9 • **Value: $9**

Bears

	Price Paid	Value
1.		
2.		
3.		
4.		
5.		
6.		
7.		
8.		
9.		
10.		
11.		
Totals		

1

Caroline Mayflower
6" • #913958 • TJ
Issued: 2000 • Current
Orig. Price: $14 • **Value: $14**

2

Carter M. Bearington
10" • #590050-08 • MB
Issued: 1998 • Retired: 1999
Orig. Price: $31 • **Value: $55**

3

Cavendish
12" • #5701-02 • AS
Issued: 1994 • Retired: 1996
Orig. Price: $20 • **Value: $53**

4

Cecil
5.5" • #5726 • AS
Issued: 1993 • Retired: 1996
Orig. Price: $7 • **Value: $33**

5

Chamberlain
16" • #5709 • AS
Issued: 1990 • Retired: 1992
Orig. Price: $32 • **Value: $155**

6

Chamomille Q. Quignapple
10" • #91004 • TJ
Issued: 1997 • Retired: 2000
Orig. Price: $24 • **Value: $32**

7

Chan
6" • #9153 • TJ
Issued: 1994 • Retired: 1998
Orig. Price: $12 • **Value: $32**

8

Chanel de la Plumtete
6" • #9184 • TJ
Issued: 1995 • Retired: 1999
Orig. Price: $9 • **Value: $18**

9

Chase Bearimore
6" • #913930 • TJ
Issued: 2000 • Current
Orig. Price: $15 • **Value: $15**

10

Chauncey Fitzbruin
6" • #912033 • TJ
Issued: 1997 • Retired: 1999
Orig. Price: $12 • **Value: $25**

11

Chipper
8" • #5642-05 • BA
Issued: 1996 • Retired: 1997
Orig. Price: $11 • **Value: $28**

12

Christian
8" • #9190 • TJ
Issued: 1992 • Retired: 2000
Orig. Price: $18 • **Value: $29**

Bears

	Price Paid	Value
1.		
2.		
3.		
4.		
5.		
6.		
7.		
8.		
9.		
10.		
11.		
12.		
Totals		

Value Guide — Boyds Plush Animals

1

Christmas Bear
info unavailable
Orig. Price: N/A • **Value: N/E**

2

Christopher
10" • #9161 • TJ
Issued: 1993 • Retired: 1998
Orig. Price: $20 • **Value: $40**

3

Chuck Woodbeary
10" • #917366 • TJ
Issued: 2000 • Current
Orig. Price: $24 • **Value: $24**

4

Churchill
12" • #5700 • AS
Issued: 1990 • Retired: 1999
Orig. Price: $20 • **Value: $85**

5

Claire
10" • #9179 • TJ
Issued: 1994 • Retired: 1998
Orig. Price: $20 • **Value: $35**

6

Clara
14" • #911061 • TJ
Issued: 1996 • Retired: 1998
Orig. Price: $20 • **Value: $35**

Bears

	Price Paid	Value
1.		
2.		
3.		
4.		
5.		
6.		
7.		
8.		
9.		
10.		
11.		
12.		
Totals		

7

Clarissa
16" • #91202 • TJ
Issued: 1996 • Retired: 1999
Orig. Price: $58 • **Value: $82**

8

Clark S. Bearhugs
6" • #918055 • TJ
Issued: 2000 • Retired: 2000
Orig. Price: $10 • **Value: $15**

9

Cleason
10" • #5121N • JB
Issued: 1992 • Retired: 1996
Orig. Price: $14 • **Value: $40**

10
New

Clem Cladiddlebear
30" • #500070-08 • JB
Issued: 2001 • Current
Orig. Price: $59 • **Value: $59**

11

Clement
16" • #5710 • AS
Issued: 1990 • Retired: 1992
Orig. Price: $32 • **Value: $130**

12

Clementine
6" • #913953 • TJ
Issued: 1998 • To Be Retired: 2001
Orig. Price: $12 • **Value: $12**

1

Cleveland G. Bearington
12" • #590042-03 • MB
Issued: 2000 • To Be Retired: 2001
Orig. Price: $48 • **Value: $48**

2

Clinton B. Bean
14" • #5109 • JB
Issued: 1993 • Retired: 1998
Orig. Price: $20 • **Value: $42**

3

Clover L. Buzzoff
10" • #91772 • TJ
Issued: 1999 • To Be Retired: 2001
Orig. Price: $18 • **Value: $18**

4

Coco
10" • #5121 • JB
Issued: 1991 • Retired: 1995
Orig. Price: $14 • **Value: $47**

5

Colette Dubeary
6" • #918439 • TJ
Issued: 2000 • Current
Orig. Price: $10 • **Value: $10**

6

Colleen O'Bruin
6" • #91805 • TJ
Issued: 1995 • Retired: 1997
Orig. Price: $12 • **Value: $38**

7

Constance
16" • #91202-01 • TJ
Issued: 1998 • Retired 2000
Orig. Price: $48 • **Value: $53**

8
New

Cooper T. Wishkabibble
8" • #90502 • TJ
Issued: 2001 • Current
Orig. Price: $18 • **Value: $18**

9

Corey Allen Bearsmoore
14" • #912616 • TJ
Issued: 2000 • Current
Orig. Price: $31 • **Value: $31**

10

Cori Beariburg
8.5" • #915211 • TJ
Issued: 2000 • To Be Retired: 2001
Orig. Price: $14 • **Value: $14**

11

Corinna
16" • #91201 • TJ
Issued: 1996 • Retired: 1999
Orig. Price: $45 • **Value: $56**

12

Corinna II
16" • #912011 • TJ
Issued: 1997 • Retired: 1998
Orig. Price: $45 • **Value: $90**

Bears

	Price Paid	Value
1.		
2.		
3.		
4.		
5.		
6.		
7.		
8.		
9.		
10.		
11.		
12.		
Totals		

1

Cornwallis
16" • #9126 • TJ
Issued: 1994 • Retired: 1996
Orig. Price: $45 • **Value: $85**

2

Cornwallis
16" • #9126-01 • TJ
Issued: 1996 • Retired: 1997
Orig. Price: $53 • **Value: $78**

3

Courtney
16" • #912021 • TJ
Issued: 1997 • Retired: 2000
Orig. Price: $45 • **Value: $56**

4

Cranberry N. Bear
8.5" • #500100-02 • JB
Issued: 2000 • Current
Orig. Price: $9 • **Value: $9**

5

Craxton B. Bean
10" • #510300-11 • JB
Issued: 1998 • To Be Retired: 2001
Orig. Price: $14 • **Value: $14**

6

D.L. Merrill
16" • #51100-05 • JB
Issued: 1999 • Retired: 2000
Orig. Price: $29 • **Value: $32**

7
New

Daisy Bloomengrows
6" • #913964 • TJ
Issued: 2001 • Current
Orig. Price: $14 • **Value: $14**

8

Darby Beariburg
6" • #913960 • TJ
Issued: 2000 • Current
Orig. Price: $12 • **Value: $12**

9

Daryl Bear
16" • #5114 • JB
Issued: pre-1990 • Retired: 1993
Orig. Price: $27 • **Value: $185**

10
New

Dawson B. Bearsworth
16" • #57150-08 • AS
Issued: 2001 • Current
Orig. Price: $30 • **Value: $30**

11

Delaney And The Duffer (LE-500)
N/A • N/A • N/A
Issued: 1993 • Retired: 1994
Orig. Price: $74 • **Value: $290**

12

Delanie B. Beansford
16" • #51101-10 • JB
Issued: 1999 • Retired: 2000
Orig. Price: $29 • **Value: $32**

Bears

	Price Paid	Value
1.		
2.		
3.		
4.		
5.		
6.		
7.		
8.		
9.		
10.		
11.		
12.		
Totals		

1

Delbert Quignapple
10" • #91003 • TJ
Issued: 1996 • Retired: 2000
Orig. Price: $24 • **Value: N/E**

2

Delmarva V. Crackenpot
10" • #91002 • TJ
Issued: 1997 • Retired: 1999
Orig. Price: $29 • **Value: $40**

3

Denton P. Jodibear
9" • #92000-06 • AR
Issued: 1999 • To Be Retired: 2001
Orig. Price: $20 • **Value: $20**

4

Derry O. Beary
6.5" • #57252-05 • AS
Issued: 2000 • Current
Orig. Price: $8 • **Value: $8**

5

Desdemona T. Witebred
10" • #912075 • TJ
Issued: 1997 • Retired: 1998
Orig. Price: $21 • **Value: $33**

6

Devin Fallsbeary
14" • #912621 • TJ
Issued: 1999 • To Be Retired: 2001
Orig. Price: $40 • **Value: $40**

7

Dexter
8" • #91331 • TJ
Issued: 1996 • Retired: 1998
Orig. Price: $25 • **Value: $45**

8

Photo Unavailable

Diana (w/boy cub)
info unavailable
Orig. Price: N/A • **Value: N/E**

9

Photo Unavailable

Diana (w/girl cub)
info unavailable
Orig. Price: N/A • **Value: N/E**

10

Dilly McDoodle
9" • #51710-12 • BY
Issued: 1999 • Retired: 1999
Orig. Price: $8 • **Value: $16**

11

Dink
16" • #5641 • BA
Issued: 1992 • Retired: 1994
Orig. Price: $21 • **Value: $52**

12

Dink
16" • #5641-08 • BA
Issued: 1995 • Retired: 1997
Orig. Price: $24 • **Value: $45**

Bears

	Price Paid	Value
1.		
2.		
3.		
4.		
5.		
6.		
7.		
8.		
9.		
10.		
11.		
12.		
Totals		

1

Disreali
5.5" • #5716 • AS
Issued: 1991 • Retired: 1993
Orig. Price: $7 • **Value: $86**

2

Doolittle Buckshot
12" • #51200-08 • JB
Issued: 1999 • To Be Retired 2001
Orig. Price: $20 • **Value: $20**

3

Doomoore Buckshot
13" • #51200-03 • JB
Issued: 2000 • Current
Orig. Price: $20 • **Value: $20**

4

Dover D. Windsor
8" • #57051-03 • AS
Issued: 2000 • Current
Orig. Price: $13 • **Value: $13**

5

Dufus Bear
16" • #5112 • JB
Issued: pre-1990 • Retired: 1997
Orig. Price: $27 • **Value: $52**

6

Dunston J. Bearsford
6" • #57251-07 • AS
Issued: 1999 • Retired: 2000
Orig. Price: $8 • **Value: $22**

7

Dwight D. Bearington
6" • #590081-03 • MB
Issued: 2000 • To Be Retired: 2001
Orig. Price: $14 • **Value: $14**

8

Eastwick Bearington
4.5" • #590101 • MB
Issued: 1999 • Retired: 2000
Orig. Price: $11 • **Value: $25**

9
New

Ebenezer S. Jodibear
9" • #92000-09 • AR
Issued: 2000 • Current
Orig. Price: $23 • **Value: $23**

10

Eddie Beanberger
(formerly "Eddie Beanbauer")
10" • #9119 • TJ
Issued: 1995 • Retired: 1999
Orig. Price: $27 • **Value: $43**

11

Eddie Beanberger
10" • #9119-01 • TJ
Issued: 1996 • Retired: 1997
Orig. Price: $30 • **Value: $45**

Bears

	Price Paid	Value
1.		
2.		
3.		
4.		
5.		
6.		
7.		
8.		
9.		
10.		
11.		
Totals		

1

Eden
5.5" • #5708 • AS
Issued: 1990 • Retired: 1996
Orig. Price: $7 • **Value: $32**

2

Eden
6" • #9139 • TJ
Issued: 1994 • Retired: 1996
Orig. Price: $13 • **Value: $45**

3

Eden II
6" • #91391 • TJ
Issued: 1996 • Retired: 1997
Orig. Price: $13 • **Value: $32**

4

Edmund (Fall 1993)
8" • #9175 • TJ
Issued: 1993 • Retired: 1994
Orig. Price: N/A • **Value: $290**

5

Edmund (Spring 1994)
8" • #9175-01 • TJ
Issued: 1994 • Retired: 1995
Orig. Price: $26 • **Value: $155**
Variation: black & white shirt
Value: $235

6

Edmund (Fall 1994)
8" • #9175-02 • TJ
Issued: 1994 • Retired: 1995
Orig. Price: $24 • **Value: $145**

7

Edmund (Spring 1995)
8" • #9175-03 • TJ
Issued: 1995 • Retired: 1996
Orig. Price: $24 • **Value: $62**

8

Edmund (Fall 1995)
8" • #9175-04 • TJ
Issued: 1995 • Retired: 1996
Orig. Price: $24 • **Value: $53**

9

Edmund (Spring 1996)
8" • #9175-05 • TJ
Issued: 1996 • Retired: 1997
Orig. Price: $26 • **Value: $50**

10

Edmund (Fall 1996)
8" • #9175-06 • TJ
Issued: 1996 • Retired: 1997
Orig. Price: $24 • **Value: $45**

11

Edmund (Spring 1997)
8" • #9175-07 • TJ
Issued: 1997 • Retired: 1998
Orig. Price: $24 • **Value: $40**

12

Edmund (Fall 1997)
8" • #9175-08 • TJ
Issued: 1997 • Retired: 1998
Orig. Price: $24 • **Value: $37**

Bears

	Price Paid	Value
1.		
2.		
3.		
4.		
5.		
6.		
7.		
8.		
9.		
10.		
11.		
12.		
Totals		

1

Edmund (Spring 1998)
8" • #9175-09 • TJ
Issued: 1998 • Retired: 1999
Orig. Price: $26 • **Value: $39**

2

Edmund (Fall 1998)
8" • #9175-10 • TJ
Issued: 1998 • Retired: 1999
Orig. Price: $27 • **Value: $35**

3

Edmund (Spring 1999)
8" • #9175-11 • TJ
Issued: 1999 • Retired: 1999
Orig. Price: $26 • **Value: $39**

4

Edmund (Fall 1999)
8" • #9175-12 • TJ
Issued: 1999 • Retired: 1999
Orig. Price: $27 • **Value: $35**

5

Edmund (Spring 2000)
8" • #9175-14 • TJ
Issued: 2000 •Retired: 2000
Orig. Price: $26 • **Value: $33**

6

Edmund (Fall 2000)
8" • #9175-15 • TJ
Issued: 2000 • To Be Retired: 2001
Orig. Price: $26 • **Value: $26**

7
New

Edmund (Spring 2001)
8" • #9175-16 • TJ
Issued: 2001 • To Be Retired: 2001
Orig. Price: $25 • **Value: $25**

8
New

Egbert Q. Bearsford
10" • #81510 • HQ
Issued: 2001 • To Be Retired: 2001
Orig. Price: $20 • **Value: $20**

9

Einstein Q. ScaredyBear
10" • #917368 • TJ
Issued: 2000 • Current
Orig. Price: $28 • **Value: $28**

10

Eldora
14" • #91615 • TJ
Issued: 1996 • Retired: 1998
Orig. Price: $31 • **Value: $48**

11

Photo Unavailable

Eleanor Bear (set/3, Eleanor, baby and chair)
N/A • #6102 • TJ
Issued: 1990 • Retired: 1990
Orig. Price: N/A • **Value: $575**

12

Eleanore Bearsevelt
16" • #912010 • TJ
Issued: 2000 • Current
Orig. Price: $58 • **Value: $58**

Bears

	Price Paid	Value
1.		
2.		
3.		
4.		
5.		
6.		
7.		
8.		
9.		
10.		
11.		
12.		
Totals		

1

Elfwood Bearington
4.5" • #590100 • MB
Issued: 1999 • Retired: 2000
Orig. Price: $11 • **Value: $23**

2

Elgin
6.5" • #9129 • TJ
Issued: 1994 • Retired: 1997
Orig. Price: $12 • **Value: $30**

3

Elijah Bearringer
14" • #912073 • TJ
Issued: 2000 • Current
Orig. Price: $31 • **Value: $31**

4

Elliot B. Bean
14" • #5108 • JB
Issued: pre-1990 • Retired: 1998
Orig. Price: $20 • **Value: $37**

5

Elly Mae
9" • #5850-10 • BB
Issued: 1995 • Retired: 1997
Orig. Price: $14 • **Value: $43**

6

Elmer O. Bearroad
12" • #911931 • TJ
Issued: 2000 • To Be Retired: 2001
Orig. Price: $27 • **Value: $27**

7

Elmore Flatski
8" • #5680-08 • FL
Issued: 1995 • Retired: 1997
Orig. Price: $13 • **Value: $36**

8

Eloise Willoughby
6" • #918402 • TJ
Issued: 1999 • Retired: 2000
Orig. Price: $14 • **Value: $24**

9

Elsworth
12" • #1107-05 • CC
Issued: 1997 • Retired: 1999
Orig. Price: $12 • **Value: $23**

10

Elton Elfberg
10" • #917306 • TJ
Issued: 1997 • Retired: 1998
Orig. Price: $21 • **Value: $33**

11

Elvin Q. Elfberg
10" • #917301 • TJ
Issued: 1997 • Retired: 1999
Orig. Price: $25 • **Value: $33**

12

Emma
14" • #9101 • TJ
Issued: 1995 • Retired: 1997
Orig. Price: $27 • **Value: $60**

Bears

	Price Paid	Value
1.		
2.		
3.		
4.		
5.		
6.		
7.		
8.		
9.		
10.		
11.		
12.		
Totals		

Value Guide — Boyds Plush Animals

1

Emmett Elfberg
10" • #917305 • TJ
Issued: 1996 • Retired: 1999
Orig. Price: $21 • **Value: $28**

2

Emmie Bramblebeary
14" • #912628 • TJ
Issued: 2000 • Current
Orig. Price: $35 • **Value: $35**

3

Emmy Lou
10" • #91001 • TJ
Issued: 1996 • Retired: 1999
Orig. Price: $24 • **Value: $35**

4

Endora Spellbound
10" • #81004 • BB
Issued: 2000 • Retired: 2000
Orig. Price: $27 • **Value: $38**

5

Erin K. Bear
7" • #91562 • TJ
Issued: 1996 • Retired: 1999
Orig. Price: $11 • **Value: $27**

6

Essex
12" • #5701-10 • AS
Issued: 1994 • Retired: 1996
Orig. Price: $20 • **Value: $40**

7

Ethan
9" • #917322 • TJ
Issued: 1998 • Retired: 1999
Orig. Price: $21 • **Value: $42**

8

Ethel B. Bruin
12" • #912051 • TJ
Issued: 1997 • Retired: 1998
Orig. Price: $25 • **Value: $45**

9

Eudemia Q. Quignapple
9" • #91006 • TJ
Issued: 1997 • Retired: 1999
Orig. Price: $16 • **Value: $30**

10

Eugenia
16" • #9120 • TJ
Issued: 1994 • Retired: 1996
Orig. Price: $45 • **Value: $80**

11

Eugenia The Apple Seller
16" • #9120-01 • AS
Issued: 1995 • Retired: 1995
Orig. Price: $53 • **Value: $120**

Bears

	Price Paid	Value
1.		
2.		
3.		
4.		
5.		
6.		
7.		
8.		
9.		
10.		
11.		
Totals		

1

Eunice P. Snowbeary
9" • #9137-01 • TJ
Issued: 1997 • Retired: 1999
Orig. Price: $20 • **Value: $32**

2

Evelyn
10" • #91614 • TJ
Issued: 1997 • Retired: 1998
Orig. Price: $24 • **Value: $50**

3

Everest
8.5" • #5844-05 • GB
Issued: 1996 • Retired: 1999
Orig. Price: $17 • **Value: $30**

4

Ewell
8" • #9127 • TJ
Issued: 1994 • Retired: 1999
Orig. Price: $17 • **Value: $25**

5
New

F.E.B.B. First Ever Bean Bear
10" • #510001-08 • PE
Issued: 2001 • Current
Orig. Price: $14 • **Value: $14**

6

Fairbanks
6" • #58070-10 • AS
Issued: 2000 • Current
Orig. Price: $8 • **Value: $8**

7

Father Chrisbear
info unavailable
Orig. Price: N/A • **Value: $195**

8

Photo Unavailable

Father Christmas
info unavailable
Orig. Price: N/A • **Value: N/E**

9

Father Christmas
info unavailable
Orig. Price: N/A • **Value: N/E**

10

Father Kristmas
16" • #917310-01 • TJ
Issued: 2000 • Retired: 2000
Orig. Price: $30 • **Value: $40**

11

Federico
11" • #1100-08 • CC
Issued: 1993 • Retired: 1997
Orig. Price: $10 • **Value: $32**

12

Federico
11" • #98039 • TJ
Issued: 1996 • Retired: 1997
Orig. Price: $21 • **Value: $45**

Bears

	Price Paid	Value
1.		
2.		
3.		
4.		
5.		
6.		
7.		
8.		
9.		
10.		
11.		
12.		
Totals		

1
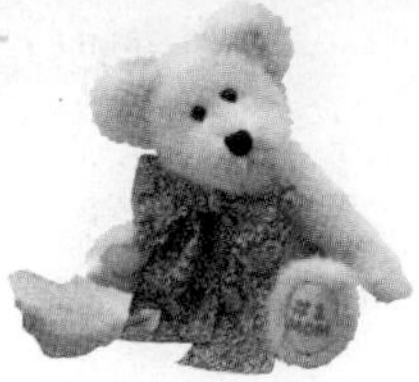
Felicity N. Hugs
10" • #510301-01 • MM
Issued: 2000 • Retired: 2000
Orig. Price: $11 • **Value: $20**

2

Felicity S. Elfberg
5.5" • #917300 • TJ
Issued: 1997 • Retired: 1998
Orig. Price: $13 • **Value: $28**

3

Fetchen P. Patch
12" • #81005 • BB
Issued: 2000 • Retired: 2000
Orig. Price: $27 • **Value: $34**

4

Fidelity B. Morgan IV
17" • #5110-05 • JB
Issued: 1997 • Retired: 1999
Orig. Price: $29 • **Value: $40**

5

Fifi Farklefrost
9" • #91361 • TJ
Issued: 2000 • Current
Orig. Price: $20 • **Value: $20**

6

Fiona Fitzbruin
14" • #91203 • TJ
Issued: 1997 • Retired: 1998
Orig. Price: $26 • **Value: $42**

7

Fitz Farklefrost
6" • #91360 • TJ
Issued: 2000 • Current
Orig. Price: $13 • **Value: $13**

8

Fitzgerald D. Bearington
12" • #590040-03 • MB
Issued: 1997 • Retired: 1997
Orig. Price: $48 • **Value: $77**

9

Fitzgerald O'Bruin
6" • #91802 • TJ
Issued: 1995 • Retired: 1997
Orig. Price: $12 • **Value: $32**

10

Fitzroy
N/A • #5795 • TJ
Issued: 1992 • Retired: 1992
Orig. Price: $18 • **Value: $76**

11

Fitzroy
7.5" • #9195 • TJ
Issued: 1992 • Retired: 1994
Orig. Price: $16 • **Value: $65**

12

Fleurette
12" • #6103B • AS
Issued: 1991 • Retired: 1991
Orig. Price: N/A • **Value: N/E**

Bears

	Price Paid	Value
1.		
2.		
3.		
4.		
5.		
6.		
7.		
8.		
9.		
10.		
11.		
12.		
Totals		

1
New

Flora B. Flutterby
10" • #917720 • TJ
Issued: 2001 • Current
Orig. Price: $18 • **Value: $18**

2

Floyd
9" • #917321 • TJ
Issued: 1998 • Retired: 1999
Orig. Price: $21 • **Value: $32**

3

Foodle McDoodle
9" • #51710-05 • BY
Issued: 1999 • Retired: 2000
Orig. Price: $8 • **Value: $12**

4

Forrest B. Bearsley
10" • #91744 • TJ
Issued: 1999 • To Be Retired: 2001
Orig. Price: $20 • **Value: $20**

5

Francesca LaFlame
16" • #912026 • TJ
Issued: 2000 • Current
Orig. Price: $59 • **Value: $59**

6

Franklin
8" • #1050-06 • DB
Issued: 1995 • Retired: 1996
Orig. Price: $11 • **Value: $58**

7

Franz Von Bruin
6" • #5010-06 • WB
Issued: 1994 • Retired: 1995
Orig. Price: $10 • **Value: $48**

8

Freddy Beanberger
10" • #911901 • TJ
Issued: 1998 • Retired: 1998
Orig. Price: $27 • **Value: $42**

9

Freezy T. Frostman
6" • #913962 • TJ
Issued: 2000 • Current
Orig. Price: $13 • **Value: $13**

10
New

G.P. Hugabunch
8" • #903000 • TJ
Issued: 2001 • Current
Orig. Price: $14 • **Value: $14**

11

Gabriel
9" • #5825 • CB
Issued: 1991 • Retired: 1997
Orig. Price: $14 • **Value: $53**

12

Photo Unavailable

Gardner
N/A • #6162B • TJ
Issued: 1991 • Retired: 1991
Orig. Price: $63 • **Value: N/E**

Bears

	Price Paid	Value
1.		
2.		
3.		
4.		
5.		
6.		
7.		
8.		
9.		
10.		
11.		
12.		
Totals		

1

Gary M. Bearenthal
16" • #912500 • TJ
Issued: 1999 • To Be Retired: 2001
Orig. Price: $53 • **Value: $53**

2

General P.D.Q. Pattington
14.5" • #92001-05 • AR
Issued: 2000 • To Be Retired: 2001
Orig. Price: $41 • **Value: $41**

3

Geneva
8" • #9162 • TJ
Issued: 1994 • Retired: 1994
Orig. Price: $18 • **Value: $105**

4

George
11" • #1100-03 • CC
Issued: 1996 • Retired: 1997
Orig. Price: $10 • **Value: $36**

5

Geraldo
8" • #912441 • TJ
Issued: 1996 • Retired: 1997
Orig. Price: $19 • **Value: $36**

6

Ginger Snap
8" • #91523 • TJ
Issued: 2000 • Current
Orig. Price: $18 • **Value: $18**

Bears

	Price Paid	Value
1.		
2.		
3.		
4.		
5.		
6.		
7.		
8.		
9.		
10.		
11.		
12.		
Totals		

7

Ginnie Higgenthorpe
6" • #918442 • TJ
Issued: 2000 • To Be Retired: 2001
Orig. Price: $10 • **Value: $11**

8
New

Ginnie Witebred
14" • #912074 • TJ
Issued: 2001 • Current
Orig. Price: $34 • **Value: $34**

9

Gladstone
12" • #5701 • AS
Issued: 1990 • Retired: 1993
Orig. Price: $20 • **Value: $110**

10

Glenda
12" • #91891-04 • TJ
Issued: 1998 • Retired: 1999
Orig. Price: $21 • **Value: $30**

11
New

Gloria Bearsevelt
14" • #912631 • TJ
Issued: 2001 • Current
Orig. Price: $38 • **Value: $38**

12

Glynnis
8" • #918910-02 • TJ
Issued: 1998 • Retired: 1999
Orig. Price: $17 • **Value: $23**

1

Goober Padoodle
6" • #517010-05 • BY
Issued: 1999 • Retired: 2000
Orig. Price: $5 • **Value: $15**

2

Gorden B. Bean
10" • #5105 • JB
Issued: pre-1990 • Retired: 1998
Orig. Price: $14 • **Value: $50**

3

Photo Unavailable

Grace
N/A • #6163B • TJ
Issued: 1991 • Retired: 1991
Orig. Price: $63 • **Value: N/E**

4

Grace
10" • #91742 • TJ
Issued: 1997 • Retired: 1998
Orig. Price: $20 • **Value: $30**

5

Grace Bedlington
16" • #912072 • TJ
Issued: 1999 • Retired: 2000
Orig. Price: $40 • **Value: $45**

6

Gram
18" • #5775 • HD
Issued: 1991 • Retired: 1991
Orig. Price: $39 • **Value: $300**

7

Gramps
18" • #5770 • HD
Issued: 1991 • Retired: 1991
Orig. Price: $39 • **Value: $340**

8

Photo Unavailable

Grandma Bearburg
14" • N/A • N/A
Issued: 1992 • Retired: 1992
Orig. Price: N/A • **Value: N/E**

9

Grenville
16" • #5715 • AS
Issued: 1992 • Retired: 1999
Orig. Price: $32 • **Value: $73**

10
New

Griffin W. Bearsley
21" • #572210-08 • AS
Issued: 2001 • Current
Orig. Price: $55 • **Value: $55**

11

Grover
8" • #91739 • TJ
Issued: 1997 • Retired: 1998
Orig. Price: $12 • **Value: $23**

12

Grumps
9" • #5766 • HD
Issued: 1991 • Retired: 1994
Orig. Price: $14 • **Value: $76**

Bears

	Price Paid	Value
1.		
2.		
3.		
4.		
5.		
6.		
7.		
8.		
9.		
10.		
11.		
12.		
Totals		

1

Guinevere
12" • #91891-09 • TJ
Issued: 1996 • Retired: 1999
Orig. Price: $21 • **Value: $32**

2

Gunnar
8" • #9123 • TJ
Issued: 1995 • Retired: 1996
Orig. Price: $24 • **Value: $38**

3

Gunther Von Bruin
6" • #5012 • WB
Issued: 1993 • Retired: 1994
Orig. Price: N/A • **Value: $135**

4

Gus Ghoulie
12" • #919640 • TJ
Issued: 1999 • Retired: 1999
Orig. Price: $20 • **Value: $50**

5

Gustav Von Bruin
10" • #5011 • WB
Issued: 1993 • Retired: 1994
Orig. Price: $21 • **Value: $60**

6

Gwain
12" • #91891-06 • TJ
Issued: 1997 • Retired: 1999
Orig. Price: $21 • **Value: $24**

Bears

	Price Paid	Value
1.		
2.		
3.		
4.		
5.		
6.		
7.		
8.		
9.		
10.		
11.		
12.		
Totals		

7

Gwen Marie Bear
12" • #912055 • TJ
Issued: 2000 • Current
Orig. Price: $27 • **Value: $27**

8

Gwendina
11" • #91891-12 • TJ
Issued: 1999 • Retired: 1999
Orig. Price: $21 • **Value: $30**

9

Gwendolyn
12" • #91891-02 • TJ
Issued: 1997 • Retired: 1999
Orig. Price: $21 • **Value: $30**

10

Gwinton
8" • #918910-06 • TJ
Issued: 1998 • Retired: 1999
Orig. Price: $17 • **Value: $30**

11

Gwynda
8" • #918910-09 • TJ
Issued: 1998 • Retired: 1999
Orig. Price: $17 • **Value: $28**

12
New

H.B. Bearwish
8" • #903003 • TJ
Issued: 2001 • Current
Orig. Price: $14 • **Value: $14**

1

Hadley Flatski
8" • #5680-05 • FL
Issued: 1994 • Retired: 1997
Orig. Price: $12 • **Value: $30**

2

Hampton T. Bearington
10" • #590052-08 • MB
Issued: 2000 • To Be Retired: 2001
Orig. Price: $36 • **Value: $36**

3

Hancock
8" • #1050-11 • DB
Issued: 1995 • Retired: 1996
Orig. Price: $11 • **Value: $45**

4

Hans Q. Berriman
6" • #91392 • TJ
Issued: 1997 • Retired: 1999
Orig. Price: $13 • **Value: $32**

5

Harding
8" • #1051-06 • DB
Issued: 1996 • Retired: 1998
Orig. Price: $13 • **Value: $31**

6

Harding G. Bearington
10" • #590051-01 • MB
Issued: 1999 • Retired: 1999
Orig. Price: $28 • **Value: $40**

7

Harrison
10" • #9176 • TJ
Issued: 1993 • Retired: 1997
Orig. Price: $20 • **Value: $38**

8

Harry S. Pattington
16" • #92001-01 • AR
Issued: 1999 • Retired: 1999
Orig. Price: $45 • **Value: $48**

9

Hartley B. Mine
8.5" • #91521 • TJ
Issued: 1999 • Retired: 2000
Orig. Price: $14 • **Value: $24**

10

Hastings P. Bearsford
6" • #57250-11 • AS
Issued: 2000 • Retired: 2000
Orig. Price: $7 • **Value: N/E**

11

Photo Unavailable

Hattie & Annie
info unavailable
Orig. Price: N/A • **Value: N/E**

12

Hawley Flatski
8" • #56801-03 • FL
Issued: 1998 • Retired: 1999
Orig. Price: $13 • **Value: $18**

Bears

	Price Paid	Value
1.		
2.		
3.		
4.		
5.		
6.		
7.		
8.		
9.		
10.		
11.		
12.		
Totals		

1

Hayden T. Bearsford
6" • #57250-10 • AS
Issued: 2000 • To Be Retired: 2001
Orig. Price: $7 • **Value: $7**

2

Hazel
8" • #1000-03 • CC
Issued: 1993 • Retired: 1996
Orig. Price: $6 • **Value: $36**

3

Hazelnut B. Bean
8.25" • #500100-05 • JB
Issued: 2000 • To Be Retired: 2001
Orig. Price: $7 • **Value: $9**

4

Heath
10" • #5703 • AS
Issued: 1990 • Retired: 1992
Orig. Price: $18 • **Value: $105**

5

Heath II
10" • #5703N • AS
Issued: 1992 • Retired: 1997
Orig. Price: $18 • **Value: $30**

6

Hemingway K. Grizzman
14" • #91263 • TJ
Issued: 1999 • To Be Retired: 2001
Orig. Price: $40 • **Value: $40**

7

Henley Fitzhampton
6" • #912034 • TJ
Issued: 1999 • To Be Retired: 2001
Orig. Price: $13 • **Value: $13**

8

Henry
8" • #1000-05 • CC
Issued: 1993 • Retired: 1995
Orig. Price: $6 • **Value: $45**

9

Henson
10" • #58011-05 • SB
Issued: 1998 • Retired: 2000
Orig. Price: $20 • **Value: $40**

10

Herbert Henry Jodibear
9" • #92000-05 • AR
Issued: 1999 • To Be Retired: 2001
Orig. Price: $20 • **Value: $20**

11
New

Herbie Bearlove
6" • #82001 • LS
Issued: 2001 • To Be Retired: 2001
Orig. Price: $10 • **Value: $10**

12

Hermine Grisslin
16" • #91206 • TJ
Issued: 1995 • Retired: 1997
Orig. Price: $45 • **Value: $66**

Bears

	Price Paid	Value
1.		
2.		
3.		
4.		
5.		
6.		
7.		
8.		
9.		
10.		
11.		
12.		
Totals		

1

Hershal
16" • #5125 • JB
Issued: 1991 • Retired: 1992
Orig. Price: $27 • **Value: $145**

2

Hillary B. Bean
14" • #5123-10 • JB
Issued: 1993 • Retired: 1998
Orig. Price: $20 • **Value: $30**

3

Hockley
16" • #5640 • BA
Issued: 1992 • Retired: 1996
Orig. Price: $21 • **Value: $55**

4

Homer
14" • #5760 • HD
Issued: 1991 • Retired: 1994
Orig. Price: $27 • **Value: $225**

5

Photo Unavailable

Homer
N/A • #6166B • TJ
Issued: 1991 • Retired: 1991
Orig. Price: $63 • **Value: $180**

6

Homer
8" • #9177 • TJ
Issued: 1993 • Retired: 1996
Orig. Price: $26 • **Value: $52**

7

Honey P. Snicklefritz (musical)
8" • #51760-08 • BY
Issued: 1999 • Retired: 1999
Orig. Price: $12 • **Value: $20**

8

Honeypot
14" • #5761 • HD
Issued: 1991 • Retired: 1994
Orig. Price: $27 • **Value: $200**

9

Hubbard W. Growler
12" • #5721-01 • AS
Issued: 1997 • Retired: 1998
Orig. Price: $21 • **Value: $40**

10

Huck
6" • #918051 • TJ
Issued: 1996 • Retired: 1998
Orig. Price: $12 • **Value: $33**

11
New

Hucklebeary B. Bear
8.25" • #500100-06 • JB
Issued: 2001 • Current
Orig. Price: $9 • **Value: $9**

Bears

	Price Paid	Value
1.		
2.		
3.		
4.		
5.		
6.		
7.		
8.		
9.		
10.		
11.		
Totals		

1
New

Huggleby B. Bearikind
8" • #82003 • LS
Issued: 2001 • To Be Retired: 2001
Orig. Price: $10 • **Value: $10**

2

Humboldt
6" • #5840-05 • GB
Issued: 1996 • To Be Retired: 2001
Orig. Price: $9 • **Value: $9**

3

Hume
info unavailable
Orig. Price: N/A • **Value: $210**

4
New

Humphrey T. Bigfoot
18" • #51110-05 • JB
Issued: 2001 • Current
Orig. Price: $40 • **Value: $40**

5
New

Huney
16" • #600001 • HF
Issued: 2001 • Current
Orig. Price: $29 • **Value: $29**

6

Huney B. Keeper
9" • #91774 • TJ
Issued: 2000 • To Be Retired: 2001
Orig. Price: $24 • **Value: $24**

7

Hunter Bearsdale With Greenspan
14" & 5" • #912625 • TJ
Issued: 2000 • Retired: 2000
Orig. Price: $32 • **Value: $38**

8

Hurshel
12" • #5639-05 • BA
Issued: 1996 • Retired: 1999
Orig. Price: $16 • **Value: $26**

9
New

Ido Loveya
8" • #903004 • TJ
Issued: 2001 • Current
Orig. Price: $14 • **Value: $14**

10

Isaiah
10" • #917304 • TJ
Issued: 1996 • Retired: 1998
Orig. Price: $19 • **Value: $42**

11

J.B. Bean
10" • #5106 • JB
Issued: pre-1990 • Retired: 1997
Orig. Price: $14 • **Value: $38**

12

J.P. Huttin III
17" • #5110-08 • JB
Issued: 1995 • Retired: 1998
Orig. Price: $29 • **Value: $45**

Bears

	Price Paid	Value
1.		
2.		
3.		
4.		
5.		
6.		
7.		
8.		
9.		
10.		
11.		
12.		
Totals		

1

J.P. Locksley
12" • #57002-08 • AS
Issued: 1999 • Retired: 2000
Orig. Price: $20 • **Value: $26**

2

Jackson R. Bearington
16" • #590021-05 • MB
Issued: 1998 • Retired: 1999
Orig. Price: $100 • **Value: $160**

3

Jameson J. Bearsford
6" • #57251-10 • AS
Issued: 1999 • Retired: 2000
Orig. Price: $8 • **Value: $22**

4
New

Jasper McBobble
10" • #510305-05 • JB
Issued: 2001 • Current
Orig. Price: $15 • **Value: $15**

5

Jaxton D. Bear
10" • #510300-10 • JB
Issued: 2000 • To Be Retired: 2001
Orig. Price: $14 • **Value: $14**

6

Jed Bruin
14" • #5123W • JB
Issued: 1992 • Retired: 1992
Orig. Price: $20 • **Value: $108**

7

Jefferson
8" • #1050-02 • DB
Issued: 1995 • Retired: 1996
Orig. Price: $11 • **Value: $52**

8

Jesse
11" • #1100-05 • CC
Issued: 1993 • Retired: 1995
Orig. Price: $10 • **Value: $62**

9

Jethro
9" • #5630 • BA
Issued: 1995 • Retired: 1997
Orig. Price: $10 • **Value: $37**

10
New

Jocelyn Bloomengrows
16" • #912012 • TJ
Issued: 2001 • Current
Orig. Price: $58 • **Value: $58**

11

Jody
16" • #5641-09 • BA
Issued: 1995 • Retired: 1996
Orig. Price: $24 • **Value: $44**

12

John
13" • #5828 • CB
Issued: 1992 • Retired: 1997
Orig. Price: $20 • **Value: $48**

Bears

	Price Paid	Value
1.		
2.		
3.		
4.		
5.		
6.		
7.		
8.		
9.		
10.		
11.		
12.		

Totals

1

Joshua
9" • #5826 • CB
Issued: 1992 • Retired: 1997
Orig. Price: $14 • **Value: $36**

2

Julia Angelbrite
10" • #91776 • TJ
Issued: 2000 • Current
Orig. Price: $19 • **Value: $19**

3

Juliella T. Frostfire
8" • #83002 • JJ
Issued: 2000 • Retitred: 2000
Orig. Price: $15 • **Value: $25**

4

Juliet S. Bearlove
12" • #912651 • FH
Issued: 2000 • Retired: 2000
Orig. Price: $24 • **Value: $40**

5

Karen A. Mulberry
10" • #917364 • TJ
Issued: 2000 • Current
Orig. Price: $23 • **Value: $23**

6

Karla Mulbeary
8" • #915500 • TJ
Issued: 1999 • Retired: 2000
Orig. Price: $18 • **Value: $30**

7

Katie B. Berrijam
10" • #910062 • TJ
Issued: 1999 • To Be Retired: 2001
Orig. Price: $23 • **Value: $23**

8

Photo Unavailable

Katy Bear
info unavailable
Orig. Price: N/A • **Value: N/E**

9

Kayla Mulbeary
6" • #913941 • TJ
Issued: 1999 • To Be Retired: 2001
Orig. Price: $14 • **Value: $14**

10

Kelly O. Beary
6.5" • #57252-08 • AS
Issued: 2000 • Current
Orig. Price: $8 • **Value: $8**

11

Kelsey M. Jodibear With Arby B. Tugalong
7.5" • #900209 • UB
Issued: 1999 • Retired: 2000
Orig. Price: $61 • **Value: $66**

12

Kemper Forbes
16" • #51102-03 • JB
Issued: 2000 • Current
Orig. Price: $29 • **Value: $29**

Bears

	Price Paid	Value
1.		
2.		
3.		
4.		
5.		
6.		
7.		
8.		
9.		
10.		
11.		
12.		
Totals		

1

Kevin G. Bearsley
10" • #917362 • TJ
Issued: 2000 • Retired: 2000
Orig. Price: $23 • **Value: $30**

2

Kip
8" • #5642-08 • BA
Issued: 1993 • Retired: 1997
Orig. Price: $11 • **Value: $34**

3

Klaus Von Fuzzner
14" • #91262 • TJ
Issued: 1998 • To Be Retired: 2001
Orig. Price: $40 • **Value: $40**

4

Klondike
14" • #912820 • TJ
Issued: 2000 • Retired 2000
Orig. Price: $27 • **Value: $43**

5

Knut V. Berriman
8" • #91231 • TJ
Issued: 1997 • Retired: 1999
Orig. Price: $24 • **Value: $33**

6

Kookie Snicklefritz
10" • #51770-12 • BY
Issued: 2000 • Current
Orig. Price: $14 • **Value: $14**

7

Kringle Bear
10" • #9163 • TJ
Issued: 1993 • Retired: 1996
Orig. Price: $19 • **Value: $60**

8

Kringle Bear
14" • #9191 • TJ
Issued: 1993 • Retired: 1996
Orig. Price: $27 • **Value: $85**

9

Kyle L. Berriman
10" • #917401 • TJ
Issued: 2000 • To Be Retired: 2001
Orig. Price: $20 • **Value: $20**

10

Lacy
10" • #6100B • TJ
Issued: pre-1990 • Retired: 1992
Orig. Price: $16 • **Value: $115**

11

Lacy
10" • #6100DB • TJ
Issued: pre-1990 • Retired: 1991
Orig. Price: N/A • **Value: $122**

12

Lacy
14" • #6101B • TJ
Issued: pre-1990 • Retired: 1992
Orig. Price: $21 • **Value: $150**

Bears

	Price Paid	Value
1.		
2.		
3.		
4.		
5.		
6.		
7.		
8.		
9.		
10.		
11.		
12.		
Totals		

1

Lacy
14" • #6101DB • TJ
Issued: pre-1990 • Retired: 1991
Orig. Price: N/A • **Value: $135**

2

Lady B. Bug
10" • #91775 • TJ
Issued: 2000 • Current
Orig. Price: $20 • **Value: $20**

3

Lady B. Lovebug
5" • #595104 • TF
Issued: 2000 • Retired: 2000
Orig. Price: $9 • **Value: $25**

4

Lancaster
8" • #57051-08 • AS
Issued: 1998 • Retired: 2000
Orig. Price: $13 • **Value: $19**

5

Lancelot
21" • #5722-11 • AS
Issued: 1996 • Retired: 1999
Orig. Price: $53 • **Value: N/E**

6

Lars
8" • #91735 • TJ
Issued: 1996 • Retired: 1997
Orig. Price: $18 • **Value: $32**

7

Latte O. Bear
8.25" • #500100-01 • JB
Issued: 2000 • Current
Orig. Price: $9 • **Value: $9**

8

Laurel S. Berrijam
6" • #913954 • TJ
Issued: 1999 • Retired: 2000
Orig. Price: $13 • **Value: $25**

9
New

Leiselle Bloomengrows
8" • #915502 • TJ
Issued: 2001 • Current
Orig. Price: $17 • **Value: $17**

10

Lem Bruin
14" • #5123 • JB
Issued: pre-1990 • Retired: 1993
Orig. Price: $20 • **Value: $123**

11

Leo Bruinski
10" • #918320 • TJ
Issued: 1998 • Retired: 2000
Orig. Price: $31 • **Value: $38**

12

Leon
8" • #1001-08 • CC
Issued: 1993 • Retired: 1999
Orig. Price: $6 • **Value: $22**

Bears

	Price Paid	Value
1.		
2.		
3.		
4.		
5.		
6.		
7.		
8.		
9.		
10.		
11.		
12.		
Totals		

1

Libby B. Bunster
10" • #916502 • TJ
Issued: 2000 • Retired 2000
Orig. Price: $20 • **Value: $50**

2

Lillian K. Bearsley
10" • #91743 • TJ
Issued: 1998 • To Be Retired: 2001
Orig. Price: $20 • **Value: $20**

3

Lincoln B. Bearington
16" • #590022-08 • MB
Issued: 1999 • Retired: 1999
Orig. Price: $100 • **Value: $138**

4

Linkin
6" • #5811 • SB
Issued: 1992 • Retired: 1995
Orig. Price: $7 • **Value: $60**

5

Lisa T. Bearringer
16" • #911950 • TJ
Issued: 1998 • To Be Retired: 2001
Orig. Price: $58 • **Value: $58**

6
New

Little Bearpeep And Friends
12" • #912056 • TJ
Issued: 2001 • Current
Orig. Price: $46 • **Value: $46**

7

Liza J. Berrijam
10" • #910061 • TJ
Issued: 1999 • To Be Retired: 2001
Orig. Price: $17 • **Value: $17**

8

Lizzie McBee
8" • #91005 • TJ
Issued: 1996 • Retired: 1997
Orig. Price: $20 • **Value: $43**

9

Lizzie Wishkabibble
10" • #50002 • TJ
Issued: 2000 • Retired: 2000
Orig. Price: $20 • **Value: $42**

10

Lloyd
10" • #5714 • AS
Issued: 1991 • Retired: 1992
Orig. Price: $18 • **Value: $225**

11

Logan Fremont
8" • #919611 • TJ
Issued: 1999 • Retired: 2000
Orig. Price: $13 • **Value: $24**

12

Lois B. Bearlove
6" • #913956 • TJ
Issued: 2000 • Retired: 2000
Orig. Price: $13 • **Value: $20**

Bears

	Price Paid	Value
1.		
2.		
3.		
4.		
5.		
6.		
7.		
8.		
9.		
10.		
11.		
12.		
Totals		

1

Lou Bearig
6" • #91771-06 • TJ
Issued: 1998 • Retired: 2000
Orig. Price: $14 • **Value: $35**

2

Louella
10" • #91242 • TJ
Issued: 1996 • Retired: 1998
Orig. Price: $24 • **Value: $50**

3

Louie B. Bear
16" • #5114-11 • JB
Issued: 1995 • Retired: 1997
Orig. Price: $27 • **Value: $46**

4

Lydia Fitzbruin
14" • #9182 • TJ
Issued: 1993 • Retired: 1996
Orig. Price: $27 • **Value: $85**

5

Lynette Bearlove
6" • #918433 • TJ
Issued: 2000 • Retired 2000
Orig. Price: $10 • **Value: $48**

6

MacMillan
8" • #5705-10 • AS
Issued: 1995 • Retired: 1997
Orig. Price: $13 • **Value: $30**

7
New

Macy Sunbeary
16" • #911952 • TJ
Issued: 2001 • Current
Orig. Price: $41 • **Value: $41**

8

Madeline Willoughby
10" • #918333 • TJ
Issued: 1999 • To Be Retired: 2001
Orig. Price: $30 • **Value: $30**

9

Madison L. Bearington
6" • #590080-08 • MB
Issued: 1997 • Retired: 1997
Orig. Price: $18 • **Value: $42**

10
New

Mae B. Bearlove
6" • #82002 • LS
Issued: 2001 • To Be Retired: 2001
Orig. Price: $11 • **Value: $11**

11

Major
10" • #5717 • AS
Issued: 1991 • Retired: 1992
Orig. Price: $18 • **Value: $95**

12

Major II
10" • #5703B • AS
Issued: 1992 • Retired: 1995
Orig. Price: $18 • **Value: $46**

Bears

	Price Paid	Value
1.		
2.		
3.		
4.		
5.		
6.		
7.		
8.		
9.		
10.		
11.		
12.		
Totals		

1

Malcolm
16" • #5711 • AS
Issued: 1992 • Retired: 1999
Orig. Price: $32 • **Value: $50**

2

Margaret T. Pattington
12" • #92001-03 • AR
Issued: 1999 • Retired: 1999
Orig. Price: $32 • **Value: $42**

3

Margarita
14" • #911062 • TJ
Issued: 1998 • To Be Retired: 2001
Orig. Price: $20 • **Value: $20**

4

Marie B. Bearlove
14" • #912626 • MM
Issued: 2000 • Retired: 2000
Orig. Price: $10 • **Value: $45**

5

Maris G. Pattington
12" • #92001-04 • AR
Issued: 2000 • To Be Retired: 2001
Orig. Price: $49 • **Value: $49**

6

Marla Sprucebeary
8" • #915501 • TJ
Issued: 2000 • Current
Orig. Price: $20 • **Value: $20**

7

Marlowe Snoopstein
11" • #91871 • TJ
Issued: 1999 • Retired: 2000
Orig. Price: $23 • **Value: $38**

8
New

Martha S. McBruin
10" • #910063 • TJ
Issued: 2001 • Current
Orig. Price: $29 • **Value: $29**

9

Marvin P. Snowbeary
6" • #9136-01 • TJ
Issued: 1997 • Retired: 2000
Orig. Price: $12 • **Value: $20**

10

Matilda
N/A • #6161B • TJ
Issued: 1991 • Retired: 1991
Orig. Price: $63 • **Value: N/E**

11

Matthew (Fall 1996)
8" • #91756 • TJ
Issued: 1996 • Retired: 1997
Orig. Price: $26 • **Value: $44**

12

Matthew (Fall 1997)
8" • #91756-08 • TJ
Issued: 1997 • Retired: 1998
Orig. Price: $26 • **Value: $36**

Bears

	Price Paid	Value
1.		
2.		
3.		
4.		
5.		
6.		
7.		
8.		
9.		
10.		
11.		
12.		
Totals		

1

Matthew (Fall 1998)
8" • #91756-10 • TJ
Issued: 1998 • Retired: 1999
Orig. Price: $27 • **Value: $37**

2

Matthew (Fall 1999)
8" • #91756-12 • TJ
Issued: 1999 • Retired: 1999
Orig. Price: $26 • **Value: $35**

3

Matthew (Fall 2000)
8" • #91756-15 • TJ
Issued: 2000 • Retired 2000
Orig. Price: $26 • **Value: $32**

4

Matthew Bear
10" • #5070 • N/A
Issued: N/A • Retired: N/A
Orig. Price: N/A • **Value: N/E**

5

Matthew Bear (Anniversary Edition)
11" • N/A • N/A
Issued: 1999 • Retired: 1999
Orig. Price: $14 • **Value: $20**

6

Matthew H. Growler
12" • #5721 • AS
Issued: 1996 • Retired: 1999
Orig. Price: $21 • **Value: $50**

7

Maximillian
21" • #572210-05 • AS
Issued: 2000 • To Be Retired: 2001
Orig. Price: $55 • **Value: $55**

8

Maya Berriman
6" • #91394 • TJ
Issued: 1999 • To Be Retired: 2001
Orig. Price: $14 • **Value: $14**

9

McKenzie
6" • #5840-03 • GB
Issued: 1997 • To Be Retired: 2001
Orig. Price: $9 • **Value: $9**

10

McKinley
12" • #5848-05 • GB
Issued: 1996 • Retired: 1999
Orig. Price: $21 • **Value: $30**

11
New

McKinley Bearington
12" • #590043-01 • MB
Issued: 2001 • To Be Retired: 2001
Orig. Price: $52 • **Value: $52**

12

McMullen
12" • #5702 • AS
Issued: 1990 • Retired: 1991
Orig. Price: $20 • **Value: $160**

Bears

	Price Paid	Value
1.		
2.		
3.		
4.		
5.		
6.		
7.		
8.		
9.		
10.		
11.		
12.		
Totals		

1

McShamus O'Growler
9" • #91732 • TJ
Issued: 1997 • Retired: 1998
Orig. Price: $21 • **Value: $40**

2

Megan Berriman
14" • #912623 • TJ
Issued: 2000 • Current
Orig. Price: $32 • **Value: $32**

3
New

Melanie McRind
12" • #912658 • TJ
Issued: 2001 • Current
Orig. Price: $28 • **Value: $28**

4

Melbourne
12" • #5719 • AS
Issued: 1992 • Retired: 1994
Orig. Price: $20 • **Value: $80**

5

Melinda S. Willoughby
6" • #913961 • TJ
Issued: 2000 • Retired: 2000
Orig. Price: $12 • **Value: $20**

6

Memsy
12" • N/A • N/A
Issued: N/A • Retired: N/A
Orig. Price: N/A • **Value: $440**

7

Mercedes Fitzbruin
8" • #91204 • TJ
Issued: 1998 • To Be Retired: 2001
Orig. Price: $19 • **Value: $19**

8
New

Merci Bearcoo
8" • #903001 • TJ
Issued: 2001 • Current
Orig. Price: $14 • **Value: $14**

9

Meredith K. Pattington
14" • #900204 • UB
Issued: 1999 • Retired: 2000
Orig. Price: $116 • **Value: $125**

10
New

Meridian Wishkabibble
12" • #90500 • TJ
Issued: 2001 • Current
Orig. Price: $31 • **Value: $31**

11

Photo Unavailable

Merlin
N/A • #6167B • TJ
Issued: 1991 • Retired: 1991
Orig. Price: $63 • **Value: N/E**

12

Photo Unavailable

Mickey
8" • #9157-01 • TJ
Issued: 1993 • Retired: 1994
Orig. Price: $14 • **Value: $65**

Bears

	Price Paid	Value
1.		
2.		
3.		
4.		
5.		
6.		
7.		
8.		
9.		
10.		
11.		
12.		
Totals		

1

Mikayla Springbeary
14" • #912624 • TJ
Issued: 2000 • Retired: 2000
Orig. Price: $32 • **Value: N/E**

2

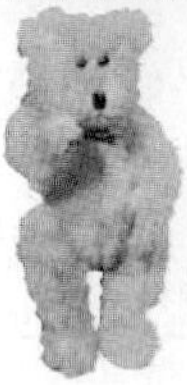

Milo
9" • #5767 • HD
Issued: 1992 • Retired: 1994
Orig. Price: $14 • **Value: $120**

3

Minnie Higgenthorpe
6" • #918441 • TJ
Issued: 1999 • Retired: 1999
Orig. Price: $10 • **Value: $23**

4

Photo Unavailable

Miss Ashley
info unavailable
Orig. Price: N/A • **Value: N/E**

5

Miss Hedda Bearimore
10" • #918453 • TJ
Issued: 2000 • Current
Orig. Price: $23 • **Value: $23**

6
New

Miss Macintosh
12" • #912652 • TJ
Issued: 2001 • Current
Orig. Price: $34 • **Value: $34**

7

Missy
8" • #5642-10 • BA
Issued: 1995 • Retired: 1996
Orig. Price: $11 • **Value: $45**

8

Mistle
8.5" • #5151-04 • JB
Issued: 1994 • Retired: 1997
Orig. Price: $12 • **Value: $43**

9

Mitchell Bearsdale
14" • #912615 • TJ
Issued: 1999 • To Be Retired: 2001
Orig. Price: $40 • **Value: $40**

10

Mohley
N/A • #5771 • HD
Issued: 1992 • Retired: 1992
Orig. Price: N/A • **Value: $135**

11

Photo Unavailable

Molly R. Berriman & Nathan
N/A • N/A • TJ
Issued: 2000 • Current
Orig. Price: N/A • **Value: N/E**

12

Momma McBear And Delmar
10" & 6" • #91007 • TJ
Issued: 1997 • Retired: 2000
Orig. Price: $25 • **Value: $40**

Bears

	Price Paid	Value
1.		
2.		
3.		
4.		
5.		
6.		
7.		
8.		
9.		
10.		
11.		
12.		
Totals		

1
New

Momma McNew And Huglsey
10" • #910021 • TJ
Issued: 2001 • Current
Orig. Price: $27 • **Value: $27**

2

Monroe J. Bearington
16" • #590023-11 • MB
Issued: 1999 • Retired: 2000
Orig. Price: $100 • **Value: $110**

3

Moriarity
11" • #9171 • TJ
Issued: 1993 • Retired: 1995
Orig. Price: $21 • **Value: $95**

4

Morris
8" • #1003-05 • CC
Issued: 1997 • Retired: 1999
Orig. Price: $7 • **Value: $20**

5

Mr. Baybeary
10" • #917314 • TJ
Issued: 2000 • Current
Orig. Price: $27 • **Value: $27**

6

Mr. BoJingles
14" • #91264 • TJ
Issued: 2000 • Current
Orig. Price: $20 • **Value: $20**

7
New

Mr. Everlove
12" • #912655 • TJ
Issued: 2001 • Current
Orig. Price: $39 • **Value: $39**

8

Mr. Jones
16" • #5869-08 • AR
Issued: 1997 • Retired: 1998
Orig. Price: $37 • **Value: $50**

9

Mr. McFarkle
14" • #912640• TJ
Issued: 2000 • Current
Orig. Price: $26 • **Value: $26**

10
New

Mr. McSnickers
14" • #912641 • TJ
Issued: 2001 • Current
Orig. Price: $30 • **Value: $30**

11

Mr. Noah and Friends
14" • #900100 •LE
Issued: 2000 • To Be Retired: 2001
Orig. Price: $61 • **Value: $61**

12

Mr. Smythe
12" • #58691-05 • AR
Issued: 1998 • Retired: 1998
Orig. Price: $27 • **Value: $43**

Bears

	Price Paid	Value
1.		
2.		
3.		
4.		
5.		
6.		
7.		
8.		
9.		
10.		
11.		
12.		
Totals		

1

Mr. Trumbull
10" • #918330 • TJ
Issued: 1998 • To Be Retired: 2001
Orig. Price: $25 • **Value: $25**

2

Mrs. Baybeary
10" • #917312 • TJ
Issued: 2000 • Current
Orig. Price: $30 • **Value: $30**

3

Photo Unavailable
Mrs. Bearberry
info unavailable
Orig. Price: N/A • **Value: N/E**

4

Photo Unavailable
Mrs. Bearburg
info unavailable
Orig. Price: N/A • **Value: $400**

5
New

Mrs. Everlove
12" • #912654 • TJ
Issued: 2001 • Current
Orig. Price: $39 • **Value: $39**

6

Mrs. Fezziwig Jodibear
9" • #92000-10 • AR
Issued: 2000 • Current
Orig. Price: $23 • **Value: $23**

7

Photo Unavailable
Mrs. Fiedler
info unavailable
Orig. Price: N/A • **Value: N/E**

8

Mrs. Mertz
10" • #918331 • TJ
Issued: 1999 • To Be Retired: 2001
Orig. Price: $30 • **Value: $30**

9

Mrs. Northstar
13" • #917303-03 • TJ
Issued: 1999 • Retired: 1999
Orig. Price: $31 • **Value: $70**

10

Mrs. Trumbull
10" • #91833 • TJ
Issued: 1998 • Current
Orig. Price: $30 • **Value: $30**

11

Muffin
8" • #56421-03 • BA
Issued: 1998 • Retired: 2000
Orig. Price: $11 • **Value: $18**

12

Nadia Berriman
10" • #917420 • TJ
Issued: 1999 • To Be Retired: 2001
Orig. Price: $30 • **Value: $30**

Bears

	Price Paid	Value
1.		
2.		
3.		
4.		
5.		
6.		
7.		
8.		
9.		
10.		
11.		
12.		

Totals

1
New

Nana Bearhugs
40" • #500050-08 • JB
Issued: 2001 • Current
Orig. Price: $209 • **Value: $209**

2

Nanette Dubeary
6" • #918432 • TJ
Issued: 2000 • Current
Orig. Price: $10 • **Value: $11**

3

Nanny Bear
info unavailable
Orig. Price: N/A • **Value: N/E**

4

Nantucket P. Bearington
4.5" • #590102 • MB
Issued: 2000 • Retired: 2000
Orig. Price: $11 • **Value: $18**

5

Naomi Bearlove
6" • #913957 • TJ
Issued: 2000 • To Be Retired: 2001
Orig. Price: $14 • **Value: $14**

6

Natasha Berriman
6" • #918050 • TJ
Issued: 1998 • To Be Retired: 2001
Orig. Price: $12 • **Value: $12**

7

Nellie
14" • #91105 • TJ
Issued: 1995 • Retired: 1997
Orig. Price: $20 • **Value: $48**

8

Nelson
16" • #91261 • TJ
Issued: 1997 • Retired: 1999
Orig. Price: $45 • **Value: $72**

9

Neville
5.5" • #5707 • AS
Issued: 1990 • Retired: 1999
Orig. Price: $7 • **Value: $30**

10

Newton
8" • #9133 • TJ
Issued: 1994 • Retired: 1996
Orig. Price: $25 • **Value: $50**

11

Nicholas
8" • #9173 • TJ
Issued: 1993 • Retired: 1997
Orig. Price: $20 • **Value: $45**

12

Nicholas Bearington
10" • #590107 • MB
Issued: 2000 • Retired: 2000
Orig. Price: $11 • **Value: N/E**

Bears

	Price Paid	Value
1.		
2.		
3.		
4.		
5.		
6.		
7.		
8.		
9.		
10.		
11.		
12.		
Totals		

1

Nicklas T. Jodibear
5" • #92000-12 • AR
Issued: 2000 • Retired: 2000
Orig. Price: $24 • **Value: $32**

2

Nickleby S. Claus
16" • #83005 • JJ
Issued: 2000 • Retired: 2000
Orig. Price: $31 • **Value: $38**

3

Niki
6" • #91730 • TJ
Issued: 1996 • Retired: 1997
Orig. Price: $13 • **Value: $33**

4

Niki II
6" • #91730-1 • TJ
Issued: 1998 • Retired: 2000
Orig. Price: $13 • **Value: $24**

5

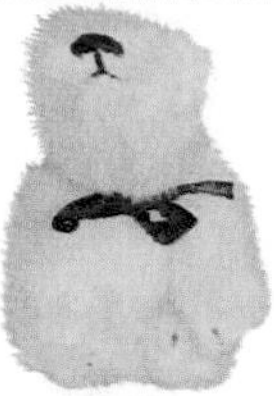

Nod
6" • #5810 • SB
Issued: 1991 • Retired: 1992
Orig. Price: $7 • **Value: $53**

6

Nod II
6" • #5810 • SB
Issued: 1992 • Retired: 1999
Orig. Price: $7 • **Value: $25**

7

Photo Unavailable

North Pole Bear
info unavailable
Orig. Price: N/A • **Value: N/E**

8
New

O. Howie Luvsya
12" • #82005 • LS
Issued: 2001 • To Be Retired: 2001
Orig. Price: $17 • **Value: $17**

9

Olaf
12" • #9138 • TJ
Issued: 1994 • Retired: 1996
Orig. Price: $27 • **Value: $50**

10

Photo Unavailable

Olivia Thornberry
info unavailable
Orig. Price: N/A • **Value: $80**

11

Omega T. Legacy & Alpha
16" & 5" • #900099 • LE
Issued: 1999 • Retired: 1999
Orig. Price: $70 • **Value: $78**

12

Ophelia
16" • #91207-01 • TJ
Issued: 1997 • Retired: 1997
Orig. Price: $40 • **Value: $63**

Bears

	Price Paid	Value
1.		
2.		
3.		
4.		
5.		
6.		
7.		
8.		
9.		
10.		
11.		
12.		
Totals		

1

Ophelia W. Witebred
16" • #91207 • TJ
Issued: 1996 • Retired: 1998
Orig. Price: $40 • **Value: $52**

2

Orville Bearington
4.5" • #590085-03 • MB
Issued: 1998 • Retired: 1999
Orig. Price: $10 • **Value: $23**

3

Otis B. Bean
14" • #5107 • JB
Issued: pre-1990 • Retired: 1997
Orig. Price: $20 • **Value: $57**

4

Otto Von Bruin
6" • #5010 • WB
Issued: 1992 • Retired: 1994
Orig. Price: $9 • **Value: $48**

5

Oxford T. Bearrister
12" • #57001-05 • AS
Issued: 1999 • Retired: 1999
Orig. Price: $20 • **Value: $27**

6

Paddy McDoodle
9" • #51710 • BY
Issued: 1998 • Retired: 2000
Orig. Price: $8 • **Value: $22**

7

Paige Willoughby
8" • #918351 • TJ
Issued: 2000 • Retired: 2000
Orig. Price: $19 • **Value: N/E**

8

Patches B. Beariluved
10" • #61000 • JB
Issued: 2000 • Current
Orig. Price: $18 • **Value: $18**

9

Patrick
8" • #9901 • TJ
Issued: 1995 • Retired: 1995
Orig. Price: $18 • **Value: $66**

10
New

Patrick Bearsevelt
6" • #913966 • TJ
Issued: 2001 • Current
Orig. Price: $13 • **Value: $13**

11

Patsy
10" • #9100 • TJ
Issued: 1995 • Retired: 1996
Orig. Price: $20 • **Value: $56**

12

Paxton P. Bean
10" • #510300-05 • JB
Issued: 1998 • To Be Retired: 2001
Orig. Price: $14 • **Value: $14**

Bears

	Price Paid	Value
1.		
2.		
3.		
4.		
5.		
6.		
7.		
8.		
9.		
10.		
11.		
12.		
Totals		

1

Peary
16" • #5807-10 • SB
Issued: 1998 • Retired: 2000
Orig. Price: $29 • **Value: $39**

2

Pendleton J. Bruin
16" • #510400-11 • JB
Issued: 1998 • Retired: 2000
Orig. Price: $27 • **Value: $35**

3

Photo Unavailable

Penny Whistlebeary
info unavailable
Orig. Price: N/A • **Value: $62**

4

Peppermint P. Bear
10" • #510305-01 • JB
Issued: 2000 • Retired: 2000
Orig. Price: $14 • **Value: $28**

5

Perceval
10" • #5703-08 • AS
Issued: 1992 • Retired: 1999
Orig. Price: $18 • **Value: $30**

6

Percy
5.5" • #5725-11 • AS
Issued: 1994 • To Be Retired: 2001
Orig. Price: $7 • **Value: $7**

7

Perriwinkle P. Snicklefritz (musical)
8" • #51760-06 • BY
Issued: 1999 • Retired: 1999
Orig. Price: $12 • **Value: $16**

8

Perry
8" • #1000-11 • CC
Issued: 1994 • Retired: 1997
Orig. Price: $6 • **Value: $30**

9
New

Peter Potter
12" • #515211-10 • JB
Issued: 2001 • Current
Orig. Price: $21 • **Value: $21**

10

Phillip Bear Hop
11" • #9189 • TJ
Issued: 1991 • Retired: 1992
Orig. Price: $27 • **Value: $365**

11

Philomena
14" • #91106 • TJ
Issued: 1995 • Retired: 1997
Orig. Price: $20 • **Value: $42**

12

Photo Unavailable

Pinecone
info unavailable
Orig. Price: N/A • **Value: N/E**

Bears

	Price Paid	Value
1.		
2.		
3.		
4.		
5.		
6.		
7.		
8.		
9.		
10.		
11.		
12.		
Totals		

1
New

Pipley McRind
6" • #913965 • TJ
Issued: 2001 • Current
Orig. Price: $13 • **Value: $13**

2

Pohley
9" • #5768 • HD
Issued: 1991 • Retired: 1994
Orig. Price: $14 • **Value: $155**

3

Polly Quignapple
10" • #910020 • TJ
Issued: 1999 • Current
Orig. Price: $27 • **Value: $27**

4

Poof Pufflebeary & Blankie
15" • #51780-03 • BA
Issued: 2000 • Current
Orig. Price: $24 • **Value: $26**

5

Pop Bruin
16" • #5124 • JB
Issued: pre-1990 • Retired: 1995
Orig. Price: $27 • **Value: $88**

6

Poppa Bear & Noelle
10" & 5.5" • #917302 • JB
Issued: 1997 • Retired: 1999
Orig. Price: $27 • **Value: $48**

7

Prudence Bearimore
12" • #912053 • TJ
Issued: 1999 • Current
Orig. Price: $31 • **Value: $31**

8

Puck
8" • #9172 • TJ
Issued: 1993 • Retired: 1997
Orig. Price: $17 • **Value: $44**

9

Punkie Boobear
10" • #919630 • TJ
Issued: 1999 • Retired: 2000
Orig. Price: $24 • **Value: $30**

10
New

Putnam P. Bearsley
6" • #57250-08 • AS
Issued: 2001 • Current
Orig. Price: $7 • **Value: $7**

11

Quaker O. Brimley
16" • #57150-10 • AS
Issued: 2000 • Current
Orig. Price: $32 • **Value: $32**

12

Quincy B. Bibbly
8.5" • #915611 • TJ
Issued: 1999 • Retired: 1999
Orig. Price: $12 • **Value: $15**

Bears

	Price Paid	Value
1.		
2.		
3.		
4.		
5.		
6.		
7.		
8.		
9.		
10.		
11.		
12.		
Totals		

Bears

Value Guide — Boyds Plush Animals

1

Rachel And B. Bearilove
10" • #910070 • TJ
Issued: 2000 • Retired: 2000
Orig. Price: $19 • **Value: $32**

2

Radcliffe Fitzbruin
16" • #912020 • TJ
Issued: 2000 • To Be Retired: 2001
Orig. Price: $45 • **Value: $45**

3

Raleigh
10" • #5703M • AS
Issued: 1994 • Retired: 1997
Orig. Price: $18 • **Value: $40**

4

Reagan V. Bearington
8" • #590070-05 • MB
Issued: 1997 • Retired: 1997
Orig. Price: $24 • **Value: $60**

5

Rebecca Bearimore
16" • #912028 • TJ
Issued: 2000 • Current
Orig. Price: $59 • **Value: $59**

6

Remington Braveheart
18" • #57210-05 • AS
Issued: 1999 • Retired: 1999
Orig. Price: $42 • **Value: $46**

7

Reva
9" • #5630-02 • BA
Issued: 1995 • Retired: 1997
Orig. Price: $10 • **Value: $32**

8

Rex
8" • #912440 • TJ
Issued: 1996 • Retired: 1998
Orig. Price: $18 • **Value: $30**

9

Rockwell B. Bruin
18" • #57211-05 • AS
Issued: 2000 • To Be Retired: 2001
Orig. Price: $41 • **Value: $41**

10

Rohley
9" • #5769 • HD
Issued: 1991 • Retired: 1992
Orig. Price: $14 • **Value: $165**

11

Roosevelt
14" • #6108B • JB
Issued: 1991 • Retired: 1992
Orig. Price: $27 • **Value: $220**

12

Roosevelt
8" • #9902 • TJ
Issued: 1995 • Retired: 1996
Orig. Price: $18 • **Value: $52**

Bears

	Price Paid	Value
1.		
2.		
3.		
4.		
5.		
6.		
7.		
8.		
9.		
10.		
11.		
12.		
Totals		

1

Roosevelt P. Bearington
16" • #590020-08 • MB
Issued: 1997 • Retired: 1997
Orig. Price: $100 • **Value: $165**

2

Ross G. Jodibear
9" • #92000-08 • AR
Issued: 2000 • To Be Retired: 2001
Orig. Price: $21 • **Value: $21**

3

Roxanne K. Bear
10" • #91741 • TJ
Issued: 1996 • Retired: 1998
Orig. Price: $20 • **Value: $30**

4

Royce
14" • #6107B • TJ
Issued: 1990 • Retired: 1992
Orig. Price: $32 • **Value: $280**

5

Rudolf
18" • #5807B • SB
Issued: 1992 • Retired: 1992
Orig. Price: N/A • **Value: $510**

6
New

Rudy McRind
14" • #912630 • TJ
Issued: 2001 • Current
Orig. Price: $29 • **Value: $29**

7

Rudy Pitoody
11" • #91880 • TJ
Issued: 2000 • Retired: 2000
Orig. Price: $21 • **Value: $29**

8

Rufus Bear
16" • #5111 • JB
Issued: pre-1990 • Retired: 1998
Orig. Price: $27 • **Value: $47**

9

Rupert
8" • #9142 • TJ
Issued: 1994 • Retired: 1996
Orig. Price: $18 • **Value: $50**

10
New

Ruskin K. Woodruff
6" • #57052-07 • AS
Issued: 2001 • Current
Orig. Price: $13 • **Value: $13**

11

Rutherford
16" • #912610 • TJ
Issued: 1998 • Retired: 2000
Orig. Price: $58 • **Value: $63**

12

S.C. Northstar
14" • #917303 • TJ
Issued: 1997 • Retired: 1999
Orig. Price: $27 • **Value: $62**

Bears

	Price Paid	Value
1.		
2.		
3.		
4.		
5.		
6.		
7.		
8.		
9.		
10.		
11.		
12.		
Totals		

1

St. Niklas
10" • #917311 • TJ
Issued: 1998 • Retired: 2000
Orig. Price: $21 • **Value: $28**

2

Sally Quignapple And Annie
10" & 5" • #91009 • TJ
Issued: 2000 • Current
Orig. Price: $25 • **Value: $25**

3

Samuel
6" • #918052 • TJ
Issued: 1998 • Retired: 2000
Orig. Price: $12 • **Value: $22**

4

Samuel Adams
8.5" • #915210 • TJ
Issued: 2000 • Current
Orig. Price: $14 • **Value: $14**

5

Sandy Claus
16" • #91731 • TJ
Issued: 1995 • Retired: 1998
Orig. Price: $29 • **Value: $60**

6

Sandy Claus II
16" • #917310 • TJ
Issued: 1998 • Retired: 2000
Orig. Price: $29 • **Value: $35**

7

Photo Unavailable

Santa Bear
info unavailable
Orig. Price: N/A • **Value: N/E**

8

Sarah Beth Jodibear
9" • #92000-04 • AR
Issued: 1999 • To Be Retired: 2001
Orig. Price: $20 • **Value: $20**

9

Sasha
10" • #9174 • TJ
Issued: 1995 • Retired: 1998
Orig. Price: $20 • **Value: $36**

10

Scooter
8" • #5642-03 • BA
Issued: 1993 • Retired: 1995
Orig. Price: $11 • **Value: $47**

11

Scruffy S. Beariluved
10" • #51000-05 • JB
Issued: 2000 • Current
Orig. Price: $18 • **Value: $18**

12

Sebastian
13" • #5827 • CB
Issued: 1991 • Retired: 1997
Orig. Price: $20 • **Value: $45**

Bears

	Price Paid	Value
1.		
2.		
3.		
4.		
5.		
6.		
7.		
8.		
9.		
10.		
11.		
12.		
Totals		

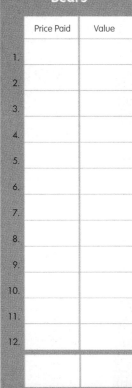

1
New

Serendipity Wishkabibble
10" • #90501 • TJ
Issued: 2001 • Current
Orig. Price: $21 • **Value: $21**

2

Sergei Bearskov
14" • #912619 • TJ
Issued: 2000 • Retired: 2000
Orig. Price: $40 • **Value: N/E**

3

Seymour P. Snowbeary
12" • #9138-01 • TJ
Issued: 1997 • Retired: 1999
Orig. Price: $27 • **Value: $36**

4

Sheldon Bearchild
6" • #918061 • TJ
Issued: 1998 • Retired: 2000
Orig. Price: $8 • **Value: $16**

5

Sherlock
11" • #5821 • TJ
Issued: 1992 • Retired: 1992
Orig. Price: $20 • **Value: $120**

6

Sherlock
11" • #9188 • TJ
Issued: 1993 • Retired: 1997
Orig. Price: $21 • **Value: $60**

7

Sigmund Von Bruin
6" • #5010-08 • WB
Issued: 1994 • Retired: 1995
Orig. Price: $10 • **Value: $60**

8

Simon Beanster And Andy
10" • #910090 • TJ
Issued: 2000 • Current
Orig. Price: $25 • **Value: $25**

9

Simone de Bearvoir
6" • #9180 • TJ
Issued: 1993 • Retired: 1996
Orig. Price: $9 • **Value: $39**

10

Sinclair Bearsford
16" • #57150-03 • AS
Issued: 2000 • Retired: 2000
Orig. Price: $32 • **Value: $48**

11

Sinkin
18" • #5808 • SB
Issued: 1991 • Retired: 1992
Orig. Price: $32 • **Value: $86**

12

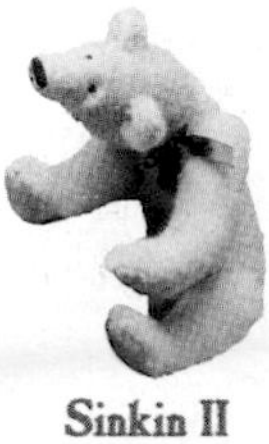

Sinkin II
18" • #5808 • SB
Issued: 1992 • Retired: 1997
Orig. Price: $32 • **Value: $52**

Bears

	Price Paid	Value
1.		
2.		
3.		
4.		
5.		
6.		
7.		
8.		
9.		
10.		
11.		
12.		
Totals		

1

Sir Henry
12" • #5720 • AS
Issued: 1991 • Retired: 1992
Orig. Price: $20 • **Value: $128**

2

Skidoo
11" • #9193 • TJ
Issued: 1992 • Retired: 1998
Orig. Price: $24 • **Value: $40**

3

Skip
12" • #5638 • BA
Issued: 1992 • Retired: 1996
Orig. Price: $16 • **Value: $50**

4

Skylar Thistlebeary
16" • #911951 • TJ
Issued: 1999 • To Be Retired: 2001
Orig. Price: $45 • **Value: $45**

5

Slugger
8" • #9177-01 • TJ
Issued: 1996 • Retired: 1999
Orig. Price: $26 • **Value: $47**

6

Smith Witter II
17" • #5110 • JB
Issued: 1994 • Retired: 1998
Orig. Price: $29 • **Value: $45**

7
New

Snickersnoodle
8" • #91770 • TJ
Issued: 2001 • Current
Orig. Price: $18 • **Value: $18**

8

Sniffles
9" • #5773 • HD
Issued: 1991 • Retired: 1992
Orig. Price: $14 • **Value: $158**

9

Snookie Snicklefritz
10" • #51770-09 • BA
Issued: 2000 • To Be Retired: 2001
Orig. Price: $14 • **Value: $14**

10

Snowball
14" • #5123W • JB
Issued: 1992 • Retired: 1993
Orig. Price: N/A • **Value: $98**

11

Spencer
5.5" • #5725 • AS
Issued: 1993 • Retired: 2000
Orig. Price: $7 • **Value: $16**

12

Spunky Boobear
8" • #81003 • TJ
Issued: 2000 • Retired: 2000
Orig. Price: $15 • **Value: $20**

Bears

	Price Paid	Value
1.		
2.		
3.		
4.		
5.		
6.		
7.		
8.		
9.		
10.		
11.		
12.		
Totals		

1

Squeeky
8" • #5615 • SQ
Issued: 1991 • Retired: 1991
Orig. Price: $10 • **Value: $120**

2

Squeeky
8" • #5616 • SQ
Issued: 1992 • Retired: 1992
Orig. Price: $10 • **Value: $120**

3

Photo Unavailable

Stella Seamstress
info unavailable
Orig. Price: N/A • **Value: N/E**

4

Stevenson Q. Bearitage
10" • #91736 • TJ
Issued: 1999 • Retired: 2000
Orig. Price: $24 • **Value: $29**

5

Photo Unavailable

Stilton
info unavailable
Orig. Price: N/A • **Value: N/E**

6

Photo Unavailable

Stonewall Bear
info unavailable
Orig. Price: N/A • **Value: N/E**

7

Stumper A. Potter
12" • #515211-11 • JB
Issued: 2000 • Current
Orig. Price: $21 • **Value: $21**

8
New

Sturbridge Q. Patriot
8" • #91524 • TJ
Issued: 2001 • Current
Orig. Price: $15 • **Value: $15**

9
New

Sugar McRind
10" • #91746 • TJ
Issued: 2001 • Current
Orig. Price: $24 • **Value: $24**

10

Sutton
8" • #57051 • AS
Issued: 2000 • Current
Orig. Price: $13 • **Value: $13**

11

Sven
8" • #9122 • TJ
Issued: 1994 • Retired: 1996
Orig. Price: $18 • **Value: $48**

12

Sylvia G. Bearimore
6" • #918438 • TJ
Issued: 2000 • Current
Orig. Price: $11 • **Value: $11**

Bears

	Price Paid	Value
1.		
2.		
3.		
4.		
5.		
6.		
7.		
8.		
9.		
10.		
11.		
12.		
Totals		

1

T. Farley Wuzzie
5" • #595100-11 • TF
Issued: 1998 • Retired: 1999
Orig. Price: $9 • **Value: $22**

2

T. Frampton Wuzzie
5" • #595100-05 • TF
Issued: 1999 • Retired: 2000
Orig. Price: $9 • **Value: $15**

3

T. Frasier Wuzzie
5" • #595100-08 • TF
Issued: 1998 • Retired: 2000
Orig. Price: $9 • **Value: $18**

4

T. Fulton Wuzzie
5" • #595100-06 • TF
Issued: 1998 • Retired: 2000
Orig. Price: $9 • **Value: $18**

5

Tabitha J. Spellbinder With Midnight Sneakypuss
16" & 6" • #900201 • UB
Issued: 1999 • Retired: 1999
Orig. Price: $69 • **Value: $75**

6

Tami P. Rally
10" • #917367 • TJ
Issued: 2000 • To Be Retired: 2001
Orig. Price: $30 • **Value: $30**

7

Tasha B. Frostbeary
14" & 6" & 3" • #900205 • UB
Issued: 1999 • Retired: 2000
Orig. Price: $69 • **Value: $75**

8

Tassel F. Wuzzie
3" • #596004 • TF
Issued: 1999 • Retired: 1999
Orig. Price: $8 • **Value: $18**

9

Tatum F. Wuzzie
3" • #596001 • TF
Issued: 1999 • Retired: 1999
Orig. Price: $8 • **Value: $18**

10

Ted
8" • #9156 • TJ
Issued: 1993 • Retired: 1996
Orig. Price: $16 • **Value: $48**

11

Teddy Beanberger (formerly "Teddy Beanbauer")
16" • #9118 • TJ
Issued: 1995 • Retired: 1997
Orig. Price: $53 • **Value: $88**

Bears

	Price Paid	Value
1.		
2.		
3.		
4.		
5.		
6.		
7.		
8.		
9.		
10.		
11.		
Totals		

1

Thatcher
5.5" • #5706 • AS
Issued: 1990 • Retired: 1997
Orig. Price: $7 • **Value: $32**

2

Thayer
8.5" • #91570 • TJ
Issued: 1997 • To Be Retired: 2001
Orig. Price: $18 • **Value: $18**

3

Theodore
7.5" • #9196 • TJ
Issued: 1992 • Retired: 1994
Orig. Price: $16 • **Value: $60**

4

Thinkin
6" • #5809 • SB
Issued: 1991 • Retired: 1994
Orig. Price: $7 • **Value: $75**

5

Thisbey F. Wuzzie
2.5" • #595160-02 • TF
Issued: 1999 • Retired: 2000
Orig. Price: $7 • **Value: $12**

6

Thor M. Berriman
12" • #91734 • TJ
Issued: 1998 • Retired: 1998
Orig. Price: $30 • **Value: $46**

7

Tilly F. Wuzzie
3" • #596000 • TF
Issued: 1999 • To Be Retired: 2001
Orig. Price: $8 • **Value: $8**

8
New

Timothy & Tiny Jodibear
7" • #92000-14 • AR
Issued: 2001 • Current
Orig. Price: $17 • **Value: $17**

9

Timothy F. Wuzzie
3.5" • #595140 • TF
Issued: 1998 • Retired: 2000
Orig. Price: $8 • **Value: $14**

10

Tinkin
10" • #5801 • SB
Issued: 1991 • Retired: 1992
Orig. Price: $20 • **Value: $70**

11

Tinkin II
10" • #5801 • SB
Issued: 1992 • Retired: 1997
Orig. Price: $20 • **Value: $70**

12

Tiny T. Jodibear
5" • #92000-11 • AR
Issued: 2000 • Current
Orig. Price: $13 • **Value: $13**

Bears

	Price Paid	Value
1.		
2.		
3.		
4.		
5.		
6.		
7.		
8.		
9.		
10.		
11.		
12.		

Totals

1

Tipton F. Wuzzie
2.5" • #595160-07 • TF
Issued: 1999 • To Be Retired: 2001
Orig. Price: $7 • **Value: $7**

2

Toe
8.5" • #5151-02 • JB
Issued: 1994 • Retired: 1997
Orig. Price: $12 • **Value: $50**

3

Tomba Bearski
14" • #912620 • TJ
Issued: 1999 • Current
Orig. Price: $42 • **Value: $42**

4

Toodle Padoodle
6" • #517010-03 • BY
Issued: 1999 • Retired: 2000
Orig. Price: $5 • **Value: $13**

5

Tootie F. Wuzzie
2.5" • #595160-01 • TF
Issued: 1999 • Retired: 2000
Orig. Price: $7 • **Value: $14**

6

Townsend Q. Bearrister
12" • #57001-03 • AS
Issued: 1999 • Retired: 2000
Orig. Price: $20 • **Value: $23**

Bears

	Price Paid	Value
1.		
2.		
3.		
4.		
5.		
6.		
7.		
8.		
9.		
10.		
11.		
12.		
Totals		

7

Travis B. Bean
16" • #5114-05 • JB
Issued: 1993 • Retired: 1998
Orig. Price: $27 • **Value: $47**

8

Photo Unavailable

Travis Bear
info unavailable
Orig. Price: N/A • **Value: N/E**

9

Treat F. Wuzzie
3" • #596002 • TF
Issued: 1999 • Retired: 1999
Orig. Price: $8 • **Value: $12**

10

Tremont
16" • #56411-08 • BA
Issued: 1997 • Retired: 2000
Orig. Price: $26 • **Value: $32**

11

Trevor F. Wuzzie
2.5" • #595160-08 • TF
Issued: 1997 • Retired: 1999
Orig. Price: $7 • **Value: $15**

12

Truman S. Bearington
18" • #590010-05 • MB
Issued: 1998 • Retired: 1998
Orig. Price: $126 • **Value: $170**

1

Trundle B. Bear
12" • #56391-10 • BA
Issued: 2000 • Retired: 2000
Orig. Price: $23 • **Value: $29**

2

Tumble F. Wuzzie
3" • #596005 • TF
Issued: 2000 • Current
Orig. Price: $8 • **Value: $8**

3

Tundra Northpole
12" • #912810 • TJ
Issued: 1999 • Retired: 2000
Orig. Price: $24 • **Value: $30**

4

Tutu
16" • #6169B • TJ
Issued: 1991 • Retired: 1991
Orig. Price: $63 • **Value: N/E**

5

Twas F. Wuzzie
3" • #596003 • TF
Issued: 1999 • Retired: 1999
Orig. Price: $8 • **Value: $20**

6

Twila Higgenthorpe
6" • #91843 • TJ
Issued: 1997 • Retired: 2000
Orig. Price: $10 • **Value: $25**

7

Twilight F. Wuzzie
2.5" • #595160-06 • TF
Issued: 1999 • Retired: 2000
Orig. Price: $7 • **Value: $12**

8

Twizzle F. Wuzzie
3.5" • #595141 • TF
Issued: 1998 • Retired: 1999
Orig. Price: $8 • **Value: $14**

9

Tylar F. Wuzzie
2.5" • #595160-11 • TF
Issued: 1997 • Retired: 1999
Orig. Price: $7 • **Value: $14**

10

Tyler Summerfield
12" • #9124 • TJ
Issued: 1996 • Retired: 1997
Orig. Price: $37 • **Value: $73**

11

Tyrone F. Wuzzie
2.5" • #595160-05 • TF
Issued: 1997 • Retired: 2000
Orig. Price: $7 • **Value: $12**

12

Uncle Ben Bearington
4.5" • #590103 • MB
Issued: 2000 • Retired: 2000
Orig. Price: $11 • **Value: $18**

Bears

	Price Paid	Value
1.		
2.		
3.		
4.		
5.		
6.		
7.		
8.		
9.		
10.		
11.		
12.		
Totals		

1
New

Uncle Sam
16" • #51100-01 • JB
Issued: 2001 • Current
Orig. Price: $29 • **Value: $29**

2

Ursa
14" • #5720-07 • AS
Issued: 1995 • Retired: 1998
Orig. Price: $24 • **Value: $37**

3

Valerie B. Bearhugs
10" • #510301 • FH
Issued: 2000 • Retired: 2000
Orig. Price: $11 • **Value: $35**

4

Varsity Bear
info unavailable
Orig. Price: N/A • **Value: $140**

5

Varsity Bear
N/A • #9198 • N/A
Issued: 1992 • Retired: 1992
Orig. Price: N/A • **Value: $275**

6

Vincent
11" • #1100-11 • CC
Issued: 1995 • Retired: 1997
Orig. Price: $10 • **Value: $42**

7

Waldo Bearsworth
11" • #912045 • TJ
Issued: 1999 • Current
Orig. Price: $27 • **Value: $27**

8

Walpole
8" • #5705M • AS
Issued: 1993 • Retired: 1997
Orig. Price: $13 • **Value: $34**

9

Walton
11" • #9128 • TJ
Issued: 1994 • Retired: 1997
Orig. Price: $21 • **Value: $50**

10
New

Warner Von Bruin
16" • #57151-05 • AS
Issued: 2001 • Current
Orig. Price: $32 • **Value: $32**

11

Warren
8" • #1002-01 • CC
Issued: 1993 • Retired: 1997
Orig. Price: $6 • **Value: $32**

Bears

	Price Paid	Value
1.		
2.		
3.		
4.		
5.		
6.		
7.		
8.		
9.		
10.		
11.		
Totals		

1

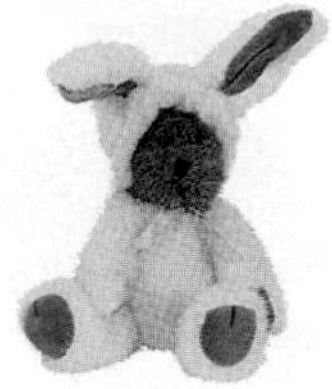

Watson
8" • #9187 • TJ
Issued: 1993 • Retired: 1999
Orig. Price: $17 • **Value: $27**

2

Wayfer North
10" • #917360 • TJ
Issued: 1999 • Retired: 2000
Orig. Price: $26 • **Value: $30**

3

Weaver Berrybrook
12" • #911930 • TJ
Issued: 1999 • Retired: 1999
Orig. Price: $20 • **Value: $38**

4

Webber Vanguard
16" • #51100-07 • JB
Issued: 2000 • To Be Retired: 2001
Orig. Price: $29 • **Value: $29**

5

Wellington
21" • #5722 • AS
Issued: 1992 • Retired: 1997
Orig. Price: $53 • **Value: $75**

6

Werner Von Bruin
6" • #5010-11 • WB
Issued: 1993 • Retired: 1995
Orig. Price: $10 • **Value: $46**

7

Wesley Bearimore
16" • #912027 • TJ
Issued: 2000 • Current
Orig. Price: $51 • Value: $51

8

Wheaton Flatski
8" • #5680-10 • FL
Issued: 1996 • Retired: 1996
Orig. Price: $13 • **Value: $50**

9

Whitaker Q. Bruin
5.5" • #91806 • TJ
Issued: 1996 • Retired: 1998
Orig. Price: $11 • **Value: $32**

10

Photo Unavailable

White Bean Bear
info unavailable
Orig. Price: N/A • **Value: N/E**

11

Wilbur Bearington
4.5" • #590085-10 • MB
Issued: 1998 • Retired: 1999
Orig. Price: $10 • **Value: $18**

12

Wilcox J. Beansford
14" • #51081-05 • JB
Issued: 1999 • To Be Retired: 2001
Orig. Price: $20 • **Value: $20**

Bears

	Price Paid	Value
1.		
2.		
3.		
4.		
5.		
6.		
7.		
8.		
9.		
10.		
11.		
12.		
Totals		

1

Willa Bruin
11" • #91205 • TJ
Issued: 1995 • Retired: 1997
Orig. Price: $30 • **Value: $50**

2

William P.
12" • #1107-03 • CC
Issued: 1998 • Retired: 1999
Orig. Price: $12 • **Value: $17**

3

Willmar Flatski
8" • #56801-05 • FL
Issued: 1998 • Retired: 1999
Orig. Price: $13 • **Value: $24**

4

Wilson
8" • #5705 • AS
Issued: 1990 • Retired: 1997
Orig. Price: $12 • **Value: $40**

5

Winifred Witebred
14" • #912071 • TJ
Issued: 1998 • Current
Orig. Price: $34 • **Value: $34**

6

Winkie II
12" • #5639-08 • BA
Issued: 1992 • Retired: 1998
Orig. Price: $16 • **Value: $34**

7

Winkin
10" • #5800 • SB
Issued: 1991 • Retired: 1993
Orig. Price: $20 • **Value: $98**

8

Winnie II
14" • #912071-01 • TJ
Issued: 1998 • To Be Retired: 2001
Orig. Price: $34 • **Value: $34**

9

Winnie Stillwithus
14" • #912071-03 • TJ
Issued: 2000 • Retired: 2000
Orig. Price: $34 • Value: $44

10

Winnie Wuzzwhite
14" • #912071-02 • TJ
Issued: 1999 • Retired: 1999
Orig. Price: $34 • **Value: $38**

11

Winstead P. Bear
15" • #515210-03 • JB
Issued: 1998 • Retired: 2000
Orig. Price: $24 • **Value: $29**

12

Winston B. Bean
10" • #5104 • JB
Issued: pre-1990 • Retired: 1996
Orig. Price: $14 • **Value: $45**

Bears

	Price Paid	Value
1.		
2.		
3.		
4.		
5.		
6.		
7.		
8.		
9.		
10.		
11.		
12.		
Totals		

1

Witch-A-Ma-Call-It
info unavailable
Orig. Price: N/A • **Value: N/E**

2

Woodrow T. Bearington
12" • #590041-03 • MB
Issued: 1999 • Retired: 1999
Orig. Price: $48 • **Value: $65**

3

Woodruff K. Bearsford
6" • #57251-05 • AS
Issued: 1999 • To Be Retired: 2001
Orig. Price: $8 • **Value: $8**

4

Wookie Snicklefritz
10" • #51770-06 • BA
Issued: 2000 • To Be Retired: 2001
Orig. Price: $14 • **Value: $14**

5

Worthington Fitzbruin
8.5" • #912032 • TJ
Issued: 1997 • Retired: 2000
Orig. Price: $14 • **Value: $24**

6

Yardley Fitzhampton
14" • #912030 • TJ
Issued: 1999 • Retired: 2000
Orig. Price: $27 • **Value: N/E**

7

Yeager Bearington
4.5" • #590085-05 • MB
Issued: 1999 • Retired: 2000
Orig. Price: $10 • **Value: $15**

8

Yogi
6" • #91771-02 • TJ
Issued: 1997 • Retired: 2000
Orig. Price: $14 • **Value: $22**

9

York
8" • #57051-05 • AS
Issued: 1998 • Retired: 2000
Orig. Price: $13 • **Value: $16**

10

Yvette Dubeary
6" • #918431 • TJ
Issued: 1999 • Current
Orig. Price: $10 • **Value: $11**

11

Zazu
16" • #5641-05 • BA
Issued: 1996 • Retired: 2000
Orig. Price: $26 • **Value: $33**

12

Ziggy Bear
12" • #5060 • N/A
Issued: N/A • Retired: N/A
Orig. Price: N/A • **Value: N/E**

Bears

	Price Paid	Value
1.		
2.		
3.		
4.		
5.		
6.		
7.		
8.		
9.		
10.		
11.		
12.		
Totals		

Camels

1
New

Sir Humpsley
8.5" • #57850 • AS
Issued: 2001 • Current
Orig. Price: $18 • **Value: $18**

Cats

2

Allie Fuzzbucket
9" • #51720 • BY
Issued: 1998 • Retired: 2000
Orig. Price: $8 • **Value: $18**

3
New

Amy Z. Sassycat
11" • #590250-10 • MB
Issued: 2001 • Current
Orig. Price: $41 • **Value: $41**

4

Armstrong Cattington
4.5" • #590087-07 • MB
Issued: 1999 • Retired: 2000
Orig. Price: $10 • **Value: $15**

5
New

Auden S. Penworthy
8" • #57410-11 • AS
Issued: 2001 • Current
Orig. Price: $13 • **Value: $13**

6

Baby
11" • #6105C • TJ
Issued: 1990 • Retired: 1990
Orig. Price: N/A • **Value: $280**

7

Blake B. Wordsworth
5.5" • #5745-06 • AS
Issued: 2000 • Current
Orig. Price: $8 • **Value: $8**

8

Boots Alleyruckus
14" • #5308-07 • JB
Issued: 1999 • Current
Orig. Price: $23 • **Value: $23**

9

Bronte
5.5" • #5742-10 • AS
Issued: 1994 • Retired: 1996
Orig. Price: $8 • **Value: $60**

	Price Paid	Value
Camels		
1.		
Cats		
2.		
3.		
4.		
5.		
6.		
7.		
8.		
9.		
Totals		

1

Browning
8" • #5741 • AS
Issued: 1992 • Retired: 1999
Orig. Price: $12 • **Value: $27**

2

Byron
8" • #5740 • AS
Issued: 1992 • Retired: 1999
Orig. Price: $12 • **Value: $27**

3

Photo Unavailable

Cabin Cat
info unavailable
Orig. Price: N/A • **Value: N/E**

4

Callaway Flatcat
8" • #56951-06 • FL
Issued: 1998 • Retired: 1999
Orig. Price: $13 • **Value: $23**

5

Callie Fuzzbucket
6" • #517020-06 • BY
Issued: 2000 • Retired: 2000
Orig. Price: $5 • **Value: $11**

6

Candy Corn Cat
8" • #91971 • TJ
Issued: 1995 • Retired: 1997
Orig. Price: $18 • **Value: $58**

7

Carlyle Wordsworth
5.5" • #57440-01 • AS
Issued: 2000 • Current
Orig. Price: $8 • **Value: $8**

8

Catherine Q. Fuzzberg
8" • #5303-08 • JB
Issued: 1997 • To Be Retired: 2001
Orig. Price: $10 • **Value: $11**

9

Catia Clawford
8" • #91712 • TJ
Issued: 2000 • Current
Orig. Price: $18 • **Value: $18**

10

Chaucer
8" • #9135 • TJ
Issued: 1994 • Retired: 1995
Orig. Price: $20 • **Value: $64**

11

Chaucer
8" • #9135-01 • TJ
Issued: 1994 • Retired: 1995
Orig. Price: $20 • **Value: $55**

12
New

Claudette Prissypuss
12" • #912091-08 • TJ
Issued: 2001 • Current
Orig. Price: $27 • **Value: $27**

Cats

	Price Paid	Value
1.		
2.		
3.		
4.		
5.		
6.		
7.		
8.		
9.		
10.		
11.		
12.		
Totals		

1

Claudine de la Plumtete
6" • #91710 • TJ
Issued: 1999 • Current
Orig. Price: $9 • **Value: $9**

2

Cleo P. Pussytoes
16" • #91209 • TJ
Issued: 1997 • Retired: 1999
Orig. Price: $40 • **Value: $50**

3

Coalcracker Ninelives
11" • #53040-07 • JB
Issued: 2000 • Current
Orig. Price: $17 • **Value: $17**

4

Cookie Grimilkin
11" • #5306 • JB
Issued: 1991 • To Be Retired: 2001
Orig. Price: $14 • **Value: $17**

5

Cuthbert Catberg
16" • #5314 • JB
Issued: 1992 • Retired: 1993
Orig. Price: N/A • **Value: $110**

6

Dewey Q. Grimilkin
info unavailable
Orig. Price: N/A • **Value: $118**

7

Dewey R. Cat
11" • #5302T • JB
Issued: 1990 • Retired: 1990
Orig. Price: N/A • **Value: $130**

8

Dickens Q. Wordsworth
5.5" • #5745-03 • AS
Issued: 2000 • Current
Orig. Price: $8 • **Value: $8**

9

Dorchester Catsworth With Artie
10" • #919760 • TJ
Issued: 2000 • To Be Retired: 2001
Orig. Price: $30 • **Value: $30**

10
New

Dreyfus Q. Wordsworth
5.5" • #5745-07 • AS
Issued: 2001 • Current
Orig. Price: $8 • **Value: $8**

11

Photo Unavailable

Eleanor
info unavailable
Orig. Price: N/A • **Value: N/E**

12

Ellsworth Flatcat II
8" • #5695-08 • FL
Issued: 1994 • Retired: 1999
Orig. Price: $12 • **Value: $25**

Cats

	Price Paid	Value
1.		
2.		
3.		
4.		
5.		
6.		
7.		
8.		
9.		
10.		
11.		
12.		
Totals		

1

Emerson T. Penworthy
8" • #57410-03 • AS
Issued: 2000 • Current
Orig. Price: $13 • **Value: $13**

2

Ernest Q. Grimilkin
11" • #5304 • JB
Issued: pre-1990 • Retired: 2000
Orig. Price: $14 • **Value: $25**

3

Felicia Fuzzbuns
12" • #912090 • TJ
Issued: 2000 • Current
Orig. Price: $30 • **Value: $30**

4

Felina B. Catterwall
8" • #919701 • TJ
Issued: 1998 • Retired: 1999
Orig. Price: $12 • **Value: $23**

5

Felina B. Catterwall
8" • #919701-01 • TJ
Issued: 1999 • Retired: 2000
Orig. Price: $14 • **Value: $23**

6
New

Finicky Snottykat
8" • #53030-10 • JB
Issued: 2001 • Current
Orig. Price: $11 • **Value: $11**

7

Fraid E. Cat
5.5" • #9198 • TJ
Issued: 1994 • Retired: 1997
Orig. Price: $12 • **Value: $38**

8

Gae Q. Grimilkin
14" • #5324 • JB
Issued: pre-1990 • Retired: 1992
Orig. Price: $20 • **Value: $135**

9

Photo Unavailable

Gardner
info unavailable
Orig. Price: $63 • **Value: N/E**

10

Garner J. Cattington
10" • #590250-11 • MB
Issued: 1998 • Retired: 1998
Orig. Price: $31 • **Value: $55**

11

Glenwood Flatcat
8" • #56951-08 • FL
Issued: 1998 • Retired: 1999
Orig. Price: $13 • **Value: $23**

12
New

Golda Meow
8" • #53030-08 • JB
Issued: 2001 • Current
Orig. Price: $11 • **Value: $11**

Cats

	Price Paid	Value
1.		
2.		
3.		
4.		
5.		
6.		
7.		
8.		
9.		
10.		
11.		
12.		
Totals		

1

Photo Unavailable

Grace
info unavailable
Orig. Price: $63 • **Value: N/E**

2

Greybeard
16" • #5312 • JB
Issued: 1991 • Retired: 1993
Orig. Price: $29 • **Value: $182**

3

Hattie
6" • #9105 • TJ
Issued: 1995 • Retired: 1997
Orig. Price: $12 • **Value: $36**

4

Heranamous
16" • #5311-07 • JB
Issued: 1996 • Retired: 1999
Orig. Price: $29 • **Value: $36**

5

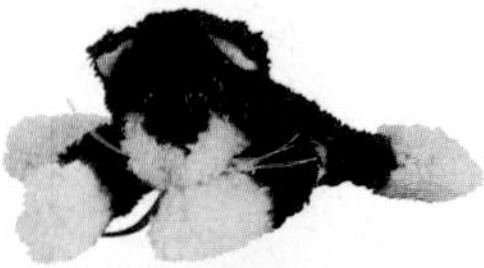

Holloway Flatcat
8" • #5695-07 • FL
Issued: 1994 • Retired: 1999
Orig. Price: $12 • **Value: $25**

6

Huxley W. Penworthy
8" • #57411-08 • AS
Issued: 2000 • Current
Orig. Price: $13 • **Value: $13**

7

Inky Catterwall
8" • #91972 • TJ
Issued: 1998 • Retired: 1999
Orig. Price: $18 • **Value: $26**

8

Java B. Bean
8.25" • #500102-07 • JB
Issued: 2000 • Current
Orig. Price: $9 • **Value: $9**

9

Kattelina Purrsley
11" • #91978 • TJ
Issued: 1999 • To Be Retired: 2001
Orig. Price: $20 • **Value: $20**

10

Keats
5.5" • #5743 • AS
Issued: 1992 • Retired: 2000
Orig. Price: $8 • **Value: $20**

11

Kitt Purrsley
8" • #91711 • TJ
Issued: 1999 • Retired: 2000
Orig. Price: $18 • **Value: $22**

12

Lacy
10" • #6100C • TJ
Issued: 1990 • Retired: 1992
Orig. Price: $16 • **Value: $120**

Cats

	Price Paid	Value
1.		
2.		
3.		
4.		
5.		
6.		
7.		
8.		
9.		
10.		
11.		
12.		
Totals		

1

Lacy
14" • #6101C • TJ
Issued: 1990 • Retired: 1991
Orig. Price: $21 • **Value: $100**

2

Lindbergh Cattington
4.5" • #590087-03 • MB
Issued: 1999 • Retired: 2000
Orig. Price: $10 • **Value: $17**

3

Lindsey P. Pussytoes
12" • #912091 • TJ
Issued: 1998 • Retired: 2000
Orig. Price: $31 • **Value: $35**

4

Lola Ninelives
9" • #919751 • TJ
Issued: 1999 • To Be Retired: 2001
Orig. Price: $24 • **Value: $24**

5

Marissa P. Pussyfoot
14" • #912093 • TJ
Issued: 1999 • To Be Retired: 2001
Orig. Price: $36 • **Value: $36**

6

Marmalade Sneakypuss
14" • #530800-08 • JB
Issued: 2000 • Current
Orig. Price: $23 • **Value: $23**

7

Midnight C. Sneakypuss
5.25" • #81002 • BB
Issued: 2000 • Retired: 2000
Orig. Price: $11 • **Value: $20**

8

Millicent P. Pussytoes
11" • #91976 • TJ
Issued: 1997 • Retired: 1998
Orig. Price: $20 • **Value: $33**

9

Milton R. Penworthy
8" • #57410-07 • AS
Issued: 2000 • Current
Orig. Price: $13 • **Value: $13**

10

Miss Prissy Fussybuns
14" • #912094 • TJ
Issued: 2000 • Current
Orig. Price: $30 • **Value: $30**

11

Momma McFuzz And Missy
12" & 5" • #910080 • TJ
Issued: 2000 • To Be Retired: 2001
Orig. Price: $30 • **Value: $30**

12

Mondale W. Cattington
10" • #590250-05 • MB
Issued: 1999 • Retired: 1999
Orig. Price: $29 • **Value: N/E**

Cats

	Price Paid	Value
1.		
2.		
3.		
4.		
5.		
6.		
7.		
8.		
9.		
10.		
11.		
12.		
Totals		

1

Mrs. Partridge
9" • #919750 • TJ
Issued: 1998 • Retired: 2000
Orig. Price: $30 • **Value: $37**

2

Mrs. Petrie
9" • #919752 • TJ
Issued: 1999 • Retired: 2000
Orig. Price: $30 • **Value: $37**

3

Ned
12" • #5656-03 • BA
Issued: 1993 • Retired: 1995
Orig. Price: $16 • **Value: $68**

4

Opel Catberg
14" • #5324-10 • JB
Issued: 1995 • Retired: 1999
Orig. Price: $20 • **Value: $34**

5

Ophilia Q. Grimilkin
14" • #5323 • JB
Issued: pre-1990 • Retired: 1990
Orig. Price: $20 • **Value: $180**

6
New

Ozzie N. Harrycat
11" • #53060-11 • JB
Issued: 2001 • Current
Orig. Price: $17 • **Value: $17**

Cats

	Price Paid	Value
1.		
2.		
3.		
4.		
5.		
6.		
7.		
8.		
9.		
10.		
11.		
12.		
Totals		

7

Pearl Catberg
14" • #5324-01 • JB
Issued: 1994 • Retired: 1995
Orig. Price: $20 • **Value: $95**

8
New

Penny P. Copperpuss
14" • #53080-06 • JB
Issued: 2001 • Current
Orig. Price: $23 • **Value: $23**

9

Phoebe Purrsmore
5.5" • #917101 • TJ
Issued: 2000 • Retired: 2000
Orig. Price: $12 • **Value: $18**

10

Poe
5.5" • #5742-07 • AS
Issued: 1993 • Retired: 1999
Orig. Price: $8 • **Value: $24**

11

Punkin Puss
8" • #9197 • TJ
Issued: 1992 • Retired: 1997
Orig. Price: $18 • **Value: $47**

12

Purrsnicitty Snottykat
11" • #53050-10 • JB
Issued: 2000 • Current
Orig. Price: $17 • **Value: $17**

1

Puss N. Boo
8" • #9164 • TJ
Issued: 1993 • Retired: 1995
Orig. Price: $18 • **Value: $55**

2

Quayle D. Cattington
6" • #590270-07 • MB
Issued: 1999 • Retired: 1999
Orig. Price: $16 • **Value: $24**

3

Robyn Purrsmore
8" • #915600 • TJ
Issued: 2000 • To Be Retired: 2001
Orig. Price: $12 • **Value: $12**

4
New

Rowena Prissypuss
8" • #915601 • TJ
Issued: 2001 • Current
Orig. Price: $15 • **Value: $15**

5

Photo Unavailable

Royce
Info unavailable
Orig. Price: $32 • **Value: N/E**

6

Sabrina P. Catterwall
8" • #919700 • TJ
Issued: 1998 • Retired: 1999
Orig. Price: $12 • **Value: N/E**

7

Sabrina P. Catterwall
8" • #919700-01 • TJ
Issued: 1999 • Retired: 2000
Orig. Price: $14 • **Value: $19**

8

Samantha Sneakypuss
11" • #91979 • TJ
Issued: 1999 • Retired: 2000
Orig. Price: $20 • **Value: $23**

9

Photo Unavailable

Samuel Catberg
info unavailable
Orig. Price: N/A • **Value: N/E**

10

Shelly
5.5" • #5742 • AS
Issued: 1992 • Retired: 2000
Orig. Price: $8 • **Value: $16**

11
New

Sly Alleyruckus
11" • #53041-07 • JB
Issued: 2001 • Current
Orig. Price: $17 • **Value: $17**

12

Socks Grimilkin
14" • #5324-07 • JB
Issued: 1993 • Retired: 1998
Orig. Price: $20 • **Value: $48**

Cats

	Price Paid	Value
1.		
2.		
3.		
4.		
5.		
6.		
7.		
8.		
9.		
10.		
11.		
12.		
Totals		

1

Spiro T. Cattington
12" • #590240-07 • MB
Issued: 1998 • Retired: 1998
Orig. Price: $51 • **Value: $72**

2

Spooky Tangaween
11" • #91975 • TJ
Issued: 1996 • Retired: 1998
Orig. Price: $20 • **Value: $32**

3

Suzie Purrkins
11" • #91977 • TJ
Issued: 1998 • Retired: 1998
Orig. Price: $20 • **Value: $33**

4

Sweetpea Catberg
11" • #5305 • JB
Issued: pre-1990 • Retired: 1992
Orig. Price: $14 • **Value: $68**

5

Sweetpea Catberg
11" • #5307 • JB
Issued: 1992 • Retired: 1998
Orig. Price: $14 • **Value: $34**

6

T. Frankel Wuzzie
5" • #595103 • TF
Issued: 1999 • Retired: 2000
Orig. Price: $9 • **Value: $12**

7

Tabby F. Wuzzie
3" • #595240-07 • TF
Issued: 1999 • Retired: 2000
Orig. Price: $7 • **Value: N/E**

8

Taylor Purrski
14" • #912095 • TJ
Issued: 2000 • To Be Retired: 2001
Orig. Price: $36 • **Value: $36**

9

Tennyson
5.5" • #5744 • AS
Issued: 1992 • Retired: 1999
Orig. Price: $8 • **Value: $22**

10

Tessa Fluffypaws
14" • #5309-01 • JB
Issued: 2000 • Current
Orig. Price: $20 • **Value: $23**

11

Thom
12" • #5656-07 • BA
Issued: 1993 • Retired: 1995
Orig. Price: $16 • **Value: $53**

12

Thoreau
8" • #5740-08 • AS
Issued: 1995 • Retired: 1999
Orig. Price: $12 • **Value: $28**

Cats

	Price Paid	Value
1.		
2.		
3.		
4.		
5.		
6.		
7.		
8.		
9.		
10.		
11.		
12.		
Totals		

1

Tigerlily
16" • #5311 • JB
Issued: pre-1990 • Retired: 1995
Orig. Price: $29 • **Value: $45**

2

Turner F. Wuzzie
3" • #595240-06 • TF
Issued: 1998 • Retired: 2000
Orig. Price: $7 • **Value: $10**

3
New

Vanessa V. Fluffypaws
16" • #53110-01 • JB
Issued: 2001 • Current
Orig. Price: $30 • **Value: $30**

4

Walter Q. Fuzzberg
8" • #5303-07 • JB
Issued: 1997 • To Be Retired: 2001
Orig. Price: $10 • **Value: $10**

5

Zachariah Alleyruckus
14" • #5308-06 • JB
Issued: 1999 • To Be Retired: 2001
Orig. Price: $20 • **Value: $23**

6

Zap Catberg
14" • #5325 • JB
Issued: 1992 • Retired: 1992
Orig. Price: $20 • **Value: N/E**

7

Zelda Catberg
14" • #5324-06 • JB
Issued: 1993 • Retired: 1993
Orig. Price: N/A • **Value: $85**

8

Zenus W. Grimilkin
11" • #5303 • JB
Issued: pre-1990 • Retired: 1991
Orig. Price: $14 • **Value: $180**

9

Zip Catberg
14" • #5325 • JB
Issued: pre-1990 • Retired: 1992
Orig. Price: $20 • **Value: $130**

10

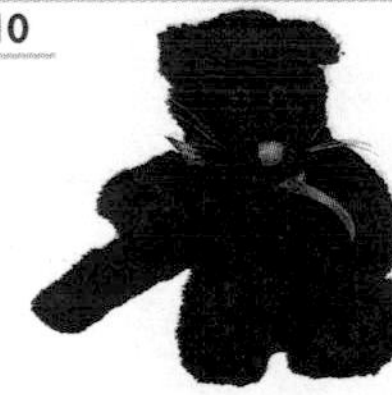

Zoe R. Grimilkin
11" • #5304-07 • JB
Issued: 1994 • Retired: 1999
Orig. Price: $14 • **Value: $26**

11

Zoom Catberg
14" • #5326 • JB
Issued: 1992 • Retired: 1993
Orig. Price: $20 • **Value: $140**

Cats

	Price Paid	Value
1.		
2.		
3.		
4.		
5.		
6.		
7.		
8.		
9.		
10.		
11.		
Totals		

Cows

1

Angus MacMoo
11" • #91341 • TJ
Issued: 1999 • Retired: 2000
Orig. Price: $20 • **Value: $28**

2

Bertha Utterberg
8" • #5758 • AS
Issued: 1996 • Retired: 1996
Orig. Price: $13 • **Value: $55**

3

Bessie Moostein
11" • #5532 • AM
Issued: 1991 • Retired: 2000
Orig. Price: $14 • **Value: $35**

4
New

Butch Hoofenutter
14" • #55330-07 • AM
Issued: 2001 • Current
Orig. Price: $20 • **Value: $20**

5
New

Corabelle Hoofenutter
11" • #55320-11 • AM
Issued: 2001 • Current
Orig. Price: $15 • **Value: $15**

Cows

	Price Paid	Value
1.		
2.		
3.		
4.		
5.		
6.		
7.		
8.		
9.		
10.		
11.		
Totals		

6

Elford Bullsworth
14" • #55330-05 • AM
Issued: 2000 • Current
Orig. Price: $19 • **Value: $19**

7

Elmer Beefcake
14" • #5535-11 • AM
Issued: 1995 • Retired: 1996
Orig. Price: $20 • **Value: $73**

8

Elmo Beefcake
11" • #5532-03 • AM
Issued: 1993 • Retired: 2000
Orig. Price: $14 • **Value: $40**

9

Ernestine Vanderhoof
8" • #55312-05 • AM
Issued: 1999 • Retired: 2000
Orig. Price: $11 • **Value: $16**

10
New

Fernando Uttermost
8" • #55314-05 • AM
Issued: 2001 • Current
Orig. Price: $13 • **Value: $13**

11
New

Florabelle Uttermost
8" • #55314-07 • AM
Issued: 2001 • Current
Orig. Price: $13 • **Value: $13**

Cows

1

Herman Beefcake
16" • #5534 • AM
Issued: 1992 • Retired: 1994
Orig. Price: $27 • **Value: $250**

2

Hester
12" • #5660-10 • BA
Issued: 1996 • Retired: 1997
Orig. Price: $16 • **Value: $35**

3

Hortense Moostein
16" • #5533 • AM
Issued: 1992 • Retired: 1995
Orig. Price: $29 • **Value: $128**

4

Ida Moostein
14" • #5535-10 • AM
Issued: 1994 • Retired: 1996
Orig. Price: $20 • **Value: $57**

5

Sadie Utterburg
16" • #5533-10 • AM
Issued: 1996 • Retired: 1999
Orig. Price: $29 • **Value: $40**

6

Silo Q. Vanderhoof
8" • #55312-07 • AM
Issued: 1999 • Retired: 2000
Orig. Price: $11 • **Value: $21**

7

T. Fodder Wuzzie
5" • #595105-01 • TF
Issued: 2000 • Retired: 2000
Orig. Price: $9 • **Value: $25**

Crows

8

Edgar
6" • #5864-07 • AR
Issued: 1996 • Retired: 1997
Orig. Price: $9 • **Value: $38**

9

Hank Krow Jr.
11" • #5865-07 • AR
Issued: 1995 • Retired: 1997
Orig. Price: $14 • **Value: $34**

Dogs

10
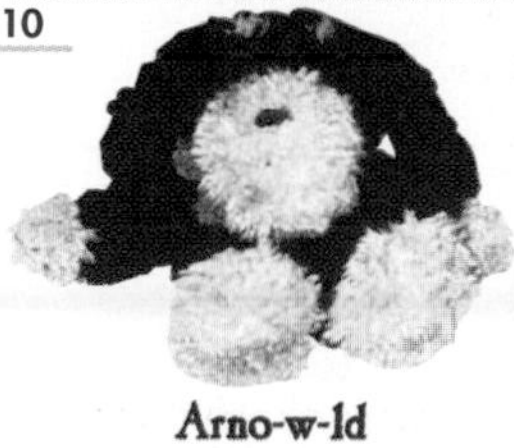
Arno-w-ld
12" • #5655-07 • BA
Issued: 1996 • Retired: 1997
Orig. Price: $16 • **Value: $50**

	Price Paid	Value
Cows		
1.		
2.		
3.		
4.		
5.		
6.		
7.		
Crows		
8.		
9.		
Dogs		
10.		
Totals		

Value Guide — Boyds Plush Animals

1

Bagley Flatberg
8" • #5690-03 • FL
Issued: 1996 • Retired: 1999
Orig. Price: $13 • **Value: $28**

2

Barkley McFarkle
9" • #51750 • BY
Issued: 1999 • Retired: 2000
Orig. Price: $8 • **Value: $15**

3

Betty Biscuit
10" • #5402-08 • JB
Issued: 1995 • Retired: 1997
Orig. Price: $14 • **Value: $38**

4

Beulah Canine
11" • #5403 • JB
Issued: pre-1990 • Retired: 1991
Orig. Price: $14 • **Value: N/E**

5

Binky McFarkle
6" • #517050-03 • BY
Issued: 2000 • Retired: 2000
Orig. Price: $5 • **Value: $11**

6

Bunky McFarkle
9" • #51750-07 • BY
Issued: 1999 • Retired: 2000
Orig. Price: $8 • **Value: $13**

7

Carson B. Barker
16" • #540300-05 • JB
Issued: 2000 • Retired: 2000
Orig. Price: $30 • **Value: $33**

8

Checkers P. Hydrant
10" • #54051-07 • JB
Issued: 2000 • To Be Retired: 2001
Orig. Price: $15 • **Value: $15**

9

Clancy G. Hydrant, Jr.
10" • #5404 • JB
Issued: 1998 • Retired: 2000
Orig. Price: $14 • **Value: $33**

10

Collier P. Hydrant II
16" • #5403 • JB
Issued: 1997 • Retired: 1999
Orig. Price: $29 • **Value: $35**

11
New

Duffy P. Hydrant
16" • #540301-07 • JB
Issued: 2001 • Current
Orig. Price: $30 • **Value: $30**

12

Fritz Von Bruin
6" • #5014 • WB
Issued: 1992 • Retired: 1992
Orig. Price: N/A • **Value: $175**

Dogs

	Price Paid	Value
1.		
2.		
3.		
4.		
5.		
6.		
7.		
8.		
9.		
10.		
11.		
12.		
Totals		

1

Hector Flatberg
8" • #5690-07 • FL
Issued: 1995 • Retired: 1996
Orig. Price: $13 • **Value: $35**

2

Hercules Von Mutt
6" • #5014-01 • WB
Issued: 1993 • Retired: 1994
Orig. Price: $10 • **Value: $70**

3

Indy (Fall 1997)
5.5" • #91757 • TJ
Issued: 1997 • Retired: 1998
Orig. Price: $12 • **Value: $25**

4

Indy (Fall 1998)
5.5" • #91757-10 • TJ
Issued: 1998 • Retired: 1999
Orig. Price: $12 • **Value: $22**

5

Indy (Fall 1999)
5" • #91757-12 • TJ
Issued: 1999 • Retired: 1999
Orig. Price: $12 • **Value: $22**

6

Indy (Spring 2000)
5" • #91757-14 • TJ
Issued: 2000 • Retired: 2000
Orig. Price: $12 • **Value: $19**

7

Indy (Fall 2000)
5" • #91757-15 • TJ
Issued: 2000 • To Be Retired: 2001
Orig. Price: $12 • Value: $12

8

Irving Poochberg
14" • #5420 • JB
Issued: pre-1990 • Retired: 1992
Orig. Price: $16 • **Value: $154**

9

Martin Muttski
11" • #5400 • JB
Issued: pre-1990 • Retired: 1992
Orig. Price: $14 • **Value: $130**

10

Merritt M. Mutt
11" • #5401 • JB
Issued: pre-1990 • Retired: 1991
Orig. Price: $14 • **Value: $125**

11

Merton Flatberg
8" • #5690-08 • FL
Issued: 1994 • Retired: 1997
Orig. Price: $12 • **Value: $32**

12

Northrop Flatberg
8" • #5690-01 • FL
Issued: 1994 • Retired: 1999
Orig. Price: $12 • **Value: $30**

Dogs

	Price Paid	Value
1.		
2.		
3.		
4.		
5.		
6.		
7.		
8.		
9.		
10.		
11.		
12.		
Totals		

1

Parker B. Pooch
10" • #54050-08 • JB
Issued: 2000 • Current
Orig. Price: $15 • **Value: $15**

2

Philo Puddlemaker
12" • #56551-07 • BA
Issued: 1999 • To Be Retired: 2001
Orig. Price: $16 • **Value: $16**

3

Preston
12" • #56961-01 • FL
Issued: 1996 • Retired: 1996
Orig. Price: N/A • **Value: $35**

4
New

Poochie
12" • #604200 • HF
Issued: 2001 • Current
Orig. Price: $19 • **Value: $19**

5

Ralph Poochstein
10" • #5400-10 • JB
Issued: 1995 • Retired: 1997
Orig. Price: $14 • **Value: $37**

6

Photo Unavailable

Roosevelt
15" • #6108D • TJ
Issued: pre-1990 • Retired: 1991
Orig. Price: $27 • **Value: $165**

7

Snuffy B. Barker
10" • #5405 • JB
Issued: 2000 • To Be Retired: 2001
Orig. Price: $15 • **Value: $15**

8

Speed Poochberg
11" • #5402 • JB
Issued: pre-1990 • Retired: 1992
Orig. Price: $14 • **Value: $138**

9

Stewart MacGregor
10" • #91400 • TJ
Issued: 2000 • Current
Orig. Price: $18 • **Value: $18**

10

T. Foley Wuzzie
5" • #595104-05 • TF
Issued: 2000 • Retired: 2000
Orig. Price: $9 • **Value: $15**

11

Toby F. Wuzzie
3" • #595500-08 • TF
Issued: 1999 • Retired: 2000
Orig. Price: $7 • **Value: $16**

12

Unidentified Dog
10" • N/A • N/A
Issued: N/A • Retired: N/A
Orig. Price: N/A • **Value: N/E**

Dogs

	Price Paid	Value
1.		
2.		
3.		
4.		
5.		
6.		
7.		
8.		
9.		
10.		
11.		
12.		
Totals		

1

Walker
12" • #5655-08 • BA
Issued: 1994 • Retired: 1997
Orig. Price: $16 • **Value: $38**

Donkeys

2

Brayburn
8" • #5670 • FL
Issued: 1996 • Retired: 1997
Orig. Price: $13 • **Value: $42**

Ducks

3
New

Quackie
12" • #607200 • HF
Issued: 2001 • Current
Orig. Price: $19 • **Value: $19**

Elephants

4
New

Hannibel Trunkster
16" • #55223 • AM
Issued: 2001 • Current
Orig. Price: $41 • **Value: $41**

5
New

Isadora T. Lightfoot
8" • #913201 • TJ
Issued: 2001 • Current
Orig. Price: $21 • **Value: $21**

6

Newton
8" • #5665 • FL
Issued: 1996 • Retired: 1997
Orig. Price: $13 • **Value: $44**

7

Nicolai A. Pachydermsky
16" • #5528-06 • AM
Issued: 1993 • Retired: 1994
Orig. Price: $28 • **Value: $230**

8

Olivia A. Pachydermsky
10" • #5527-06 • AM
Issued: 1993 • Retired: 1994
Orig. Price: $14 • **Value: $145**

9

Omar A. Pachydermsky
7.5" • #5526-06 • AM
Issued: 1993 • Retired: 1994
Orig. Price: $8 • **Value: $95**

	Price Paid	Value
Dogs		
1.		
Donkeys		
2.		
Ducks		
3.		
Elephants		
4.		
5.		
6.		
7.		
8.		
9.		
Totals		

1

P. Gallery Trunkster
10" • #55250 • AM
Issued: 2000 • Current
Orig. Price: $17 • **Value: $17**

Foxes

2

Reggie Foxworthy
8" • #55210 • AM
Issued: 1999 • Current
Orig. Price: $12 • **Value: $12**

Frogs

3

Ezra R. Ribbit
6" • #566470 • BA
Issued: 1998 • Current
Orig. Price: $5 • **Value: $5**

4

G. Kelly Ribbit (musical)
9" • #91320 • TJ
Issued: 1999 • To Be Retired: 2001
Orig. Price: $25 • **Value: $25**

5

Jacque Le Grenouille
8" • #5018 • WB
Issued: 1993 • Retired: 1995
Orig. Price: $10 • **Value: $66**

6

Jeremiah B. Ribbit
9.5" • #566450 • BA
Issued: 1997 • Retired: 1999
Orig. Price: $12 • **Value: $20**

7
New

Paddies
12" • #609200 • HF
Issued: 2001 • Current
Orig. Price: $19 • **Value: $19**

8

Racheal Q. Ribbit
12" • #566340 • BA
Issued: 1997 • Retired: 2000
Orig. Price: $21 • **Value: N/E**

9

S.C. Ribbit (musical)
12" • #917309 • TJ
Issued: 1998 • Retired: 1999
Orig. Price: $25 • **Value: $36**

	Price Paid	Value
Elephants		
1.		
Foxes		
2.		
Frogs		
3.		
4.		
5.		
6.		
7.		
8.		
9.		
Totals		

Giraffes

1
New

Wilt Stiltwalker
14" • #55221 • AM
Issued: 2001 • Current
Orig. Price: $19 • **Value: $19**

Gorillas

2

Joe Magilla
11" • #5525 • AM
Issued: 1995 • Retired: 1998
Orig. Price: $14 • **Value: $30**

3

Mike Magilla
8" • #55251 • AM
Issued: 1998 • Retired: 1999
Orig. Price: $12 • **Value: $19**

4

Viola Magillacuddy
8" • #91351 • TJ
Issued: 1999 • Retired: 1999
Orig. Price: $14 • **Value: $18**

Hares

5

Alexandra
14" • #5730 • AS
Issued: 1991 • Retired: 1995
Orig. Price: $20 • **Value: $110**

6

Alice
7.5" • #5750 • AS
Issued: 1992 • Retired: 1999
Orig. Price: $7 • **Value: $22**

7

Allison Babbit
14" • #9166 • TJ
Issued: 1994 • Retired: 1998
Orig. Price: $20 • **Value: $32**

8

Amarretto
17" • #9110 • TJ
Issued: 1995 • Retired: 1997
Orig. Price: $19 • **Value: $30**

9

Amelia R. Hare
12" • #5203 • JB
Issued: pre-1990 • Retired: 1998
Orig. Price: $14 • **Value: $31**

	Price Paid	Value
Giraffes		
1.		
Gorillas		
2.		
3.		
4.		
Hares		
5.		
6.		
7.		
8.		
9.		
Totals		

1

Photo Unavailable

Anastasia
14" • #5876 • HT
Issued: 1992 • Retired: 1992
Orig. Price: $32 • **Value: $76**

2

Anastasia
12" • #912081 • TJ
Issued: 1998 • To Be Retired: 2001
Orig. Price: $26 • **Value: $26**

3

Anisette
12" • #9109-07 • TJ
Issued: 1996 • Retired: 1996
Orig. Price: $12 • **Value: $42**

4

Anna
6" • #5870 • HT
Issued: 1992 • Retired: 1993
Orig. Price: $9 • **Value: $105**

5

Anne
7.5" • #5734 • AS
Issued: 1991 • Retired: 1997
Orig. Price: $7 • **Value: $33**

6

Archer
10" • #91544 • TJ
Issued: 1996 • Retired: 1998
Orig. Price: $24 • **Value: $45**

Hares

	Price Paid	Value
1.		
2.		
3.		
4.		
5.		
6.		
7.		
8.		
9.		
10.		
11.		
12.		
Totals		

7

Ashley
12" • #9132 • TJ
Issued: 1995 • Retired: 1998
Orig. Price: $20 • **Value: $32**

8

Aubergine
7.5" • #9107 • TJ
Issued: 1995 • Retired: 1998
Orig. Price: $12 • **Value: $26**

9

Auntie Adina (LE-500)
14" • N/A • N/A
Issued: N/A • Retired: N/A
Orig. Price: N/A • **Value: $235**

10

Auntie Babbit
12" • #91660 • JB
Issued: 1996 • Retired: 1998
Orig. Price: $30 • **Value: $46**

11

Auntie Harestein
14" • N/A • N/A
Issued: 1993 • Retired: 1993
Orig. Price: N/A • **Value: N/E**

12

Babs
12" • #5650-09 • BA
Issued: 1994 • Retired: 1998
Orig. Price: $16 • **Value: $36**

1

Baby
14" • #6105H • TJ
Issued: 1990 • Retired: 1991
Orig. Price: N/A • **Value: $280**

2

Beatrice
14" • #6168H • TJ
Issued: 1991 • Retired: 1991
Orig. Price: $63 • **Value: N/E**

3

Bedford Boneah
17" • #58291-05 • CH
Issued: 1998 • Retired: 1999
Orig. Price: $23 • **Value: N/E**

4

Bedford Boneah II
14" • #582910-05 • CH
Issued: 2000 • Retired: 2000
Orig. Price: $24 • **Value: N/E**

5

Beecher B. Bunny
10" • #5250-10 • JB
Issued: 1996 • Retired: 1998
Orig. Price: $16 • **Value: $35**

6

Bixie
12" • #56501-10 • BA
Issued: 1998 • Retired: 2000
Orig. Price: $16 • **Value: $20**

7

Bopper
14" • #5748 • HD
Issued: 1991 • Retired: 1992
Orig. Price: $27 • **Value: $150**

8

Brigette Delapain
10" • #91691 • TJ
Issued: 1996 • Retired: 1998
Orig. Price: $21 • **Value: $45**

9

Brigham Boneah
15" • #58291 • CH
Issued: 1997 • Retired: 1999
Orig. Price: $23 • **Value: N/E**

10

Brigham Boneah II
14" • #582910 • CH
Issued: 2000 • Retired: 2000
Orig. Price: $24 • **Value: $30**

11

Briton R. Hare
15" • #5204 • JB
Issued: pre-1990 • Retired: 1991
Orig. Price: $20 • **Value: $118**

12

Buffie Bunnyhop
8" • #522700-03 • JB
Issued: 2000 • Current
Orig. Price: $10 • **Value: $11**

Hares

	Price Paid	Value
1.		
2.		
3.		
4.		
5.		
6.		
7.		
8.		
9.		
10.		
11.		
12.		
Totals		

1

Bumpus
9" • #5746 • HD
Issued: 1991 • Retired: 1992
Orig. Price: $14 • **Value: $105**

2

Bunkie Hoppleby
9" • #51740-06 • BY
Issued: 2000 • Retired: 2000
Orig. Price: $8 • **Value: $10**

3

Bunnylove Rarebit
9" • #91314 • TJ
Issued: 1996 • Retired: 1998
Orig. Price: $20 • **Value: $41**

4

Camilla
7.5" • #5732 • AS
Issued: 1993 • Retired: 1998
Orig. Price: $7 • **Value: $20**

5

Cara Z. Bunnyhugs
9" • #91649 • TJ
Issued: 2000 • Retired: 2000
Orig. Price: $14 • **Value: $25**

6

Carlin Wabbit
8" • #9115 • TJ
Issued: 1995 • Retired: 1998
Orig. Price: $13 • **Value: $33**

Hares

	Price Paid	Value
1.		
2.		
3.		
4.		
5.		
6.		
7.		
8.		
9.		
10.		
11.		
12.		
Totals		

7

Cathy J. Hiphop
6" • #917030 • TJ
Issued: 2000 • Retired: 2000
Orig. Price: $12 • **Value: $22**

8

Cecilia
8" • #5648-01 • BA
Issued: 1993 • Retired: 1998
Orig. Price: $11 • **Value: $24**

9

Chardonnay
7.5" • #9106 • TJ
Issued: 1995 • Retired: 1998
Orig. Price: $12 • **Value: $30**

10

Charlotte R. Hare
14" • #5224 • JB
Issued: 1992 • Retired: 1998
Orig. Price: $20 • **Value: $45**

11

Chelsea R. Hare
14" • #5217-01 • JB
Issued: 1993 • Retired: 1998
Orig. Price: $20 • **Value: $34**

12

Chesterfield Q. Burpee
8" • #91546 • TJ
Issued: 1996 • Retired: 1998
Orig. Price: $21 • **Value: $38**

1

Chloe Fitzhare
17" • #5240-03 • JB
Issued: 1996 • Retired: 1998
Orig. Price: $29 • **Value: $39**

2

Clara R. Hare
8" • #5227-08 • JB
Issued: 1994 • Retired: 1998
Orig. Price: $10 • **Value: $26**

3

Clarisse
16" • #91208 • TJ
Issued: 1997 • Retired: 1998
Orig. Price: $40 • **Value: $53**

4

Columbine Dubois
6" • #91402 • TJ
Issued: 1996 • Retired: 1998
Orig. Price: $12 • **Value: $28**

5

Cora B. Bunny
20" • #5212 • JB
Issued: pre-1990 • Retired: 1994
Orig. Price: $29 • **Value: $145**

6

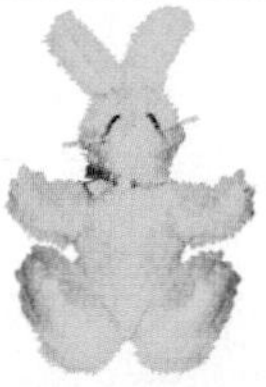

Cordillia R. Hare
15" • #5205 • JB
Issued: pre-1990 • Retired: 1992
Orig. Price: $20 • **Value: $120**

7

Cosette D. Lapine
10" • #916601 • TJ
Issued: 1997 • Retired: 1999
Orig. Price: $27 • **Value: $36**

8

Cousin Rose Anjanette
7.5" • #91112-01 • TJ
Issued: 1998 • Retired: 2000
Orig. Price: $12 • **Value: $24**

9

Curly Lapin
14" • #5207 • JB
Issued: pre-1990 • Retired: 1995
Orig. Price: $14 • **Value: $75**

10
New

Dabney P. Powderfoot
14" • #58290-10 • JB
Issued: 2001 • Current
Orig. Price: $23 • **Value:** $23

11

Daffodil de la Hoppsack
8" • #91404 • TJ
Issued: 1998 • Retired: 1999
Orig. Price: $13 • **Value: $25**

12

Daisey
12" • #9109 • TJ
Issued: 1995 • Retired: 1998
Orig. Price: $12 • **Value:** $24

Hares

	Price Paid	Value
1.		
2.		
3.		
4.		
5.		
6.		
7.		
8.		
9.		
10.		
11.		
12.		
Totals		

1

Daphne R. Hare
14" • #5225 • JB
Issued: 1992 • Retired: 1998
Orig. Price: $20 • **Value: $34**

2

Darcy Babbit
14" • #9178 • TJ
Issued: 1993 • Retired: 1995
Orig. Price: $18 • **Value: $125**

3

Photo Unavailable

Darcy Babbit II
info unavailable
Orig. Price: N/A • **Value: $135**

4
New

Delanie D. Hopplebuns
16" • #912078 • TJ
Issued: 2001 • Current
Orig. Price: $40 • **Value: $40**

5

Delia R. Hare
12" • #5202 • JB
Issued: 1992 • Retired: 1992
Orig. Price: $14 • **Value: $135**

6

Demi
10.5" • #9112 • TJ
Issued: 1995 • Retired: 1998
Orig. Price: $20 • **Value: $36**

7

Demi II
12" • #9112-00 • TJ
Issued: 1995 • Retired: 1995
Orig. Price: $21 • **Value: $36**

8

Diana
10.5" • #5738 • AS
Issued: 1991 • Retired: 1997
Orig. Price: $14 • **Value: $44**

9

Diana
8" • #9181-01 • TJ
Issued: 1996 • Retired: 1997
Orig. Price: $21 • **Value: $35**

10

Diana (also known as "Elizabeth")
7.5" • #98041 • TJ
Issued: 1996 • Retired: 1996
Orig. Price: $12 • **Value: $27**

11

Dixie
16" • #56541-08 • BA
Issued: 1996 • Retired: 1998
Orig. Price: $24 • **Value: $33**

12

Dolly Q. Bunnycombe
10" • #590150-01 • MB
Issued: 1998 • Retired: 1998
Orig. Price: $24 • **Value: $45**

Hares

	Price Paid	Value
1.		
2.		
3.		
4.		
5.		
6.		
7.		
8.		
9.		
10.		
11.		
12.		
Totals		

1

Donna
8" • #1200-01 • CC
Issued: 1994 • Retired: 1998
Orig. Price: $7 • **Value: $22**

2

Dora B. Bunny
20" • #5211 • JB
Issued: pre-1990 • Retired: 1994
Orig. Price: $29 • **Value: $160**

3

Dudley Hopson
8" • #91663 • TJ
Issued: 1999 • Retired: 2000
Orig. Price: $12 • **Value: $17**

4

Earhart Harington
4.5" • #590086-01 • MB
Issued: 1999 • Retired: 2000
Orig. Price: $10 • **Value: $14**

5

Edina Flatstein
8" • #5685-05 • FL
Issued: 1996 • Retired: 2000
Orig. Price: $13 • **Value: $28**

6

Edith Q. Harington
9" • #590160-03 • MB
Issued: 1999 • Retired: 1999
Orig. Price: $26 • **Value: $34**

7

Edith Q. Harington II
9" • #5901600-03 • MB
Issued: 2000 • To Be Retired: 2001
Orig. Price: $31 • **Value: $31**

8

Eleanor
10.5" • #5737-01 • AS
Issued: 1995 • Retired: 1997
Orig. Price: $14 • **Value: $40**

9

Elizabeth
7.5" • #5733 • AS
Issued: 1991 • Retired: 1999
Orig. Price: $7 • **Value: $22**

10

Eloise R. Hare
8.5" • #5230-10 • JB
Issued: 1994 • Retired: 1999
Orig. Price: $12 • **Value: $22**

11

Elsinore
7.5" • #5732-05 • AS
Issued: 1996 • Retired: 1999
Orig. Price: $7 • **Value: $16**

12

Photo Unavailable

Emily Babbit (Spring 1993)
8" • #9150 • TJ
Issued: 1993 • Retired: 1994
Orig. Price: $20 • **Value: $225**

Hares

	Price Paid	Value
1.		
2.		
3.		
4.		
5.		
6.		
7.		
8.		
9.		
10.		
11.		
12.		
Totals		

Value Guide — Boyds Plush Animals

1

Emily Babbit (Fall 1993)
8" • #9158 • TJ
Issued: 1993 • Retired: 1994
Orig. Price: $24 • **Value: $200**

2

Emily Babbit (Spring 1994)
10.5" • #9150 • TJ
Issued: 1994 • Retired: 1995
Orig. Price: $27 • **Value: $68**

3

Emily Babbit (Spring 1995)
10.5" • #9150-01 • TJ
Issued: 1995 • Retired: 1996
Orig. Price: $20 • **Value: $54**

4

Emily Babbit (Fall 1995)
10.5" • #9150-04 • TJ
Issued: 1995 • Retired: 1996
Orig. Price: $20 • **Value: $53**

5

Emily Babbit (Spring 1996)
10.5" • #9150-05 • TJ
Issued: 1996 • Retired: 1997
Orig. Price: $24 • **Value: $40**

6

Emily Babbit (Fall 1996)
8" • #9150-06 • TJ
Issued: 1996 • Retired: 1997
Orig. Price: $24 • **Value: $40**

Hares

	Price Paid	Value
1.		
2.		
3.		
4.		
5.		
6.		
7.		
8.		
9.		
10.		
11.		
12.		
Totals		

7

Emily Babbit (Spring 1997)
10.5" • #9150-07 • TJ
Issued: 1997 • Retired: 1998
Orig. Price: $24 • **Value: $36**

8

Emily Babbit (Fall 1997)
10.5" • #9150-08 • TJ
Issued: 1997 • Retired: 1998
Orig. Price: $25 • **Value: $35**

9

Emily Babbit (Spring 1998)
8" • #9150-09 • TJ
Issued: 1998 • Retired: 1999
Orig. Price: $27 • **Value: $34**

10

Emily Babbit (Fall 1998)
10" • #9150-10 • TJ
Issued: 1998 • Retired: 1999
Orig. Price: $27 • **Value: $36**

11

Emily Babbit (Spring 1999)
8" • #9150-11 • TJ
Issued: 1999 • Retired: 1999
Orig. Price: $27 • **Value: $36**

12

Emily Babbit (Fall 1999)
8" • #9150-12 • TJ
Issued: 1999 • Retired: 1999
Orig. Price: $27 • **Value: $35**

1

Emily Babbit (Spring 2000)
8" • #9150-14 • TJ
Issued: 2000 • Retired: 2000
Orig. Price: $27 • **Value: $33**

2

Emily Babbit (Fall 2000)
8" • #9150-15 • TJ
Issued: 2000 • To Be Retired: 2001
Orig. Price: $27 • **Value: $27**

3
New

Emily Babbit (Spring 2001)
8" • #9150-16 • TJ
Issued: 2001 • To Be Retired: 2001
Orig. Price: $27 • **Value: $27**

4

Emily R. Hare
14" • #5226 • JB
Issued: 1992 • Retired: 1993
Orig. Price: $20 • **Value: $120**

5

Emma R. Hare
14" • #5225-08 • JB
Issued: 1994 • Retired: 1996
Orig. Price: $20 • **Value: $62**

6

Farnsworth Jr.
9.5" • #5870-08 • AR
Issued: 1995 • Retired: 1998
Orig. Price: $12 • **Value: $27**

7

Farnsworth Sr.
15" • #5875-08 • AR
Issued: 1995 • Retired: 1998
Orig. Price: $20 • **Value: $35**

8

Fergie
7.5" • #5735 • AS
Issued: 1991 • Retired: 1992
Orig. Price: $7 • **Value: $125**

9

Fern Blumenshine
6" • #91692 • TJ
Issued: 1999 • Retired: 2000
Orig. Price: $12 • **Value: $24**

10

Photo Unavailable

Fleurette Hare
info unavailable
Orig. Price: N/A • **Value: N/E**

11
New

Flopsie
12" • #601100 • HF
Issued: 2001 • Current
Orig. Price: $19 • **Value: $19**

12

Flora B. Bunny
20" • #5210 • JB
Issued: 1990 • Retired: 1994
Orig. Price: $29 • **Value: $140**

Hares

	Price Paid	Value
1.		
2.		
3.		
4.		
5.		
6.		
7.		
8.		
9.		
10.		
11.		
12.		
Totals		

1

Flossie B. Hopplebuns
8" • #56481-10 • BA
Issued: 1999 • Retired: 1999
Orig. Price: $11 • **Value: N/E**

2
New

Fluff Pufflepoof
14" • #56380-01 • BA
Issued: 2001 • Current
Orig. Price: $26 • **Value: $26**

3

Fluffie Bunnyhop
8" • #522700-01 • JB
Issued: 2000 • Current
Orig. Price: $10 • **Value: $11**

4

Frangelica
12" • #9109-10 • TJ
Issued: 1996 • Retired: 1998
Orig. Price: $12 • **Value: $30**

5

G.G. Willikers
8" • #91162 • TJ
Issued: 1996 • Retired: 1998
Orig. Price: $20 • **Value: $38**

6

Gabby Bunnyhop
8" • #522700-09 • JB
Issued: 2000 • Retired: 2000
Orig. Price: $8 • **Value: $17**

Hares

	Price Paid	Value
1.		
2.		
3.		
4.		
5.		
6.		
7.		
8.		
9.		
10.		
11.		
12.		
Totals		

7

Photo Unavailable

Gardner
N/A • #6162H • TJ
Issued: 1991 • Retired: 1991
Orig. Price: $63 • **Value: N/E**

8

Giselle de la Fleur
6" • #91703 • TJ
Issued: 1998 • Retired: 1999
Orig. Price: $10 • **Value: $22**

9

Golda
10.5" • #9146 • TJ
Issued: 1994 • Retired: 1995
Orig. Price: $20 • **Value: $41**

10

Photo Unavailable

Grace
N/A • #6163H • TJ
Issued: 1991 • Retired: 1991
Orig. Price: $63 • **Value: N/E**

11

Grace Agnes
11" • #5830-01 • CB
Issued: 1994 • Retired: 1995
Orig. Price: $21 • **Value: $75**

12
New

Graham Quackers
8" • 81509 • HQ
Issued: 2001 • To Be Retired: 2001
Orig. Price: $18 • **Value: $18**

1

Grayson R. Hare
9" • #5230-06 • JB
Issued: 1997 • Retired: 1999
Orig. Price: $12 • **Value: $26**

2

Greta de la Fleur
6" • #91704 • TJ
Issued: 1999 • Retired: 1999
Orig. Price: $9 • **Value: $18**

3

Gretchen
10" • #911210 • TJ
Issued: 1998 • Retired: 1999
Orig. Price: $17 • **Value: $27**

4

Hailey
8" • #9168 • TJ
Issued: 1995 • Retired: 1998
Orig. Price: $11 • **Value: $28**

5

Hannah
7.5" • #91111 • TJ
Issued: 1997 • Retired: 1999
Orig. Price: $12 • **Value: $24**

6

Harriett R. Hare
12" • #5200-08 • JB
Issued: 1994 • Retired: 1996
Orig. Price: $14 • **Value: $45**

7

Harry Lapin II
14" • #5217 • JB
Issued: 1992 • Retired: 1993
Orig. Price: N/A • **Value: $200**

8

Harry R. Hare
17" • #5217-03 • JB
Issued: 1993 • Retired: 1994
Orig. Price: $20 • **Value: $120**

9

Harvey P. Hoppleby
9" • #51740 • BY
Issued: 1999 • Retired: 2000
Orig. Price: $8 • **Value: $10**

10
New

Hattie Hopsalot
16" • #52401-01 • JB
Issued: 2001 • Current
Orig. Price: $31 • **Value: $31**

11

Hedy
10.5" • #9186-01 • TJ
Issued: 1994 • Retired: 1998
Orig. Price: $20 • **Value: $40**

12

Higgins
10" • #5877-06 • AR
Issued: 1995 • Retired: 1997
Orig. Price: $21 • **Value: $48**

Hares

	Price Paid	Value
1.		
2.		
3.		
4.		
5.		
6.		
7.		
8.		
9.		
10.		
11.		
12.		
Totals		

1
New

Higgins D. Nibbleby
8" • #58330 • AS
Issued: 2001 • Current
Orig. Price: $13 • **Value: $13**

2

Higgy
7" • #5876-03 • AR
Issued: 1996 • Retired: 1997
Orig. Price: $20 • **Value: $37**

3

Photo Unavailable

Homer
N/A • #6166H • TJ
Issued: 1991 • Retired: 1991
Orig. Price: $63 • **Value: N/E**

4

Hopkins
10.5" • #91121 • TJ
Issued: 1998 • Retired: 1999
Orig. Price: $18 • **Value: $27**

5

Iris Rosenbunny
10" • #91651 • TJ
Issued: 1999 • Retired: 2000
Orig. Price: $20 • **Value: $23**

6

Jack
20" • #5215 • JB
Issued: 1991 • Retired: 1992
Orig. Price: $29 • **Value: $242**

7

Jane
14" • #5732 • AS
Issued: 1992 • Retired: 1992
Orig. Price: $20 • **Value: $240**

8

Jane
10.5" • #5737-05 • AS
Issued: 1994 • Retired: 1998
Orig. Price: $14 • **Value: $28**

9

Janet
8" • #1200-03 • CC
Issued: 1994 • Retired: 1997
Orig. Price: $7 • **Value: $30**

10

Jenna D. Lapinne
8.5" • #916630 • TJ
Issued: 2000 • Current
Orig. Price: $16 • **Value: $16**

11

Jessica
8" • #9168-02 • TJ
Issued: 1997 • Retired: 2000
Orig. Price: $12 • **Value: $26**

12

Photo Unavailable

Jill
20" • #5216 • JB
Issued: 1991 • Retired: 1992
Orig. Price: $29 • **Value: $235**

Hares

	Price Paid	Value
1.		
2.		
3.		
4.		
5.		
6.		
7.		
8.		
9.		
10.		
11.		
12.		
Totals		

1

Josephine
6" • #91701 • TJ
Issued: 1996 • Retired: 1998
Orig. Price: $9 • **Value: $22**

2

Juliana Hopkins
8" • #91122 • TJ
Issued: 1999 • Retired: 1999
Orig. Price: $17 • **Value: $22**

3

Juliana Hopkins II
8" • #911220 • TJ
Issued: 2000 • Retired: 2000
Orig. Price: $15 • **Value: $28**

4

Julip O'Harea
12" • #91664 • TJ
Issued: 1996 • Retired: 1998
Orig. Price: $23 • **Value: $36**

5

Juniper Bunnyhugs
10" • #916501 • BE
Issued: 2000 • Retired: 2000
Orig. Price: $16 • **Value: $40**

6

Katerina
10" • #5874 • HT
Issued: 1992 • Retired: 1993
Orig. Price: $20 • **Value: $95**

7

Kathryn
7.5" • #5732-01 • AS
Issued: 1994 • Retired: 1998
Orig. Price: $7 • **Value: $25**

8
New

Keefer P. Lightfoot
12" • #52200-06 • JB
Issued: 2001 • Current
Orig. Price: $20 • **Value: $20**

9

Kerry Q. Hopgood
17" • #52401-03 • JB
Issued: 1999 • To Be Retired: 2001
Orig. Price: $29 • **Value: $29**

10
New

Key Lime Thumpster
10" • #52010-08 • JB
Issued: 2001 • Current
Orig. Price: $16 • **Value: $16**

11

Lacy
14" • #6100H • TJ
Issued: 1990 • Retired: 1994
Orig. Price: $16 • **Value: $105**

12

Lacy
17" • #6101H • TJ
Issued: 1990 • Retired: 1992
Orig. Price: $21 • **Value: $125**

Hares

	Price Paid	Value
1.		
2.		
3.		
4.		
5.		
6.		
7.		
8.		
9.		
10.		
11.		
12.		
Totals		

1

Lady Harriwell
11" • #91892-14 • TJ
Issued: 1999 • Retired: 1999
Orig. Price: $21 • **Value: $25**

2

Lady Payton
10.5" • #918921-09 • TJ
Issued: 1998 • Retired: 1999
Orig. Price: $17 • **Value: $30**

3

Lady Pembrooke
15" • #91892-09 • TJ
Issued: 1997 • Retired: 1999
Orig. Price: $21 • **Value: $28**

4

Lana
10.5" • #9186 • TJ
Issued: 1993 • Retired: 1994
Orig. Price: $20 • **Value: $65**

5

Larry Lapin
17" • #5209 • JB
Issued: pre-1990 • Retired: 1991
Orig. Price: $20 • **Value: $175**

6

Photo Unavailable

Larry Too
17" • #5217 • JB
Issued: 1992 • Retired: 1992
Orig. Price: $20 • **Value: N/E**

7

Lauren
8" • #9168-01 • TJ
Issued: 1996 • Retired: 1998
Orig. Price: $11 • **Value: $25**

8

Lavinia V. Hariweather
10" • #91661 • TJ
Issued: 1997 • Retired: 1999
Orig. Price: $20 • **Value: $29**

9

Lenora Flatstein
8" • #5685-08 • FL
Issued: 1994 • Retired: 1998
Orig. Price: $12 • **Value: $30**

10

Leona B. Bunny
20" • #5214 • JB
Issued: pre-1990 • Retired: 1992
Orig. Price: $29 • **Value: $325**

11

Libby Lapinette
6" • #91681 • TJ
Issued: 1999 • Retired: 1999
Orig. Price: $11 • **Value: $14**

12

Lila Hopkins
8" • #91124 • TJ
Issued: 2000 • Current
Orig. Price: $18 • **Value: $18**

Hares

	Price Paid	Value
1.		
2.		
3.		
4.		
5.		
6.		
7.		
8.		
9.		
10.		
11.		
12.		
Totals		

1

Lily R. Hare
8" • #5227-01 • JB
Issued: 1994 • Retired: 2000
Orig. Price: $10 • **Value: $19**

2

Livingston R. Hare
12" • #5200 • JB
Issued: pre-1990 • Retired: 1998
Orig. Price: $14 • **Value: $35**

3

Lottie de Lopear
9" • #91648 • TJ
Issued: 2000 • Retired: 2000
Orig. Price: $15 • **Value: $27**

4

Lucille
13.5" • #91141 • TJ
Issued: 1997 • Retired: 1998
Orig. Price: $24 • **Value: $45**

5

Lucinda de la Fleur
6" • #91705 • TJ
Issued: 1999 • Retired: 2000
Orig. Price: $9 • **Value: $15**

6

Lucy P. Blumenshine
6" • #91702 • TJ
Issued: 1997 • Retired: 1998
Orig. Price: $10 • **Value: $26**

7
New

Lula Mae Loppenhop
6" • #573304-08 • AS
Issued: 2001 • Current
Orig. Price: $7 • **Value: $7**

8

Magnolia O'Harea
17" • #91667 • TJ
Issued: 1996 • Retired: 1998
Orig. Price: $31 • **Value: $42**

9

Mallory
info unavailable
Orig. Price: N/A • **Value: $44**

10

Margaret Mary
11" • #5830 • CB
Issued: 1992 • Retired: 1995
Orig. Price: $21 • **Value: $80**

11

Marigold McHare
8" • #52270-08 • JB
Issued: 1999 • Retired: 2000
Orig. Price: $10 • **Value: $13**

12

Marlena
10.5" • #9154 • TJ
Issued: 1994 • Retired: 1997
Orig. Price: $20 • **Value: $40**

Hares

	Price Paid	Value
1.		
2.		
3.		
4.		
5.		
6.		
7.		
8.		
9.		
10.		
11.		
12.		
Totals		

1

Marta M. Hare
12" • #5206 • JB
Issued: pre-1990 • Retired: 1992
Orig. Price: $14 • **Value: $140**

2

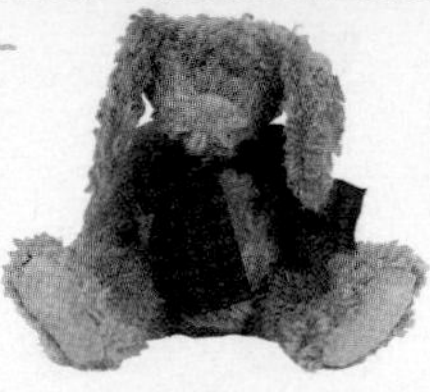

Martha T. Bunnycombe
15.5" • #590140-03 • MB
Issued: 1998 • Retired: 1998
Orig. Price: $51 • **Value: $74**

3

Mary
10.5" • #5737 • AS
Issued: 1991 • Retired: 1997
Orig. Price: $14 • **Value: $34**

4

Mary Catherine
9" • #5829 • CB
Issued: 1992 • Retired: 1995
Orig. Price: $16 • **Value: $70**

5

Mary Regina
9" • #5829-01 • CB
Issued: 1994 • Retired: 1995
Orig. Price: $16 • **Value: $72**

6

Photo Unavailable

Matilda
N/A • #6161H • TJ
Issued: 1991 • Retired: 1991
Orig. Price: $63 • **Value: N/E**

7
New

Mazie Q. Lightfoot
9" • #58300-05 • AS
Issued: 2001 • Current
Orig. Price: $15 • **Value: $15**

8

Photo Unavailable

Merlin
N/A • #6167H • TJ
Issued: 1991 • Retired: 1991
Orig. Price: $63 • **Value: N/E**

9

Michelline
7.5" • #91815 • TJ
Issued: 1996 • Retired: 1997
Orig. Price: $13 • **Value: $27**

10

Mickey
8" • #1200-08 • CC
Issued: 1994 • Retired: 1995
Orig. Price: $7 • **Value: $50**

11

Mickie
16" • #5654 • BA
Issued: 1992 • Retired: 1998
Orig. Price: $21 • **Value: N/E**

12

Millie Hopkins
8" • #91123 • TJ
Issued: 1999 • Retired: 2000
Orig. Price: $18 • **Value: $24**

Hares

	Price Paid	Value
1.		
2.		
3.		
4.		
5.		
6.		
7.		
8.		
9.		
10.		
11.		
12.		
Totals		

1

Mimi Delapain
8" • #9169 • JB
Issued: 1995 • Retired: 1998
Orig. Price: $9 • **Value: $26**

2

Mimosa
17" • #9110-10 • TJ
Issued: 1996 • Retired: 1998
Orig. Price: $19 • **Value: $33**

3

Mipsie Blumenshine
6" • #917040 • TJ
Issued: 2000 • Retired: 2000
Orig. Price: $12 • **Value: $22**

4
New

Miracle Gardenglow
8" • #916632 • TJ
Issued: 2001 • Current
Orig. Price: $19 • **Value: $19**

5

Miranda Blumenshine
10" • #91142 • TJ
Issued: 1999 • Retired: 2000
Orig. Price: $23 • **Value: $25**

6

Moe Lapin
14" • #5208 • JB
Issued: 1990 • Retired: 1995
Orig. Price: $14 • **Value: $75**

7

Molly
14" • N/A • N/A
Issued: 1993 • Retired: 1993
Orig. Price: N/A • **Value: N/E**

8

Momma O'Harea & Bonnie Blue
12" & 6" • #91008 • TJ
Issued: 1998 • Retired: 1998
Orig. Price: $29 • **Value: $40**

9

Montgomery Flatstein
8" • #5685-10 • FL
Issued: 1994 • Retired: 2000
Orig. Price: $12 • **Value: $21**

10

Photo Unavailable

Mrs. Harelwig
info unavailable
Orig. Price: N/A • **Value: N/E**

11

Photo Unavailable

Mrs. Harestein
info unavailable
Orig. Price: N/A • **Value: N/E**

12

Photo Unavailable

Nanny II
info unavailable
Orig. Price: N/A • **Value: N/E**

Hares

	Price Paid	Value
1.		
2.		
3.		
4.		
5.		
6.		
7.		
8.		
9.		
10.		
11.		
12.		
Totals		

Value Guide — Boyds Plush Animals

1

Natalie Nibblenose
6" • #573300-01 • AS
Issued: 2000 • Retired: 2000
Orig. Price: $7 • **Value: $15**

2

Natasha
10" • #5873 • HT
Issued: 1992 • Retired: 1994
Orig. Price: $20 • **Value: $85**

3

Nibbie Bunnyhop
8" • #522700-06 • BE
Issued: 2000 • Retired: 2000
Orig. Price: $8 • **Value: $13**

4

Photo Unavailable

Nickie
16" • #5653 • BA
Issued: 1992 • Retired: 1993
Orig. Price: $21 • **Value: $150**

5

Nickie Nibblenose
6" • #573303-03 • AS
Issued: 2000 • Retired: 2000
Orig. Price: $7 • **Value: $16**

6
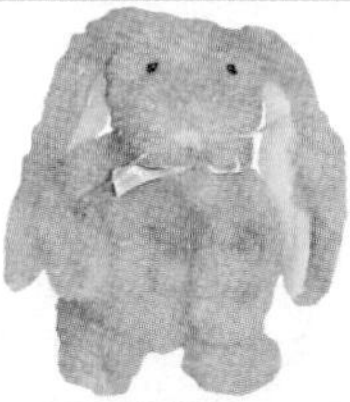

Olga
6" • #5871 • HT
Issued: 1992 • Retired: 1992
Orig. Price: $9 • **Value: $118**

7

Oliver
6" • #91110 • TJ
Issued: 1998 • Retired: 2000
Orig. Price: $12 • **Value: $17**

8

Orchid de la Hoppsack
8" • #91405 • TJ
Issued: 1998 • Retired: 1999
Orig. Price: $13 • **Value: $23**

9

Pansy Rosenbunny
10" • #91652 • TJ
Issued: 1999 • Retired: 1999
Orig. Price: $20 • **Value: $23**

10

Paula Hoppleby
8" • #91125 • TJ
Issued: 2000 • Retired: 2000
Orig. Price: $18 • **Value: N/E**

11

Peapod
6" • #91071 • TJ
Issued: 1996 • Retired: 1997
Orig. Price: $12 • **Value: $35**

12
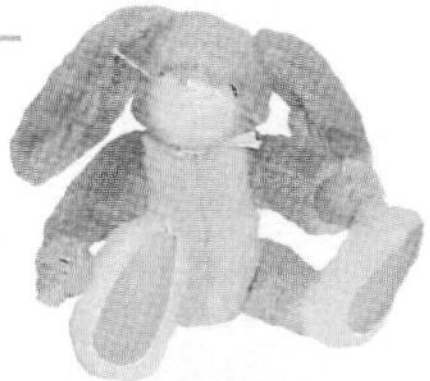

Penelope
14" • #5729 • AS
Issued: 1992 • Retired: 1995
Orig. Price: $20 • **Value: $70**

Hares

	Price Paid	Value
1.		
2.		
3.		
4.		
5.		
6.		
7.		
8.		
9.		
10.		
11.		
12.		
Totals		

1

Peter
6" • #9111 • TJ
Issued: 1995 • Retired: 1997
Orig. Price: $11 • **Value: $27**

2

Pixie
12" • #5651 • BA
Issued: 1992 • Retired: 1993
Orig. Price: $16 • **Value: $59**

3

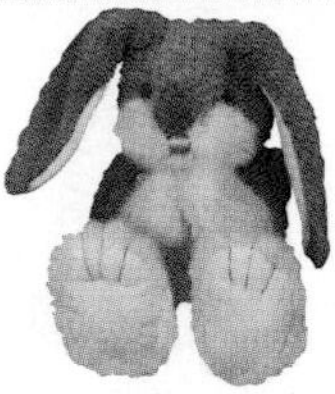

Pixie
12" • #56510-05 • BA
Issued: 1998 • Retired: 2000
Orig. Price: $16 • **Value: $22**

4

Pookie C. Hoppleby
6" • #517040-01 • BY
Issued: 2000 • Retired: 2000
Orig. Price: $5 • **Value: $9**

5

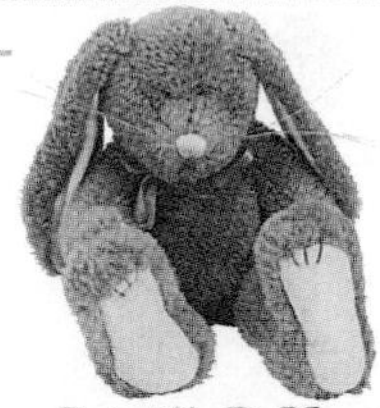

Priscilla R. Hare
14" • #5217-08 • JB
Issued: 1995 • Retired: 1997
Orig. Price: $16 • **Value: $36**

6

Priscilla R. Hare
17" • #5217-12 • JB
Issued: 1993 • Retired: 1994
Orig. Price: $20 • **Value: N/E**

7

Regena Haresford
13" • #916490 • TJ
Issued: 2000 • Current
Orig. Price: $30 • **Value: $30**

8

Regina
14" • #5731 • AS
Issued: 1991 • Retired: 1993
Orig. Price: $20 • **Value: $135**

9

Regina
10.5" • #5737-08 • AS
Issued: 1998 • Retired: 1999
Orig. Price: $14 • **Value: $25**

10

Rita
11" • #1201-08 • CC
Issued: 1994 • Retired: 1995
Orig. Price: $10 • **Value: $68**

11
New

Rosalie Bloomengrows
10" • #916500 • TJ
Issued: 2001 • Current
Orig. Price: $27 • **Value: $27**

12

Rosalynn P. Harington
12" • #590140-01 • MB
Issued: 1999 • Retired: 1999
Orig. Price: $51 • **Value: $58**

Hares

	Price Paid	Value
1.		
2.		
3.		
4.		
5.		
6.		
7.		
8.		
9.		
10.		
11.		
12.		
Totals		

Value Guide — Boyds Plush Animals

1

Rosalynn P. Harington II
12" • #5901400-01 • MB
Issued: 2000 • Retired: 2000
Orig. Price: $56 • **Value: $64**

2

Roscoe P. Bumpercrop
17" • #912079 • TJ
Issued: 1999 • To Be Retired: 2001
Orig. Price: $40 • **Value: $40**

3

Rose
7.5" • #91112 • TJ
Issued: 1997 • Retired: 1998
Orig. Price: $12 • **Value: $25**

4

Roslyn Hiphop
14" • #912080 • TJ
Issued: 2000 • To Be Retired: 2001
Orig. Price: $31 • **Value: $31**

5

Roxbunny R. Hare
14" • #5878-06 • AR
Issued: 1997 • Retired: 1998
Orig. Price: $14 • **Value: $35**

6

Photo Unavailable

Royce
N/A • #6107H • TJ
Issued: 1990 • Retired: 1992
Orig. Price: $32 • **Value: $300**

7

Rumpus
9" • #5745 • HD
Issued: 1991 • Retired: 1992
Orig. Price: $14 • **Value: $165**

8

Ruth
11" • #1201-01 • CC
Issued: 1994 • Retired: 1995
Orig. Price: $10 • **Value: $70**

9

Sangria
17" • #9110-05 • TJ
Issued: 1998 • Retired: 1999
Orig. Price: $20 • **Value: $26**

10

Sara
7.5" • #9140 • TJ
Issued: 1994 • Retired: 1996
Orig. Price: $13 • **Value: $50**

11

Sara II
6" • #91401 • TJ
Issued: 1996 • Retired: 1998
Orig. Price: $13 • **Value: $25**

Hares

	Price Paid	Value
1.		
2.		
3.		
4.		
5.		
6.		
7.		
8.		
9.		
10.		
11.		
Totals		

1

Sarah
10.5" • #5739 • AS
Issued: 1991 • Retired: 1993
Orig. Price: $14 • **Value: $82**

2

Savannah Buttercup
10" • #91650 • TJ
Issued: 2000 • Retired: 2000
Orig. Price: $27 • **Value: $33**

3

Sharona
10.5" • #5737-10 • AS
Issued: 1998 • Retired: 1999
Orig. Price: $14 • **Value: $25**

4

Sophie
12" • #9114 • TJ
Issued: 1995 • Retired: 1998
Orig. Price: $20 • **Value: $40**

5

Sophie B . Bunny
20" • #5215 • JB
Issued: 1993 • Retired: 1994
Orig. Price: $29 • **Value: $220**

6

Squeeky
8" • #5620 • SQ
Issued: 1991 • Retired: 1992
Orig. Price: $10 • **Value: $95**

7

Squeeky
8" • #5621 • SQ
Issued: 1992 • Retired: 1992
Orig. Price: $10 • **Value: $105**

8

Stanley R. Hare
12" • #5201 • JB
Issued: 1991 • Retired: 1998
Orig. Price: $14 • **Value: $27**

9

Stellina Hopswell
8" • #573700-01 • AS
Issued: 2000 • To Be Retired: 2001
Orig. Price: $14 • **Value: $14**

10

Sterling Hopswell
8" • #573701-06 • AS
Issued: 2000 • To Be Retired: 2001
Orig. Price: $14 • **Value: $14**

11

Stewart Rarebit
8" • #9116 • TJ
Issued: 1995 • Retired: 1998
Orig. Price: $13 • **Value: $30**

12

T. Farrell Wuzzie
5" • #595101-06 • TF
Issued: 2000 • Retired: 2000
Orig. Price: $9 • **Value: $11**

Hares

	Price Paid	Value
1.		
2.		
3.		
4.		
5.		
6.		
7.		
8.		
9.		
10.		
11.		
12.		
Totals		

1

T. Hopplewhite
12" • #52200-01 • JB
Issued: 2000 • Retired: 2000
Orig. Price: $19 • **Value: $26**

2

Taffy C. Hopplebuns
8" • #56481-03 • BA
Issued: 1999 • Retired: 1999
Orig. Price: $11 • **Value: $18**

3

Tami F. Wuzzie
3" • #596100 • TF
Issued: 1999 • To Be Retired: 2001
Orig. Price: $8 • **Value: $8**

4
New

Tangerine Thumpster
10" • #52031-01 • JB
Issued: 2001 • Current
Orig. Price: $16 • **Value: $16**

5

Tanner F. Wuzzie
4" • #595300-08 • TF
Issued: 1998 • Retired: 2000
Orig. Price: $7 • **Value: $9**

6

Tapper F. Wuzzie
3" • #595300-06 • TF
Issued: 1999 • Retired: 2000
Orig. Price: $7 • **Value: $9**

7

Tarragon
17" • #9110-07 • TJ
Issued: 1996 • Retired: 1997
Orig. Price: $19 • **Value: $52**

8

Tatiana
14" • #5877 • HT
Issued: 1992 • Retired: 1992
Orig. Price: $32 • **Value: $150**

9
New

Tatters T. Hareloom
10" • #52000 • JB
Issued: 2001 • Current
Orig. Price: $18 • **Value: $18**

10

Teddy Hare
info unavailable
Orig. Price: $13 • **Value: $225**

11

Teddy Hare
info unavailable
Orig. Price: N/A • **Value: $185**

12

Teddy Hare
info unavailable
Orig. Price: N/A • **Value: N/E**

Hares

	Price Paid	Value
1.		
2.		
3.		
4.		
5.		
6.		
7.		
8.		
9.		
10.		
11.		
12.		
Totals		

1

Teddy Hare
info unavailable
Orig. Price: N/A • **Value: N/E**

2
New

Tessie T. Nibblenose
6" • #917050 • TJ
Issued: 2001 • Current
Orig. Price: $12 • **Value: $12**

3

Thump
14" • #5747 • HD
Issued: 1991 • Retired: 1992
Orig. Price: $27 • **Value: $220**

4
New

Tina Marie Hopgood
6" • #81507 • HQ
Issued: 2001 • To Be Retired: 2001
Orig. Price: $12 • **Value: $12**

5

Tipper
8" • #5648-08 • BA
Issued: 1993 • Retired: 1997
Orig. Price: $11 • **Value: $42**

6

Tippy F. Wuzzie
4" • #595300-01 • TF
Issued: 1998 • Retired: 2000
Orig. Price: $7 • **Value: $9**

7

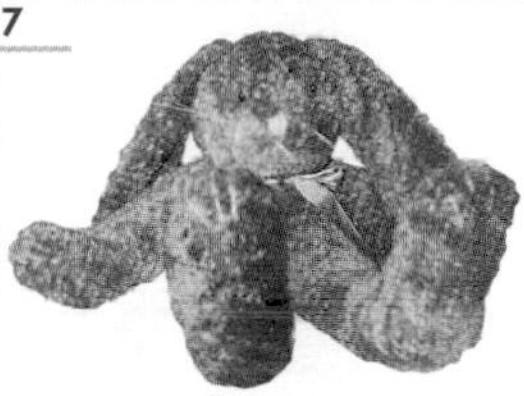

Trixie
16" • #5654-08 • BA
Issued: 1993 • Retired: 1996
Orig. Price: $24 • **Value: $90**

8

Photo Unavailable

Tutu
N/A • #6169H • TJ
Issued: 1991 • Retired: 1991
Orig. Price: $63 • **Value: $175**

9
New

Twigley Hopsalot
8" • #522701-08 • JB
Issued: 2001 • Current
Orig. Price: $11 • **Value: $11**

10

Vanessa D. LaPinne
10" • #91662 • TJ
Issued: 1999 • Retired: 2000
Orig. Price: $27 • **Value: $35**

11
New

Vanna Hopkins
6" • #91113 • TJ
Issued: 2001 • Current
Orig. Price: $12 • **Value: $12**

12

Veronica
10.5" • #9181 • TJ
Issued: 1994 • Retired: 1997
Orig. Price: $20 • **Value: $60**

Hares

	Price Paid	Value
1.		
2.		
3.		
4.		
5.		
6.		
7.		
8.		
9.		
10.		
11.		
12.		

Totals

1

Victoria
7.5" • #5736 • AS
Issued: 1991 • Retired: 1999
Orig. Price: $7 • **Value: $20**

2

Violet Dubois
6" • #91403 • TJ
Issued: 1996 • Retired: 1998
Orig. Price: $12 • **Value: $26**

3
New

Webster Hopplebuns
8" • #916631 • TJ
Issued: 2001 • Current
Orig. Price: $19 • **Value: $19**

4

Wedgewood J. Hopgood
17" • #52401-10 • JB
Issued: 1999 • Retired: 2000
Orig. Price: $29 • **Value: $35**

5

Whitney
12" • #9130 • TJ
Issued: 1995 • Retired: 1998
Orig. Price: $20 • **Value: $35**

6

Wilhelm Von Bruin
6" • #5015 • WB
Issued: 1992 • Retired: 1995
Orig. Price: $9 • **Value: $44**

Hares

	Price Paid	Value
1.		
2.		
3.		
4.		
5.		
6.		
7.		
8.		

Kangaroos

9.		

Lambs

10.		

Totals

7

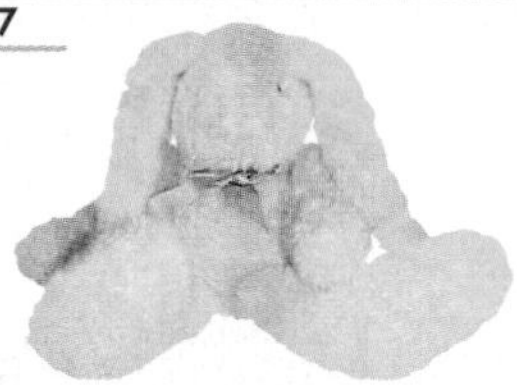

Wixie
12" • #5650 • BA
Issued: 1992 • Retired: 1998
Orig. Price: $16 • **Value: $32**

8

Zelda Fitzhare
17" • #5240-10 • JB
Issued: 1995 • Retired: 1998
Orig. Price: $29 • **Value: $41**

Kangaroos

9
New

Adelaide & Joey Downunder
12" • #55222 • AM
Issued: 2001 • Current
Orig. Price: $26 • **Value: $26**

Lambs

10

Abbey Ewe
14" • #91311-01 • TJ
Issued: 1996 • Retired: 1998
Orig. Price: $29 • **Value: $52**

1

Daisy Ewe
10" • #5500 • AM
Issued: pre-1990 • Retired: 1994
Orig. Price: $14 • **Value: $50**

2

Dick Butkus
10" • #9155 • TJ
Issued: 1994 • Retired: 1994
Orig. Price: $20 • **Value: $145**

3

Dipsey Baadoodle
9" • #51800-01 • BY
Issued: 2000 • Retired: 2000
Orig. Price: $8 • **Value: $12**

4

Elspethe Ewe
8" • #91312 • TJ
Issued: 1997 • Retired: 1998
Orig. Price: $11 • **Value: $25**

5

Embraceable Ewe
8" • #913121 • TJ
Issued: 2000 • To Be Retired: 2001
Orig. Price: $11 • **Value: $11**

6

New

Flossie
12" • #602100 • HF
Issued: 2001 • Current
Orig. Price: $19 • **Value: $19**

7

New

Liza Fuzzyfleece
14" • #55203-01 • AM
Issued: 2001 • Current
Orig. Price: $23 • **Value: $23**

8

New

Lucibelle Fuzzyfleece
14" • #55203-06 • AM
Issued: 2001 • Current
Orig. Price: $23 • **Value: $23**

9

Madabout Ewe
6" • #91312-01 • TJ
Issued: 1998 • Retired: 2000
Orig. Price: $11 • **Value: $22**

10

Maisey Ewe
10" • #5501 • AM
Issued: pre-1990 • Retired: 1994
Orig. Price: $14 • **Value: $96**

11

Matilda Baahead
10" • #55200-01 • AM
Issued: 2000 • Current
Orig. Price: $14 • **Value: $14**

12

Maude Ewe
7" • #5510-07 • AM
Issued: 1994 • Retired: 1996
Orig. Price: $7 • **Value: $45**

Lambs

	Price Paid	Value
1.		
2.		
3.		
4.		
5.		
6.		
7.		
8.		
9.		
10.		
11.		
12.		
Totals		

1

McNeil Mutton
14" • #91311-07 • TJ
Issued: 1996 • Retired: 1998
Orig. Price: $29 • **Value: $44**

2

Pansy
10" • #5501-01 • N/A
Issued: N/A • Retired: N/A
Orig. Price: N/A • **Value: $85**

3

Phoebe Ewe
7" • #5510-01 • AM
Issued: 1994 • Retired: 1996
Orig. Price: $7 • **Value: $48**

4

Rose Mutton
15" • #5520 • AM
Issued: pre-1990 • Retired: 1994
Orig. Price: $20 • **Value: $115**

5

Sadie Ewe
7" • #5510-03 • AM
Issued: 1994 • Retired: 1994
Orig. Price: $7 • **Value: $90**

6

Squeeky
8" • #5622 • SQ
Issued: 1992 • Retired: 1992
Orig. Price: $10 • **Value: $85**

Lambs

	Price Paid	Value
1.		
2.		
3.		
4.		
5.		
6.		
7.		
8.		
9.		
10.		

Lions

11.		
Totals		

7

Tallulah Baahead
14" • #5520-01 • AM
Issued: 1995 • Retired: 2000
Orig. Price: $20 • **Value: $50**

8

Photo Unavailable

Tutu
N/A • #6169L • TJ
Issued: 1991 • Retired: 1991
Orig. Price: $63 • **Value: N/E**

9

Violet Ewe
10" • #5500-07 • AM
Issued: 1996 • Retired: 1998
Orig. Price: $14 • **Value: $34**

10

Wannabee Ewe-Too
8" • #91312-02 • TJ
Issued: 1999 • Retired: 1999
Orig. Price: $11 • **Value: N/E**

Lions

11

Butch
8" • #5861 • BB
Issued: 1994 • Retired: 1994
Orig. Price: $14 • **Value: $112**

1

Dickie The Lionheart
6" • #51700 • BY
Issued: 1997 • Retired: 1999
Orig. Price: $5 • **Value: $14**

2

Elvis
12" • #5859 • AR
Issued: 1995 • Retired: 1996
Orig. Price: $20 • **Value: $45**

3

I.M. Uproarius
11" • #55220 • AM
Issued: 2000 • Current
Orig. Price: $16 • **Value: $16**

4

Lance
8" • #51900 • BY
Issued: 1997 • Retired: 1999
Orig. Price: $8 • **Value: $14**

5

Leopold Q. Lion
10" • #5530 • AM
Issued: pre-1990 • Retired: 1993
Orig. Price: $14 • **Value: $175**

6

Marley Dredlion
9" • #51735 • BY
Issued: 1999 • Retired: 2000
Orig. Price: $8 • **Value: $13**

7

Photo Unavailable

Merlin
info unavailable
Orig. Price: N/A • **Value: N/E**

8

Sampson T. Lion
14" • #5531 • AM
Issued: pre-1990 • Retired: 1992
Orig. Price: $29 • **Value: $305**

9

Spike T. Lion
14" • #5860 • BB
Issued: 1992 • Retired: 1994
Orig. Price: $20 • **Value: $116**

10

Theo F. Wuzzie
3" • #596007 • TF
Issued: 2000 • Current
Orig. Price: $7 • **Value: $7**

Mice

11

Bebe
6" • #9167 • TJ
Issued: 1994 • Retired: 1996
Orig. Price: $13 • **Value: $45**

Lions

	Price Paid	Value
1.		
2.		
3.		
4.		
5.		
6.		
7.		
8.		
9.		
10.		
Mice		
11.		
Totals		

1

Bebe
6" • #9167-01 • TJ
Issued: 1994 • Retired: 1995
Orig. Price: $13 • **Value: $45**

2

Brie
6" • #5756 • AS
Issued: 1993 • Current
Orig. Price: $8 • **Value: $8**

3
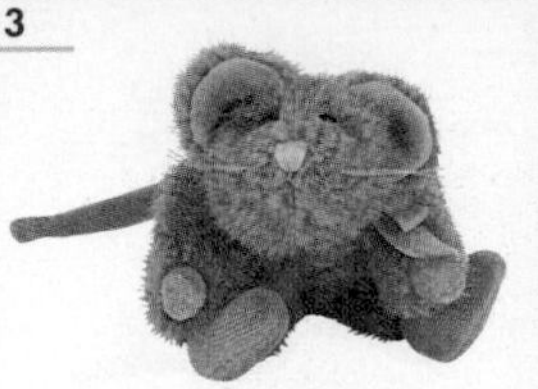

Chedda
6" • #5756-06 • AS
Issued: 1993 • Retired: 2000
Orig. Price: $8 • **Value: $11**

4

Chutney Cheeseworthy
8" • #916710 • TJ
Issued: 2000 • Current
Orig. Price: $18 • **Value: $18**

5

Colby S. Mouski
6" • #91672 • TJ
Issued: 1998 • Retired: 1999
Orig. Price: $12 • **Value: $20**

6

Cottage McNibble
6" • #91673 • TJ
Issued: 1999 • Retired: 2000
Orig. Price: $12 • **Value: $18**

7
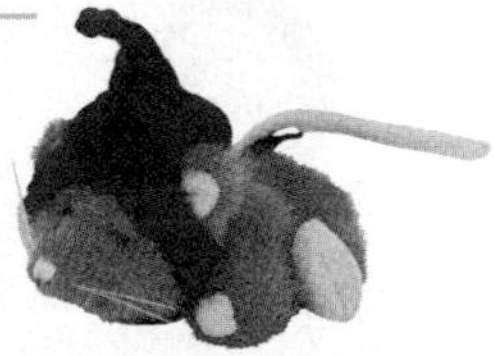

Feta
6" • #91075 • TJ
Issued: 1995 • Retired: 1996
Orig. Price: $12 • **Value: $80**

8

Gouda
6" • #91671 • TJ
Issued: 1998 • Retired: 2000
Orig. Price: $12 • **Value: $17**

9

Joy
6" • #9165-06 • TJ
Issued: 1993 • Retired: 1996
Orig. Price: $12 • **Value: $42**

10

Monterey Mouski
6" • #91675 • TJ
Issued: 1999 • To Be Retired: 2001
Orig. Price: $12 • **Value: $12**

11

Munster Q. Fondue
6" • #5755-06 • AS
Issued: 2000 • Current
Orig. Price: $8 • **Value: $8**

12
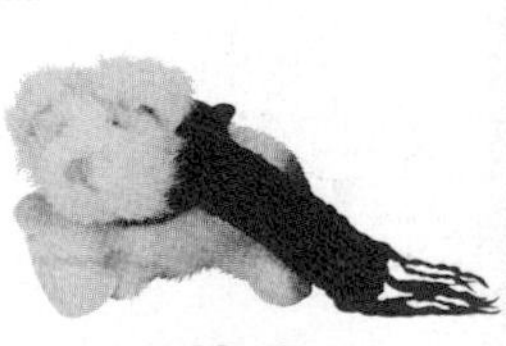

Noel
6" • #9165-01 • TJ
Issued: 1993 • Retired: 1996
Orig. Price: $12 • **Value: $44**

Mice

	Price Paid	Value
1.		
2.		
3.		
4.		
5.		
6.		
7.		
8.		
9.		
10.		
11.		
12.		
Totals		

1

Romano B. Grated
6" • #5755 • AS
Issued: 2000 • Current
Orig. Price: $8 • **Value: $8**

2

Roq
8" • #5757-01 • AS
Issued: 1994 • Retired: 1995
Orig. Price: $14 • **Value: $65**

3

Sharp McNibble
6" • #91674 • TJ
Issued: 1999 • To Be Retired: 2001
Orig. Price: $12 • **Value: $12**

4

Stilton
8" • #5757 • AS
Issued: 1993 • Retired: 1995
Orig. Price: $14 • **Value: $68**

5
New

Swiss C. Mouski
6" • #91670 • TJ
Issued: 2001 • Current
Orig. Price: $12 • **Value: $12**

6

Tidbit F. Wuzzie
2.5" • #595170 • TF
Issued: 1999 • Retired: 2000
Orig. Price: $7 • **Value: $13**

Monkeys

7

Bertha S. Simiansky
10" • #5524-11 • AM
Issued: 1993 • Retired: 1996
Orig. Price: $14 • **Value: $43**

8

Dalton Monkbury
8" • #55242-08 • AM
Issued: 1998 • To Be Retired: 2001
Orig. Price: $12 • **Value: $12**

9

Darwin Monkbury
8" • #55242-05 • AM
Issued: 1998 • To Be Retired: 2001
Orig. Price: $12 • **Value: $12**

10

Finster R. Tsuris
10" • #55241-05 • AM
Issued: 1997 • Retired: 1999
Orig. Price: $14 • **Value: $37**

11

Imogene R. Tsuris
10" • #55241-11 • AM
Issued: 1997 • Retired: 1999
Orig. Price: $14 • **Value: $35**

Mice	Price Paid	Value
1.		
2.		
3.		
4.		
5.		
6.		
Monkeys		
7.		
8.		
9.		
10.		
11.		
Totals		

1

Jim I. Swingster
10" • #55241-08 • AM
Issued: 2000 • Current
Orig. Price: $16 • **Value: $16**

2
New

Simianne Z. Jodibear
7" • #92000-15 • AR
Issued: 2001 • Current
Orig. Price: $18 • **Value: $18**

3

Simon S. Simiansky
10" • #5524-10 • AM
Issued: 1993 • Retired: 1996
Orig. Price: $14 • **Value: $58**

4

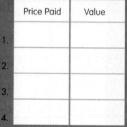

Toodles F. Wuzzie
3" • #596006 • TF
Issued: 2000 • Current
Orig. Price: $8 • **Value: $8**

Moose

5

Beatrice Von Hindenmoose
17" • #5542 • NL
Issued: 1991 • Retired: 1997
Orig. Price: $16 • **Value: $65**

6

Bismark Von Hindenmoose
20" • #5545-05 • NL
Issued: 1995 • Retired: 1996
Orig. Price: $29 • **Value: $77**

7

Edwina
14" • #9144 • TJ
Issued: 1994 • Retired: 1997
Orig. Price: $20 • **Value: $45**

8

Egon Von Hindenmoose
6" • #5546 • NL
Issued: 1993 • Retired: 1997
Orig. Price: $8 • **Value: $52**

9

Euphoria
8" • #91446 • TJ
Issued: 1995 • Retired: 1998
Orig. Price: $14 • **Value: $28**

10

Father Krismoose
info unavailable
Orig. Price: N/A • **Value: N/E**

11

Photo Unavailable

Father Moose Moss
info unavailable
Orig. Price: N/A • **Value: N/E**

Monkeys	Price Paid	Value
1.		
2.		
3.		
4.		
Moose		
5.		
6.		
7.		
8.		
9.		
10.		
11.		
Totals		

1

Father Moosemas
info unavailable
Orig. Price: N/A • **Value: N/E**

2

Festus
14" • #91444 • TJ
Issued: 1995 • Retired: 1996
Orig. Price: $21 • **Value: $55**

3

Gertrude
17" • #6108 • TJ
Issued: 1993 • Retired: 1993
Orig. Price: N/A • **Value: $300**

4

Helmut
14" • #9145 • TJ
Issued: 1994 • Retired: 1995
Orig. Price: $27 • **Value: $72**
Variation: green sweater
Value: $82

5

Irwin Mooseltoe
12" • #917296 • TJ
Issued: 2000 • Retired: 2000
Orig. Price: $27 • **Value: N/E**

6

Justina (formerly "Philomena")
14" • #91443 • TJ
Issued: 1995 • Retired: 1997
Orig. Price: $27 • **Value: $53**

7

Kris Moose (formerly "Father Krismoose")
14" • #9192 • JB
Issued: 1992 • Retired: 1996
Orig. Price: $27 • **Value: N/E**

8

Photo Unavailable

Krismoose
info unavailable
Orig. Price: N/A • **Value: N/E**

9

Maddie LaMoose
6" • #517030-05 • BY
Issued: 1999 • Retired: 2000
Orig. Price: $5 • **Value: $10**

10

Malone E. Moosetrax
10" • #554110-05 • NL
Issued: 2000 • Current
Orig. Price: $14 • **Value: $14**

11

Manheim Von Hindenmoose
20" • #5545 • NL
Issued: 1992 • Retired: 1996
Orig. Price: $29 • **Value: $65**

12

Martin V. Moosington
10" • #590301-05 • MB
Issued: 2000 • To Be Retired: 2001
Orig. Price: $32 • **Value: $32**

Moose

	Price Paid	Value
1.		
2.		
3.		
4.		
5.		
6.		
7.		
8.		
9.		
10.		
11.		
12.		
Totals		

1

Martini
12" • #91109 • TJ
Issued: 1998 • Retired: 1999
Orig. Price: $12 • **Value: $28**

2

Maurice Von Hindenmoose
14" • #5540-05 • NL
Issued: 1996 • Retired: 1999
Orig. Price: $14 • **Value: $23**

3

Maynard Von Hindenmoose
14" • #5541 • NL
Issued: 1992 • Retired: 1997
Orig. Price: $14 • **Value: $46**

4

Menachem
8.5" • #91212 • TJ
Issued: 1996 • Retired: 1998
Orig. Price: $20 • **Value: $37**

5

Mendel Von Hindenmoose
6" • #5547 • NL
Issued: 1996 • Retired: 2000
Orig. Price: $8 • **Value: $19**

6

Milhous N. Moosington
14" • #590300 • MB
Issued: 1999 • Retired: 1999
Orig. Price: $84 • **Value: $120**

7

Miliken Von Hindenmoose
17" • #55421-05 • NL
Issued: 1997 • Retired: 1999
Orig. Price: $20 • **Value: $35**

8

Millie LaMoose
9" • #51730 • BY
Issued: 1998 • Retired: 1999
Orig. Price: $8 • **Value: $18**

9

Minney Moose
14" • #91108 • TJ
Issued: 1996 • Retired: 1998
Orig. Price: $20 • **Value: $34**

10

Montague
8" • #9121 • TJ
Issued: 1994 • Retired: 1996
Orig. Price: $20 • **Value: $47**

11

Montana Mooski
12" • #917295 • TJ
Issued: 1999 • To Be Retired: 2001
Orig. Price: $30 • **Value: $30**

12

Monte Mooselton
12" • #917290 • TJ
Issued: 1998 • Retired: 1999
Orig. Price: $21 • **Value: $39**

Moose

	Price Paid	Value
1.		
2.		
3.		
4.		
5.		
6.		
7.		
8.		
9.		
10.		
11.		
12.		
Totals		

1

Mortimer Von Hindenmoose
14" • #55411-05 • NL
Issued: 1997 • Retired: 1999
Orig. Price: $14 • **Value: $24**

2

Mother Moosemas
info unavailable
Orig. Price: N/A • **Value: N/E**

3

Murgatroyd Von Hindenmoose
14" • #5540 • NL
Issued: 1991 • Retired: 1994
Orig. Price: $14 • **Value: $45**

4

Murgatroyd Von Hindenmoose II
14" • #5540 • NL
Issued: 1993 • Retired: 1997
Orig. Price: $14 • **Value: $50**

5

Murphy Mooselfluff
10" • #917291 • TJ
Issued: 1999 • Current
Orig. Price: $24 • **Value: $24**

6

Murray Moosehoofer
14" • #554210-05 • NL
Issued: 2000 • Current
Orig. Price: $20 • **Value: $20**

7

Myles Von Hindenmoose
6" • #55470-05 • NL
Issued: 2000 • Current
Orig. Price: $9 • **Value: $9**

8

Myron Von Hindenmoose
10" • #912121 • TJ
Issued: 1997 • Retired: 1998
Orig. Price: $21 • **Value: $38**

9

Nadia Von Hindenmoose
17" • #5542-01 • NL
Issued: 1994 • Retired: 1996
Orig. Price: $20 • **Value: $84**

10

Siegfried Von Hindenmoose
20" • #5544 • NL
Issued: 1991 • Retired: 1995
Orig. Price: $29 • **Value: $190**

11

T. Fargo Wuzzie
5" • #595102 • TF
Issued: 1999 • Retired: 2000
Orig. Price: $9 • **Value: $16**

12

Talbot F. Wuzzie
3.5" • #595440 • TF
Issued: 1998 • Retired: 1999
Orig. Price: $7 • **Value: $16**

Moose

	Price Paid	Value
1.		
2.		
3.		
4.		
5.		
6.		
7.		
8.		
9.		
10.		
11.		
12.		
Totals		

1

Windberg
8" • #5675-05 • FL
Issued: 1995 • Retired: 1999
Orig. Price: $13 • **Value: $23**

Pandas

2

Bamboo Bearington
14" • #590030 • MB
Issued: 2000 • To Be Retired: 2001
Orig. Price: $52 • **Value: $52**

3

C. Carryout Bearington
4.5" • #590106 • MB
Issued: 2000 • Current
Orig. Price: $10 • **Value: $10**

4

Dewey P. Wongbruin
16" • #5154 • JB
Issued: 1997 • Retired: 1999
Orig. Price: $29 • **Value: $36**

5
New

Domino
12" • #57004-07 • AS
Issued: 2001 • Current
Orig. Price: $19 • **Value: $19**

6

Hsing-Hsing Wongbruin
14" • #51540-07 • JB
Issued: 1999 • To Be Retired: 2001
Orig. Price: $20 • **Value: $20**

7

Nana
14" • #5765 • HD
Issued: 1991 • Retired: 1992
Orig. Price: $27 • **Value: $525**

8

Ogden B. Bean
8" • #5153 • JB
Issued: 1994 • Retired: 1999
Orig. Price: $12 • **Value: $28**

9

Ting F. Wuzzie
2.5" • #595161 • TF
Issued: 1999 • Retired: 2000
Orig. Price: $7 • **Value: $17**

10

Yolanda Panda
6" • #57701 • AS
Issued: 1998 • To Be Retired: 2001
Orig. Price: $9 • **Value: $9**

Moose

	Price Paid	Value
1.		

Pandas

	Price Paid	Value
2.		
3.		
4.		
5.		
6.		
7.		
8.		
9.		
10.		

Totals

Penguins

1

Tuxie Waddlewalk
8" • #55500 • NL
Issued: 1999 • To Be Retired: 2001
Orig. Price: $13 • **Value: $13**

2

Willie Waddlewalk
6" • #555001 • NL
Issued: 2000 • Current
Orig. Price: $10 • **Value: $11**

Pigs

3

Aphrodite
7" • #5537 • AM
Issued: 1994 • Retired: 1995
Orig. Price: $12 • **Value: $55**

4

Aphrodite
7" • #5539 • AM
Issued: 1995 • Retired: 1996
Orig. Price: $12 • **Value: $47**

5

Erin O'Pigg
11" • #5536-09 • AM
Issued: 1996 • Retired: 1997
Orig. Price: $14 • **Value: $38**

6

Farland O'Pigg
16" • #5538 • AM
Issued: 1992 • Retired: 1997
Orig. Price: $29 • **Value: $75**

7
New

Farley O'Pigg
8" • #55392-07 • AM
Issued: 2001 • Current
Orig. Price: $13 • **Value: $13**

8
New

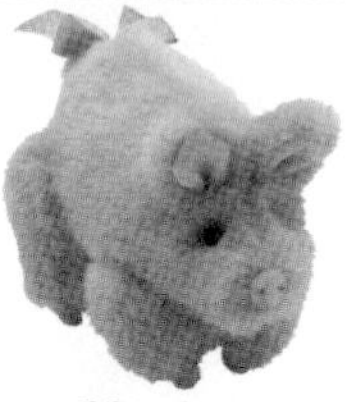

Hamlet
8" • #55360 • AM
Issued: 2001 • Current
Orig. Price: $13 • **Value: $13**

9
New

Ivy Bloomengrows
8" • #91602 • TJ
Issued: 2001 • Current
Orig. Price: $18 • **Value: $18**

10

Kaitlin K. Trufflesnout
8" • #91601-03 • TJ
Issued: 1999 • Retired: 1999
Orig. Price: $12 • **Value: N/E**

11

Kaitlin McSwine
8" • #91601 • TJ
Issued: 1997 • Retired: 1999
Orig. Price: $12 • **Value: $24**

Penguins

	Price Paid	Value
1.		
2.		

Pigs

	Price Paid	Value
3.		
4.		
5.		
6.		
7.		
8.		
9.		
10.		
11.		
Totals		

1

Kaitlin McSwine II
8" • #91601-01 • TJ
Issued: 1997 • Retired: 1999
Orig. Price: $14 • **Value: $22**

2

Kaitlin McSwine III
8" • #91601-02 • TJ
Issued: 1998 • To Be Retired: 2001
Orig. Price: $16 • **Value: $16**

3

Lofton Q. McSwine
8" • #55391-09 • AM
Issued: 1997 • Retired: 2000
Orig. Price: $11 • **Value: $16**

4

Maggie O'Pigg
11" • #5536-07 • AM
Issued: 1993 • Retired: 1999
Orig. Price: $14 • **Value: $28**

5

Mudpuddle P. Piglet
9" • #51790-09 • BY
Issued: 2000 • Retired: 2000
Orig. Price: $8 • **Value: $13**

6
New

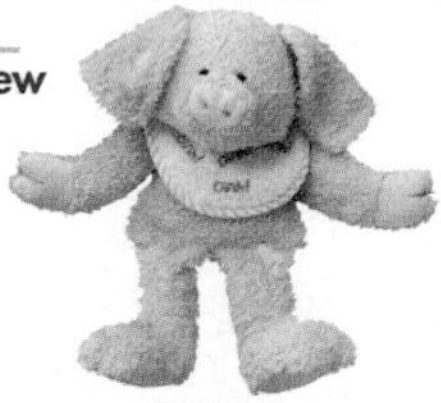

Pinkie
12" • #605200 • HF
Issued: 2001 • Current
Orig. Price: $19 • **Value: $19**

Pigs

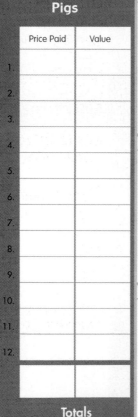

	Price Paid	Value
1.		
2.		
3.		
4.		
5.		
6.		
7.		
8.		
9.		
10.		
11.		
12.		
Totals		

7

Primrose
11" • #9160 • TJ
Issued: 1993 • Retired: 1996
Orig. Price: $20 • **Value: $66**

8

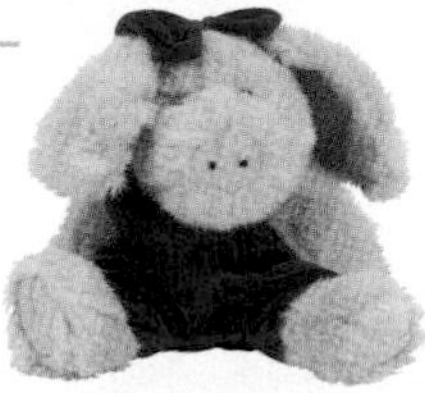

Primrose II
11" • #9160-01 • TJ
Issued: 1997 • Retired: 1997
Orig. Price: $20 • **Value: $50**

9

Primrose III
11" • #9160-02 • TJ
Issued: 1998 • Retired: 2000
Orig. Price: $23 • **Value: $27**

10

Primrose IV
11" • #9160-04 • TJ
Issued: 2000 • Current
Orig. Price: $23 • **Value: $23**

11

Primrose P. Trufflesnout
11" • #9160-03 • TJ
Issued: 1999 • Retired: 1999
Orig. Price: $23 • **Value: N/E**

12

Reilly O'Pigg
16" • #5538-07 • AM
Issued: 1993 • Retired: 1995
Orig. Price: $29 • **Value: $80**

1

Rosie O'Pigg
11" • #5536 • AM
Issued: 1992 • Retired: 1998
Orig. Price: $14 • **Value: $35**

2

Sheffield O'Swine
8" • #55391-07 • AM
Issued: 1997 • Retired: 2000
Orig. Price: $11 • **Value: $16**

3

Truffles O' Pigg
9" • #916010-01 • TJ
Issued: 2000 • Current
Orig. Price: $16 • **Value: $16**

Raccoons

4

Bandit Bushytail
6" • #55211 • AM
Issued: 2000 • Current
Orig. Price: $12 • **Value: $12**

Raggedymuffs

5

Delray
19" • #744101 • RM
Issued: 2000 • To Be Retired: 2001
Orig. Price: $19 • **Value: $19**

6
New

Kissimmee
19" • #744103 • RM
Issued: 2001 • Current
Orig. Price: $19 • **Value: $19**

7

Sanibel
19" • #744102 • TJ
Issued: 2000 • To Be Retired: 2001
Orig. Price: $19 • **Value: $19**

Skunks

8
New

Oda Perume
10" • #55212 • AM
Issued: 2001 • Current
Orig. Price: $16 • **Value: $16**

Squirrels

	Price Paid	Value
Pigs		
1.		
2.		
3.		
Raccoons		
4.		
Raggedymuffs		
5.		
6.		
7.		
Skunks		
8.		
Totals		

1
New

Merle B. Squirrel
7" • #55214 • AM
Issued: 2001 • Current
Orig. Price: $13 • **Value: $13**

Ornaments

2

Adrienne Berrifrost
5.5" • #56202-06 • OR
Issued: 1999 • Retired: 2000
Orig. Price: $9 • **Value: $13**

3

Aimee Berrifrost
5.5" • #56202-04 • OR
Issued: 1999 • Retired: 2000
Orig. Price: $9 • **Value: $13**

4

Alyssa Berrifrost
5.5" • #56202-02 • OR
Issued: 1999 • Retired: 2000
Orig. Price: $9 • **Value: $13**

5

Angelica
7" • #5611-08 • OR
Issued: 1993 • Retired: 1997
Orig. Price: $12 • **Value: $23**

6

Angelina
5.5" • #5615-07 • OR
Issued: 1995 • Retired: 1997
Orig. Price: $7 • **Value: $22**

7

Angelina II
5.5" • #56151-07 • OR
Issued: 1998 • To Be Retired: 2001
Orig. Price: $7 • **Value: $7**

8

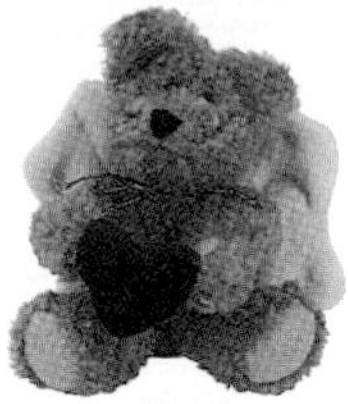

Ariel
5" • #5620-08 • OR
Issued: 1995 • Retired: 1999
Orig. Price: $7 • **Value: $19**

9

Arinna Goodnight
5.5" • #56231-04 • OR
Issued: 1997 • Retired: 1999
Orig. Price: $7 • **Value: $13**

10

Athena
5.5" • #5617-01 • OR
Issued: 1995 • Retired: 1996
Orig. Price: $7 • **Value: $30**

11

Aurora Goodnight
5.5" • #56232-12 • OR
Issued: 1999 • Retired: 1999
Orig. Price: $7 • **Value: $10**

Squirrels

	Price Paid	Value
1.		
Ornaments		
2.		
3.		
4.		
5.		
6.		
7.		
8.		
9.		
10.		
11.		
Totals		

1

Bernice Blizzard
3.5" • #56193 • OR
Issued: 1999 • Current
Orig. Price: $7 • **Value: $7**

2

Bert Blizzard
3.5" • #56192 • OR
Issued: 1999 • Current
Orig. Price: $7 • **Value: $7**

3

Bibi Buzzby
5.5" • #56220-12 • OR
Issued: 1999 • Current
Orig. Price: $8 • **Value: $8**

4

Billy Bob
5" • #56201-06 • OR
Issued: 1997 • Retired: 1999
Orig. Price: $7 • **Value: $15**

5

Biscuit B. Beggar
5.5" • #56250 • OR
Issued: 2000 • Current
Orig. Price: $9 • **Value: $9**

6
New

Brady Swingenamiss
5" • #56301 • OR
Issued: 2001 • Current
Orig. Price: $10 • **Value: $10**

7

Brendalynn Blizzard
3.5" • #56193-06 • OR
Issued: 2000 • Retired: 2000
Orig. Price: $7 • **Value: $9**

8

Bud Buzzby
5.5" • #56220-08 • OR
Issued: 1999 • Current
Orig. Price: $8 • **Value: $8**

9

Cappuccino Frenzy
5.5" • #56271 • OR
Issued: 1999 • To Be Retired: 2001
Orig. Price: $7 • **Value: $7**

10

Cassandra C. Angelflight
5.5" • #83001 • OR
Issued: 2000 • Retired: 2000
Orig. Price: $9 • **Value: $11**

11

Cassie Goodnight
5.5" • #56232-01 • OR
Issued: 1998 • Retired: 1999
Orig. Price: $7 • **Value: $12**

12

Celeste
5" • #5609-01 • OR
Issued: 1994 • Retired: 1999
Orig. Price: $7 • **Value: N/E**

Ornaments

	Price Paid	Value
1.		
2.		
3.		
4.		
5.		
6.		
7.		
8.		
9.		
10.		
11.		
12.		
Totals		

1

Celestina Goodnight
5.5" • #56231-02 • OR
Issued: 1997 • Retired: 1999
Orig. Price: $7 • **Value: $16**

2

Charity Angelbeary
5.5" • #56240-04 • OR
Issued: 2000 • Retired: 2000
Orig. Price: $9 • **Value: $14**

3

Chilly Frostbite
3.5" • #56260 • OR
Issued: 1999 • Retired: 2000
Orig. Price: $7 • **Value: $9**

4

Chillin' Sockley
5.5" • #56290-01 • OR
Issued: 2000 • To Be Retired: 2001
Orig. Price: $7 • **Value: $7**

5

Clarence
4.5" • #5608-08 • OR
Issued: 1993 • Retired: 1996
Orig. Price: $6 • **Value: $32**

6

Comet
5.5" • #5622 • OR
Issued: 1996 • Retired: 1999
Orig. Price: $7 • **Value: $18**

Ornaments

	Price Paid	Value
1.		
2.		
3.		
4.		
5.		
6.		
7.		
8.		
9.		
10.		
11.		
12.		
Totals		

7

Corona Goodspeed
5.5" • #5624-09 • OR
Issued: 1998 • Retired: 2000
Orig. Price: $7 • **Value: $16**

8

Country Angel
4.5" • #7401 • OR
Issued: 1993 • Retired: 1993
Orig. Price: N/A • **Value: $35**

9

Cowsies
5" • #5607 • OR
Issued: 1993 • Retired: 1994
Orig. Price: $5 • **Value: $42**

10

Deitrich
5.5" • #5608-06 • OR
Issued: 1996 • Retired: 1997
Orig. Price: $6 • **Value: $22**

11

Dinkle B. Bumbles
5.5" • #56221-12 • OR
Issued: 2000 • Current
Orig. Price: $8 • **Value: $8**

12

Dipper
7" • #5611-09 • OR
Issued: 1996 • Retired: 1998
Orig. Price: $12 • **Value: $22**

1

Douglas Polartrek
3.5" • #561919 • OR
Issued: 2000 • Current
Orig. Price: $7 • **Value:** $7

2

Echo Goodnight
5.5" • #56232-14 • OR
Issued: 1999 • Retired: 1999
Orig. Price: $7 • **Value:** $11

3

Edna May
5" • #56201-02 • OR
Issued: 1997 • Retired: 1999
Orig. Price: $7 • **Value:** $20

4

Espresso Frisky
5.5" • #56272 • OR
Issued: 1999 • To Be Retired: 2001
Orig. Price: $7 • **Value:** $7

5

Faith Angelbeary
5.5" • #56240-02 • OR
Issued: 2000 • Retired: 2000
Orig. Price: $9 • **Value:** $13

6
New

Flip Hopsey
3.5" • #81505 • OR
Issued: 2001 • To Be Retired: 2001
Orig. Price: $7 • **Value:** $7

7

Flit Angelwish
3.5" • #56265-01 • OR
Issued: 2000 • Current
Orig. Price: $7 • **Value:** $7

8
New

Flutter Flowerflit
5" • #562200 • OR
Issued: 2001 • Current
Orig. Price: $10 • **Value:** $10

9

Gabriella
8" • #7408 • OR
Issued: 1994 • Retired: 1995
Orig. Price: $8 • **Value:** N/E

10

Gabriella
8" • #7408-08 • OR
Issued: 1996 • Retired: 1997
Orig. Price: $8 • **Value:** N/E

11

Galaxy
7" • #56111-01 • OR
Issued: 1998 • Retired: 1999
Orig. Price: $12 • **Value:** $17

12

Gonna Luvya
5" • #56200-01 • OR
Issued: 2000 • Current
Orig. Price: $7 • **Value:** $7

Ornaments

	Price Paid	Value
1.		
2.		
3.		
4.		
5.		
6.		
7.		
8.		
9.		
10.		
11.		
12.		
Totals		

1

Gweneth
5" • #56031 • OR
Issued: 1997 • Retired: 1999
Orig. Price: $6 • **Value: $20**

2
New

Iddy Biddy Ladybug
5" • #562201 • OR
Issued: 2001 • Current
Orig. Price: $10 • **Value: $10**

3

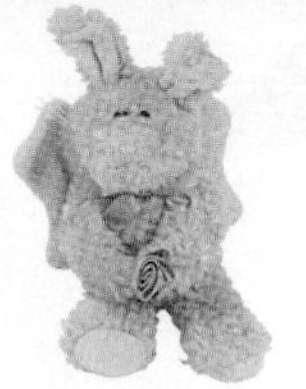

Immanuella
5" • #5609-09 • OR
Issued: 1996 • Retired: 1999
Orig. Price: $7 • **Value: $18**

4

Jeri Hopkins
5" • #56241-06 • OR
Issued: 2000 • Retired: 2000
Orig. Price: $7 • **Value: $8**

5

Jill Hopkins
5" • #56241-12 • OR
Issued: 2000 • Retired: 2000
Orig. Price: $7 • **Value: $8**

6

Josanna Java
5.5" • #56273 • OR
Issued: 2000 • Current
Orig. Price: $7 • **Value: $7**

Ornaments

	Price Paid	Value
1.		
2.		
3.		
4.		
5.		
6.		
7.		
8.		
9.		
10.		
11.		
12.		
Totals		

7

Josie Hopkins
5" • #56241-09 • OR
Issued: 2000 • Retired: 2000
Orig. Price: $7 • **Value: $8**

8

Juliette
4.5" • #5612-01 • OR
Issued: 1994 • Retired: 1999
Orig. Price: $7 • **Value: $16**

9

Jupiter Goodspeed
5.5" • #5624-06 • OR
Issued: 1998 • Retired: 1999
Orig. Price: $7 • **Value: $18**

10

Katalina Kafinata
5.5" • #56274 • OR
Issued: 2000 • Current
Orig. Price: $7 • **Value: $7**

11

Lady B. Lovebug
5" • #595104 • TF
Issued: 2000 • Retired: 2000
Orig. Price: $9 • **Value: $17**

12

Lambsies
4.5" • #5603 • OR
Issued: 1991 • Retired: 1995
Orig. Price: $5 • **Value: $27**

1
New

Lana Hoppennibble
3.5" • #561932 • OR
Issued: 2001 • Current
Orig. Price: $7 • **Value: $7**

2

Lilith Angel Ewe
5" • #56030-01 • OR
Issued: 2000 • Current
Orig. Price: $7 • **Value: $7**

3

Lilly R. Ribbit
4" • #56194 • OR
Issued: 2000 • To Be Retired: 2001
Orig. Price: $7 • **Value: $7**

4

Linnea
7" • #5610-01 • OR
Issued: 1994 • Retired: 1997
Orig. Price: $12 • **Value: $22**

5

Lionsies
4.5" • #5604 • OR
Issued: 1991 • Retired: 1994
Orig. Price: $5 • **Value: $55**

6

Lorelei
5.5" • #56141 • OR
Issued: 1997 • Retired: 2000
Orig. Price: $7 • **Value: $13**

7
New

Lula Quackenwaddle
3" • #561930 • OR
Issued: 2001 • Current
Orig. Price: $7 • **Value: $7**

8

Luna
5" • #5621-10 • OR
Issued: 1996 • Retired: 1997
Orig. Price: $6 • **Value: N/E**

9
New

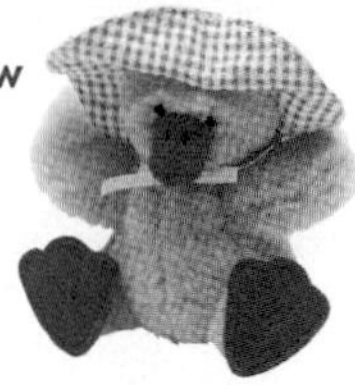

Lyla Quackenwaddle
3" • #561931 • OR
Issued: 2001 • Current
Orig. Price: $7 • **Value: $7**

10

Mabel Witmoose
5" • #56172 • OR
Issued: 1999 • Retired: 2000
Orig. Price: $8 • **Value: $8**

11

Matilda
5.5" • #5617-05 • OR
Issued: 1995 • Retired: 1999
Orig. Price: $7 • **Value: $16**

12

Meltin' Sockley
5.5" • #56290-02 • OR
Issued: 2000 • To Be Retired: 2001
Orig. Price: $7 • **Value: $7**

Ornaments

	Price Paid	Value
1.		
2.		
3.		
4.		
5.		
6.		
7.		
8.		
9.		
10.		
11.		
12.		
Totals		

1

Mercer
5.5" • #56171-03 • OR
Issued: 1998 • Retired: 2000
Orig. Price: $7 • **Value: $9**

2

Mercury
7" • #5610-09 • OR
Issued: 1996 • Retired: 1998
Orig. Price: $12 • **Value: $21**

3

Mocha Mooseby
5.5" • #56270 • OR
Issued: 1999 • To Be Retired: 2001
Orig. Price: $7 • **Value: $7**

4

Molasses
5.5" • #56280-02 • OR
Issued: 2000 • To Be Retired: 2001
Orig. Price: $7 • **Value: $7**

5

Moondust Goodspeed
5.5" • #5624-08 • OR
Issued: 1999 • Retired: 1999
Orig. Price: $7 • **Value: $14**

6

Moosies
6" • #5605 • OR
Issued: 1993 • Retired: 1996
Orig. Price: $5 • **Value: $29**

7

Narcissus
5" • #5621-08 • OR
Issued: 1996 • Retired: 1997
Orig. Price: $6 • **Value: $17**

8

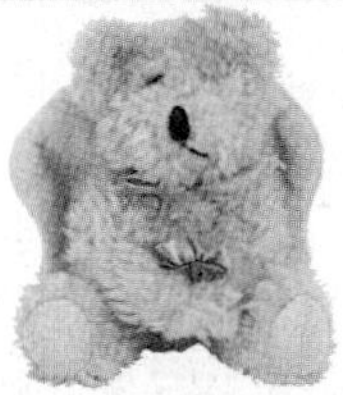

Orion
5" • #5612-09 • OR
Issued: 1996 • Retired: 2000
Orig. Price: $7 • **Value: $16**

9

Ovid
4.5" • #5614 • OR
Issued: 1994 • Retired: 1996
Orig. Price: $7 • **Value: $40**

10

Pair O'Bears
info unavailable
Orig. Price: N/A • **Value: N/E**

11

Pair O'Bears
4.5" • #5601 • OR
Issued: pre-1990 • Retired: 1996
Orig. Price: $5 • **Value: $46**

12

Pair O'Hares
6" • #5600 • OR
Issued: 1991 • Retired: 1994
Orig. Price: $5 • **Value: $45**

Ornaments

	Price Paid	Value
1.		
2.		
3.		
4.		
5.		
6.		
7.		
8.		
9.		
10.		
11.		
12.		
Totals		

1

Pair O'Hares
6" • #5602 • OR
Issued: 1990 • Retired: 1991
Orig. Price: $5 • **Value: N/E**

2

Pair O'Highland Plaid Bears
5" • #5618-02 • OR
Issued: 1996 • Retired: 1998
Orig. Price: $4 • **Value: $14**

3

Pair O'Homespun Bears
5" • #5618 • OR
Issued: 1995 • Retired: 1996
Orig. Price: $4 • **Value: $38**

4

Pair O'Piggs
6" • #5606 • OR
Issued: 1993 • Retired: 1996
Orig. Price: $5 • **Value: $55**

5
New

Perky P. Rally
5" • #56300 • OR
Issued: 2001 • Current
Orig. Price: $10 • **Value: $10**

6

Pinkle B. Bumbles
5.5" • #56221-09 • OR
Issued: 2000 • Current
Orig. Price: $8 • **Value: $8**

7

Raggedy Twins
4.5" • #7400 • OR
Issued: 1993 • Retired: 1995
Orig. Price: $6 • **Value: $85**

8

Regulus P. Roar
5" • #56041 • OR
Issued: 1997 • Retired: 1999
Orig. Price: $6 • **Value: $15**

9

Roary Manesford
5" • #56032 • OR
Issued: 2000 • Current
Orig. Price: $7 • **Value: $7**

10

Sassafrass
5.25" • #56280-01 • OR
Issued: 2000 • To Be Retired: 2001
Orig. Price: $7 • **Value: $7**

11

Seraphina
5" • #5615 • OR
Issued: 1994 • Retired: 1999
Orig. Price: $7 • **Value: $18**

12

Serena Goodnight
5.5" • #56232-08 • OR
Issued: 1998 • Retired: 2000
Orig. Price: $7 • **Value: $15**

Ornaments

	Price Paid	Value
1.		
2.		
3.		
4.		
5.		
6.		
7.		
8.		
9.		
10.		
11.		
12.		
Totals		

1

Silverton Snowbeary
5" • #56191 • OR
Issued: 1998 • Current
Orig. Price: $7 • **Value: $7**

2
New

Skip Hopsey
3.5" • #81506 • OR
Issued: 2001 • To Be Retired: 2001
Orig. Price: $7 • **Value: $7**

3

Squeek McSnoozle
3.5" • #56180-02 • OR
Issued: 2000 • Retired: 2000
Orig. Price: $10 • **Value: $13**

4

Stardust Goodspeed
5.5" • #5624-01 • OR
Issued: 1999 • Retired: 2000
Orig. Price: $7 • **Value: $12**

5

Stella Goodnight
5.5" • #5623-09 • OR
Issued: 1997 • Retired: 1999
Orig. Price: $7 • **Value: $18**

6

T.F. Buzzie Wuzzie
2.5" • #595180 • TF
Issued: 2000 • Current
Orig. Price: $8 • **Value: $8**

Ornaments

	Price Paid	Value
1.		
2.		
3.		
4.		
5.		
6.		
7.		
8.		
9.		
10.		
11.		
12.		
Totals		

7

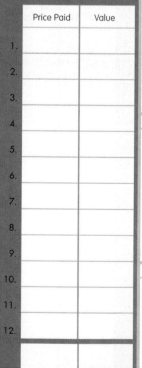

T.F. Wuzziewitch
3" • #81001 • OR
Issued: 2000 • Retired: 2000
Orig. Price: $8 • **Value: $13**

8

Tad Northpole
4" • #561940 • OR
Issued: 2000 • Retired: 2000
Orig. Price: $8 • **Value: $13**

9

Thomasina F. Wuzzie
3" • #596009 • TF
Issued: 2000 • Current
Orig. Price: $8 • **Value: $8**

10
New

Tootall F. Wuzzie
3" • #596012 • TF
Issued: 2001 • Current
Orig. Price: $8 • **Value: $8**

11

Tricky F. Wuzzie
3" • #596008 • TF
Issued: 2000 • Retired: 2000
Orig. Price: $8 • **Value: $13**

12
New

Trudy F. Wuzzie
2.5" • #595184 • TF
Issued: 2001 • Current
Orig. Price: $8 • **Value: $8**

1
New

Truelove F. Wuzzie
3" • #82000 • OR
Issued: 2001 • To Be Retired: 2001
Orig. Price: $6 • **Value: $6**

2
New

Tuttle F. Wuzzie
2.5" • #596010 • TF
Issued: 2001 • Current
Orig. Price: $8 • **Value: $8**

3
New

Tutu F. Wuzzie
3" • #596011 • TF
Issued: 2001 • Current
Orig. Price: $8 • **Value: $8**

4
New

Twaddle F. Wuzzie
2.5" • #595186 • TF
Issued: 2001 • Current
Orig. Price: $8 • **Value: $8**

5

Tweedle F. Wuzzie
2.5" • #595181 • TF
Issued: 2000 • Current
Orig. Price: $8 • **Value: $8**

6

Tweek McSnoozle
5.5" • #83000 • OR
Issued: 2000 • Retired: 2000
Orig. Price: $11 • **Value: $15**

7
New

Twickenham F. Wuzzie
2.5" • #595183 • TF
Issued: 2001 • Current
Orig. Price: $8 • **Value: $8**

8

Twiddle F. Wuzzie
2.5" • #595182 • TF
Issued: 2000 • Current
Orig. Price: $8 • **Value: $8**

9
New

Twila Twinkletoes
5" • #56302 • OR
Issued: 2001 • Current
Orig. Price: $10 • **Value: $10**

10

Venus
4.5" • #5616 • OR
Issued: 1994 • Retired: 1996
Orig. Price: $7 • **Value: $32**

11
New

Weezie Flitenfly
4" • #561941 • OR
Issued: 2001 • Current
Orig. Price: $8 • **Value: $8**

12

White Snowberry Bear
5" • #5619 • OR
Issued: 1995 • Retired: 1996
Orig. Price: $7 • **Value: $18**

Ornaments

	Price Paid	Value
1.		
2.		
3.		
4.		
5.		
6.		
7.		
8.		
9.		
10.		
11.		
12.		
Totals		

1

Willie S. Hydrant IV
5.5" • #5625 • OR
Issued: 1998 • Retired: 2000
Orig. Price: $7 • **Value: $15**

2

Winkle B. Bumbles
5.5" • #56221-06 • OR
Issued: 2000 • Current
Orig. Price: $8 • **Value: $8**

3

Zephyr Goodnight
5.5" • #5623-06 • OR
Issued: 1997 • Retired: 1999
Orig. Price: $7 • **Value: $14**

4

Zipp Angelwish
3.5" • #56265-03 • OR
Issued: 2000 • Current
Orig. Price: $7 • **Value: $7**

Pins

5

B. Burt Bundleup
2" • #599914 • WW
Issued: 2000 • Current
Orig. Price: $6 • **Value: $6**

6
New

Hopley F. Wuzzie
2" • #599919 • WW
Issued: 2001 • Current
Orig. Price: $6 • **Value: $6**

7
New

Juggles F. Wuzzie
2" • #599918 • WW
Issued: 2001 • Current
Orig. Price: $6 • **Value: $6**

8

Miss Minnie Partridge
2" • #8100 • WW
Issued: 2000 • Retired: 2000
Orig. Price: $6 • **Value: $8**

9
New

Riblet F. Wuzzie
2" • #599917 • WW
Issued: 2001 • Current
Orig. Price: $6 • **Value: $6**

10

St. Moosekins
2" • #599916 • WW
Issued: 2000 • Current
Orig. Price: $6 • **Value: $6**

11

Teedle F. Wuzzie
2" • #599911-02 • WW
Issued: 2000 • Current
Orig. Price: $6 • **Value: $6**

Ornaments

	Price Paid	Value
1.		
2.		
3.		
4.		
Pins		
5.		
6.		
7.		
8.		
9.		
10.		
11.		
Totals		

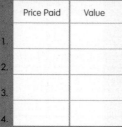

1

Tess F. Wuzzie
2" • #599901-06 • WW
Issued: 1999 • Retired: 2000
Orig. Price: $5 • **Value: $8**

2

Thistle F. Wuzzie
2" • #599912-07 • WW
Issued: 2000 • Current
Orig. Price: $6 • **Value: $6**

3

Thomas F. Wuzzie
2" • #599903-07 • WW
Issued: 1999 • Retired: 2000
Orig. Price: $5 • **Value: $8**

4

Tinger F. Wuzzie
2" • #599910-08 • WW
Issued: 2000 • Current
Orig. Price: $6 • **Value: $6**

5

Tinker F. Wuzzie
2" • #599900-02 • WW
Issued: 1999 • Retired: 2000
Orig. Price: $6 • **Value: $8**

6

Tinsel F. Wuzzie
2" • #599900-08 • WW
Issued: 1999 • Retired: 2000
Orig. Price: $6 • **Value: $8**

7

Tiny Tux Waddlewalk
2" • #599915 • WW
Issued: 2000 • Current
Orig. Price: $6 • **Value: $6**

8

Tucker F. Wuzzie
2" • #599902-08 • WW
Issued: 1999 • Retired: 2000
Orig. Price: $5 • **Value: $8**

9

Twinkle F. Wuzzie
2" • #599900-01 • WW
Issued: 1999 • Retired: 2000
Orig. Price: $6 • **Value: $8**

Puppets

10

Benny P. Chatsworth
16" • #585010-10 • IF
Issued: 2000 • Current
Orig. Price: $35 • **Value: $35**

11

Charlie P. Chatsworth
18" • #585000-08 • IF
Issued: 1999 • Retired: 2000
Orig. Price: $40 • **Value: $42**

Pins

	Price Paid	Value
1.		
2.		
3.		
4.		
5.		
6.		
7.		
8.		
9.		
Puppets		
10.		
11.		
Totals		

1

Fillabuster P. Chatsworth
18" • #585001-03 • IF
Issued: 1999 • Retired: 2000
Orig. Price: $40 • **Value: $42**

2

Howlin P. Chatsworth
18" • #585101-05 • IF
Issued: 2000 • Retired: 2000
Orig. Price: $40 • **Value: $42**

3

Katawalin P. Chatsworth
18" • #585200-07 • IF
Issued: 2000 • Retired: 2000
Orig. Price: $40 • **Value: $42**

4

Montell P. Chatsworth
16" • #585310-05 • IF
Issued: 2000 • Current
Orig. Price: $35 • **Value: $35**

5
New

Peekers
10" • #58600-05 • FM
Issued: 2001 • Current
Orig. Price: $15 • **Value: $15**

6
New

Sneekers
10" • #58601-07 • FM
Issued: 2001 • Current
Orig. Price: $15 • **Value: $15**

Puppets

	Price Paid	Value
1.		
2.		
3.		
4.		
5.		
6.		
7.		
8.		

Stringalongs

	Price Paid	Value
9.		
10.		
11.		
Totals		

7

Wiley P. Chatsworth
18" • #585000-05 • IF
Issued: 1999 • Retired: 2000
Orig. Price: $40 • **Value: $42**

8
New

Wink
10" • #58600-08 • FM
Issued: 2001 • Current
Orig. Price: $15 • **Value: $15**

Stringalongs

9

Giddyup Stringalong
3" • #596200 • SA
Issued: 2000 • Current
Orig. Price: $8 • **Value: $8**

10

Petey B. Stringalong
3" • #596201 • SA
Issued: 2000 • Current
Orig. Price: $8 • **Value: $8**

11

Squirt M. Stringalong
3" • #596202 • SA
Issued: 2000 • Current
Orig. Price: $8 • **Value: $8**

Tree Toppers

1

Angelique Angelfrost
10" • #744110-06 • TJ
Issued: 2000 • Retired: 2000
Orig. Price: $15 • **Value: $32**

2

Ariella Angelfrost
10" • #744110 • TJ
Issued: 1999 • Retired: 2000
Orig. Price: $15 • **Value: $35**

3

Holly Beary
12" • #744115-02 • TJ
Issued: 2000 • Retired: 2000
Orig. Price: $20 • **Value: $38**

Club Pieces

4
1996

Raeburn
6" • #01996-31 • F.o.B.
Issued: 1996 • Retired: 1997
Membership Gift • **Value: $33**

5
1996

Uncle Elliot
pin • #01996-11 • F.o.B.
Issued: 1996 • Retired: 1997
Membership Gift • **Value: $25**

6
1996

Uncle Elliot . . . The Head Bean Wants You
N/A • #01996-21 • F.o.B.
Issued: 1996 • Retired: 1997
Membership Gift • **Value: $90**

7
1997

Velma Q. Berriweather
11" • #01996-51 • F.o.B.
Issued: 1997 • Retired: 1997
Orig. Price: $29 • **Value: $65**

8
1997

Velma Q. Berriweather . . . The Cookie Queen
N/A • #01996-41 • F.o.B.
Issued: 1997 • Retired: 1997
Orig. Price: $19 • **Value: $83**

9
1998

Eleanor
6" • #01998-31 • F.o.B.
Issued: 1998 • Retired: 1998
Membership Gift • **Value: $20**

10
1998

Lady Libearty
pin • #01998-11 • F.o.B.
Issued: 1998 • Retired: 1998
Membership Gift • **Value: $8**

Tree Toppers	Price Paid	Value
1.		
2.		
3.		
F.o.B.		
4.		
5.		
6.		
7.		
8.		
9.		
10.		
Totals		

1
1998

Lady Libearty
N/A • #01998-21 • F.o.B.
Issued: 1998 • Retired: 1998
Membership Gift • **Value: $45**

2
1998

Ms. Berriweather's Cottage
N/A • #01998-41 • F.o.B.
Issued: 1998 • Retired: 1998
Orig. Price: $21 • **Value: $47**

3
1998

Zelma G. Berriweather
11" • #01998-51 • F.o.B.
Issued: 1998 • Retired: 1998
Orig. Price: $32 • **Value: $62**

4
1999

Bloomin' F.o.B.
pin • #01999-11 • F.o.B.
Issued: 1999 • Retired: 1999
Membership Gift • **Value: $8**

5
1999

Blossum B. Berriweather ... Bloom With Joy!
N/A • #01999-21 • F.o.B.
Issued: 1999 • Retired: 1999
Membership Gift • **Value: $32**

6
1999

Flora Mae Berriweather
6" • #01999-31 • F.o.B.
Issued: 1999 • Retired: 1999
Membership Gift • **Value: $20**

F.o.B.

	Price Paid	Value
1.		
2.		
3.		
4.		
5.		
6.		
7.		
8.		
9.		
10.		
11.		
12.		
Totals		

7
1999

Noah's Genius At Work Table
Noah's Pageant Series
N/A • #2429 • F.o.B.
Issued: 1999 • Retired: 1999
Orig. Price: $11.50 • **Value: $42**

8
1999

Plant With Hope, Grow With Love, Bloom With Joy
6" & 6" & 6" • #01999-51 • F.o.B.
Issued: 1999 • Retired: 1999
Orig. Price: $25 • **Value: $55**

9
1999

Sunny And Sally Berriweather ... Plant With Hope
N/A • #01999-41 • F.o.B.
Issued: 1999 • Retired: 1999
Orig. Price: $23 • **Value: $50**

10
2000

"Brewin' F.o.B." Official Mini-Tea Set
N/A • #02000-65 • F.o.B.
Issued: 2000 • Retired: 2000
Orig. Price: N/A • **Value: $20**

11
2000

Caitlin Berriweather
pin • #02000-11 • F.o.B.
Issued: 2000 • Retired: 2000
Membership Gift• **Value: N/E**

12
2000

Caitlin Berriweather
6" • #02000-31 • F.o.B.
Issued: 2000 • Retired: 2000
Membership Gift • **Value: $26**

1
2000

Catherine And Caitlin Berriweather . . . Fine Cup of Tea
N/A • #02000-21 • F.o.B.
Issued: 2000 • Retired: 2000
Membership Gift • **Value: N/E**

2
2000

Catherine And Caitlin Berriweather With Little Scruff . . . Family Traditions
N/A • #02000-41 • F.o.B.
Issued: 2000 • Retired: 2000
Orig. Price: $25 • **Value: $60**

3
2000

Catherine Berriweather And Little Scruff
11" & 3" • #02000-51 • F.o.B.
Issued: 2000 • Retired: 2000
Orig. Price: $26 • **Value: N/E**

4
2000

Noah's Tool Box
Noah's Pageant Series
N/A • #2434 • F.o.B.
Issued: 2000 • Retired: 2000
Orig. Price: $12 • **Value: N/E**

5
New

Gadget
5" • #02001-31 • F.o.B.
Issued: 2001 • To Be Retired: 2001
Membership Gift • **Value: N/E**

6
New

Gizmoe . . . Life's A Juggle
N/A • #02001-21 • F.o.B.
Issued: 2001 • To Be Retired: 2001
Membership Gift • **Value: N/E**

7
New

Gizmoe's Big Top With Giggle McNibble
N/A • #02001-65 • F.o.B.
Issued: 2001 • To Be Retired: 2001
Orig. Price: $13 • **Value: $13**

8
New

Greatest F.o.B. 2000 Bearwear Pin
pin • #02001-11 • F.o.B.
Issued: 2001 • To Be Retired: 2001
Membership Gift • **Value: N/E**

9
New

Gussie . . . Life Is A Balancing Act
N/A • #02001-41 • F.o.B.
Issued: 2001 • To Be Retired: 2001
Orig. Price: $25 • **Value: $25**

10
New

Melvin Sortalion
12" • #02001-51 • F.o.B.
Issued: 2001 • To Be Retired: 2001
Orig. Price: $30 • **Value: $30**

11
New

Noah's Book Shelf
Noah's Pageant Series
N/A • #2439 • F.o.B.
Issued: 2001 • To Be Retired: 2001
Orig. Price: $11 • **Value: $11**

F.o.B.

	Price Paid	Value
1.		
2.		
3.		
4.		
5.		
6.		
7.		
8.		
9.		
10.		
11.		
Totals		

Boyds Plush Exclusive Animals

The whimsical plush beasts of the Boyds Collection Ltd. have an elusive side to them. Each year, the company offers a number of pieces that are "here today, gone tomorrow" – and sometimes that's the literal truth! They also produce launches, or pieces that are created before being introduced in a regular line, just to whet the collectors' appetite. Collectors can find exclusive pieces only at specially selected retailers, or on the home shopping network QVC. So keep your eyes peeled for these items and grab 'em before they disappear – because they won't be around forever!

Exclusive Bears

1

AP Gold Bear (LE-4,800)
Canadian
10" • #BC94283
Issued: 1999
Value: $40

2

Abby Grace
Parade Of Gifts
6" • #94585POG
Issued: 2000
Value: N/E

3

Photo Unavailable

Aberdeen
QVC
Issued: 1994
Value: N/E

4

Abigail
Bon-Ton
Issued: 1996
Value: $50

5

Abigail
Elder-Beerman
Issued: 1998
Value: $50

6

Abigail A. Beanster
QVC
10"
Issued: 2000
Value: N/E

7

Abigail & Beryl Bramblebeary
QVC
6"
Issued: 2000
Value: N/E

8

Adkin
Frederick Atkins
10"
Issued: 1997
Value: $35

9

Al'Berta B. Bear (LE-10,000)
Canadian
10" • #BC94277
Issued: 1998
Value: $44

10

Aldina
Dillard's
#94714DL
Issued: 1997
Value: $50

Bears

	Price Paid	Value
1.		
2.		
3.		
4.		
5.		
6.		
7.		
8.		
9.		
10.		
Totals		

1

Alex Nicole
Dillard's
10" • #94743DL
Issued: 1999
Value: N/E

2

Alexandra & Belle
QVC
10"
Issued: 2000
Value: $35

3

Alexis Bearinsky
GCC
16" • #94862GCC
Issued: 1998
Value: $75

4

Alexis Berriman
The San Francisco Music Box Company
♪ Lara's Theme
16" • #41-72770
Issued: 1999
Value: $70

5

Allie Bearington
Welcome Home
12"
Issued: 1999
Value: N/E

6

Allison Bearburg
QVC
16"
Issued: 2000
Value: $35

7

Ally
Lord & Taylor
8"
Issued: 1997
Value: $30

8

Amelia P. Quignapple
QVC
10"
Issued: 1999
Value: $30

9

Anastasia
QVC
Issued: 1995
Value: $77

10

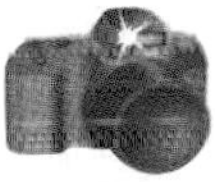

Photo Unavailable

Andrew
Dillard's
10" • #94742DL
Issued: 1999
Value: $26

11

Angel
GCC
8" • #94885GCC
Issued: 2000
Value: N/E

12

Angeline
QVC
Issued: 1997
Value: N/E

13

Anna Belle
Parade Of Gifts
14" • #94581POG
Issued: 1999
Value: $44

14

Annabella
GCC (Early Release)
12" • #912072GCC
Issued: 1998
Value: $40

Bears

	Price Paid	Value
1.		
2.		
3.		
4.		
5.		
6.		
7.		
8.		
9.		
10.		
11.		
12.		
13.		
14.		
Totals		

1

Annabelle Z. Witebred
QVC
Issued: 1998
Value: $34

2

Photo Unavailable

Arlo
Select Retailers
info unavailable
Value: N/E

3

Photo Unavailable

Artemus J. Bear
Country Living
16"
Issued: 1997
Value: $50

4

Photo Unavailable

Artie Finkmorton, Izzy Wingnut & Norton Flapjack
QVC
Issued: 1998
Value: N/E

5

Photo Unavailable

Ashley Lynn
Elder Beerman
Issued: 2000
Value: $28

6

Attie
Frederick Atkins
8"
Issued: 1997
Value: $48

7

Aubrey
Dillard's
14" • #94723DL
Issued: 1997
Value: $45

8

Aubrey
GCC
10" • #94863GCC
Issued: 1998
Value: $42

9

Aubrey T. Tippeetoes
The San Francisco Music Box Company
♪ Dance of the Sugarplum Fairy
13" • #41-72980
Issued: 2000
Value: N/E

10

Aunt Becky Bearchild
The San Francisco Music Box Company
♪ Whistle While You Work
12" • #912052SF
Issued: 1999
Value: $40

11

Aunt Mattie MacDolittle
QVC
16"
Issued: 2000
Value: N/E

12

Aunt Phiddy Bearburn (LE-3,600)
JT Webb
10"
Issued: 1998
Value: $65

13

Auntie Adeline
Carson Pirie Scott & Co.
10"
Issued: 1997
Value: $54

14

Auntie Edna, Flora & Tillie
QVC
Issued: 1998
Value: $105

Bears

	Price Paid	Value
1.		
2.		
3.		
4.		
5.		
6.		
7.		
8.		
9.		
10.		
11.		
12.		
13.		
14.		
Totals		

1

Auntie Esther & Theona DoLittle (LE-1,800)
QVC
16" & 8"
Issued: 1998
Value: $125

2

Auntie Marguerite & Beesley Honeybruin With Topaz F. Wuzzie (LE-1,800)
QVC
14" & 8" & 3"
Issued: 1999
Value: N/E

3

Autumn & Fallston (LE-3,000)
QVC
14" & 6"
Issued: 1999
Value: $88

4

Ava Marie Adorable
Select Retailers
12" • #94586SYN
Issued: 2000
Value: $42

5

Photo Unavailable

Azalea & Jordan Rosebeary
QVC
11" & 6"
Issued: 1999
Value: N/E

6

Azure Lee, Ginger C. & Sunbeam P. Snickelfritz (musical)
QVC
♪ Brahms' Lullaby (Azure)
♪ Rock A Bye Baby (Ginger & Sunbeam)
5.5" & 5.5" & 5.5"
Issued: 1999
Value: N/E

7

B.A. Bigfoot
QVC
18"
Issued: 2000
Value: N/E

8

Bailey (Spring 1996)
QVC
8"
Issued: 1996
Value: $230

9

Bailey (Spring 1997)
QVC
8"
Issued: 1997
Value: $90

10

Bailey (Spring 1998)
QVC
8"
Issued: 1998
Value: $55

11

Barbara Mary
Boscov's
10"
Issued: 1999
Value: $50

12

Barnard B. Bear
Barnes & Noble
10"
Issued: 1998
Value: $60

13

Barney B. Keeper
Bon-Ton
Issued: 1997
Value: N/E

14

Barret
Select Retailers
Issued: 1996
Value: $75

Bears

	Price Paid	Value
1.		
2.		
3.		
4.		
5.		
6.		
7.		
8.		
9.		
10.		
11.		
12.		
13.		
14.		
Totals		

1

Barston Q. Growler
QVC
Issued: 1997
Value: $50

2

Bath & Body Works Bear
Bath & Body Works
Issued: 1996
Value: N/E

3

Bauer B. Bear
Eddie Bauer
12"
Issued: 1998
Value: $65

4

Bea Beary
Longaberger
10"
Issued: 2000
Value: N/E

5

Beatrice
Elder-Beerman
10"
Issued: 1998
Value: N/E

6

Beatrice B. Bearhugs, Baileyanne Bearhugs & Tedley F. Wuzzie (LE-37,000)
QVC
16" & 10" & 3"
Issued: 1999
Value: $88

7

Beatrice Bearymore
May Department Store Company
12" • #94155MC
Issued: 1999
Value: N/E

8

Photo Unavailable

Beatrice Bearymore
May Department Store Company
12"
Issued: 2000
Value: $30

9

Beauregard
QVC
info unavailable
Value: $60

10

Beauregard
Select Retailers
Issued: 1996
Value: N/E

11

Photo Unavailable

Becky
Lord & Taylor
8"
Issued: 1999
Value: N/E

12

Beezer B. Goodlebear
QVC
16"
Issued: 1999
Value: N/E

13

Belk Bear
Belk
Issued: 1997
Value: N/E

Bears

	Price Paid	Value
1.		
2.		
3.		
4.		
5.		
6.		
7.		
8.		
9.		
10.		
11.		
12.		
13.		
Totals		

1

Benjamin & Caroline
QVC
6"
Issued: 2000
Value: $20

2

Benjamin Beanbeary
Belk
8"
Issued: 1998
Value: N/E

3

Benjamin Bear
The San Francisco Music Box Company
♪ Let Me Be Your Teddy Bear
12" • #41-72142
Issued: 1998
Value: $40

4

Benjamin W. Bear
Barnes & Noble
12"
Issued: 2000
Value: N/E

5

Bernice B. Bear
Barnes & Noble
10"
Issued: 1999
Value: N/E

6

Photo Unavailable

Berret
Select Retailers
8"
Issued: 1996
Value: N/E

7

Betty Lou
QVC
Issued: 1996
Value: $320

8

Bill
QVC
Issued: 1995
Value: N/E

9

Bingham
QVC
22"
Issued: 1998
Value: N/E

10

Blackstone
QVC
Issued: 1997
Value: $24

11

Bluebeary
Smucker's Catalog
12" • #CGS0010
Issued: 2000
Value: $44

12

Bobbi Frostbeary
Select Retailers
10" • #94589SYN
Issued: 2000
Value: $18

13

Photo Unavailable

Bobbie B. Beansford
QVC
10"
Issued: 2000
Value: $11

14

Photo Unavailable

Boo Bear
Marshall Field's
Issued: 1994
Value: N/E

Bears

	Price Paid	Value
1.		
2.		
3.		
4.		
5.		
6.		
7.		
8.		
9.		
10.		
11.		
12.		
13.		
14.		
Totals		

1

Boo B. Bear
QVC
Issued: 1997
Value: N/E

2

Boo-Boo
Select Retailers
Issued: 1998
Value: $32

3

Bosley & Chadwick
QVC
Issued: 1997
Value: N/E

4

Photo Unavailable

Brambley B. Bigfoot
QVC
Issued: 2000
Value: N/E

5

Brandie & Madeira
QVC
Issued: 1998
Value: N/E

6

Brandon
Dillard's
#94703DL
Issued: 1996
Value: $30

7

Brandon A. Bearski
GCC
16" • #94886GCC
Issued: 2000
Value: $38

8

Braxton
The San Francisco Music Box Company
♪ I Will Always Love You
14" • #41-72640
Issued: 1998
Value: N/E

Bears

	Price Paid	Value
1.		
2.		
3.		
4.		
5.		
6.		
7.		
8.		
9.		
10.		
11.		
12.		
13.		
14.		
Totals		

9

Brewster McRooster
QVC
10"
Issued: 1999
Value: $39.50

10

Bria
Select Retailers
Issued: 1998
Value: N/E

11

Brian
Canadian
12" • #BC100708
Issued: 1997
Value: $33

12

Brianna
Elder-Beerman
11"
Issued: 1999
Value: N/E

13

Photo Unavailable

Brianne
Frederick Atkins
10"
Issued: 1998
Value: N/E

14

Brighton, Salisbury & Somerset
QVC
Issued: 1998
Value: N/E

1

Brinton S. Beansford
QVC
info unavailable
Value: $16

2

Bristol, Chelsea & Cornwell
QVC
8.5" & 8.5" & 8.5"
Issued: 2000
Value: $36

3

Bronson
Select Retailers
Issued: 1996
Value: $42

4

Brumley
QVC
Issued: 1997
Value: $40

5

Bruno Bedlington
QVC
Issued: 1998
Value: $64

6

Buchanan J. Bearington
QVC
11"
Issued: 1998
Value: N/E

7

Photo Unavailable

Buckles
Lord & Taylor
Issued: 1997
Value: N/E

8

Buffy
Victoria's Secret
Issued: 1996
Value: $43

9

Buford B.
QVC
Issued: 1997
Value: $58

10

Bunker Bedlington
GCC
8" • #94869GCC
Issued: 1999
Value: $28

11

Burgess P. Bear
QVC
15"
info unavailable
Value: N/E

12

Photo Unavailable

Burt
Select Retailers
info unavailable
Value: N/E

13

C. Elbert
Dillard's
17" • #94720DL
Issued: 1997
Value: $56

14

CB The Skater (LE-3,600)
Canadian
12" • BC94285PO
Issued: 2000
Value: $60

Bears

	Price Paid	Value
1.		
2.		
3.		
4.		
5.		
6.		
7.		
8.		
9.		
10.		
11.		
12.		
13.		
14.		
Totals		

1

C.C. Cocoa Bear
Carlton Cards
8"
Issued: 2000
Value: $32

2

C.C. Goodbear
Country Clutter
10"
Issued: 1999
Value: $36

3

Photo Unavailable

Caledonia, Humboldt & Shasta
QVC
Issued: 1998
Value: N/E

4

Photo Unavailable

Carlie
Proffitt's
12"
Issued: 1999
Value: N/E

5

Carly Bearworth
Spring 2000 Gift Show
6" • #918801
Issued: 2000
Value: $28

6

Caroline
QVC
Issued: 1996
Value: $50

7

Casimir B. Bean
GCC
#94858GCC
Issued: 1998
Value: $42

8

Cass
Select Retailers
Issued: 1998
Value: N/E

Bears

	Price Paid	Value
1.		
2.		
3.		
4.		
5.		
6.		
7.		
8.		
9.		
10.		
11.		
12.		
13.		
14.		
Totals		

9

Cassidy
QVC
Issued: 1997
Value: $75

10

Ceylon Pekoe
QVC
Issued: 1997
Value: $65

11

Chamomille
The San Francisco Music Box Company
♪ *A Dream Is A Wish Your Heart Makes*
11" • #41-72645
Issued: 1998
Value: N/E

12

Chandler
Select Retailers
8"
Issued: 1997
Value: $37

13

Charlotte Tewksbeary With Hobbes
QVC
16" & 5"
Issued: 1999
Value: $45

14

Christian
Dillard's
12" • #94744DL
Issued: 1999
Value: $35

1

Christmas Bear
QVC
Issued: 1995
Value: $205

2

Cimmaron
QVC
Issued: 1997
Value: $22

3

Clara
Bon-Ton
14"
Issued: 1996
Value: $45

4

Clara
Kirlin's
Issued: 1996
Value: $48

5

Clarissa
The San Francisco Music Box Company
♪ *Make Someone Happy*
15" • #41-72584
Issued: 1998
Value: $50

6

Clark
QVC
10"
Issued: 1998
Value: $40

7

Clark II
Platinum Dealers
6" • #918055-01
Issued: 2000
Value: N/E

8

Claudette
Country Gift
info unavailable
Value: N/E

9

Claudius B. Bean
Lord & Taylor
14"
Issued: 1998
Value: $50

10

Claudius B. Bean
QVC
Issued: 1997
Value: $45

11

Clementine
Elder-Beerman
14"
Issued: 1997
Value: $50

12

Colleen
QVC
info unavailable
Value: N/E

13

Collette
Select Retailers
Issued: 1997
Value: N/E

14

Corliss & Quincy
QVC
8" & 8"
Issued: 1998
Value: $30

Bears

	Price Paid	Value
1.		
2.		
3.		
4.		
5.		
6.		
7.		
8.		
9.		
10.		
11.		
12.		
13.		
14.		
Totals		

1

Cosmos
Elder-Beerman
Issued: 1998
Value: N/E

2

Courtney
QVC
16"
Issued: 1998
Value: $50

3

Cranston
GCC
8.25" • #94855GCC
Issued: 1997
Value: $37

4

Cromwell
QVC
Issued: 1997
Value: $78

5

Crystal Icebeary & Frosty Icebeary
Welcome Home
Issued: 2000
Value: $38

6

Cynthia Berrijam
QVC
16"
Issued: 1999
Value: $32

7

Dana & Desiree de Bearvoire
QVC
6" & 6"
Issued: 2000
Value: N/E

8

Photo Unavailable

Danielle & Elizabieta de Bearvoire
QVC
Issued: 1997
Value: N/E

Bears

	Price Paid	Value
1.		
2.		
3.		
4.		
5.		
6.		
7.		
8.		
9.		
10.		
11.		
12.		
13.		
14.		
Totals		

9

Daphne
Elder-Beerman
10" • #8155914EB
Issued: 1999
Value: N/E

10

Darbey & Daniel Bearimore
QVC
8" & 8"
Issued: 1999
Value: $36

11

Darby
Select Retailers
Issued: 1997
Value: N/E

12

Daria & Dickens
QVC
8" & 8"
Issued: 1998
Value: $66

13

Dean B. Bearberg
Select Retailers
info unavailable
Value: N/E

14

Debbie Claire
Dillard's
12" • #94741DL
Issued: 1999
Value: $35

1

Debbie M. Dobbsey
Coach House Gifts
10"
Issued: 2000
Value: $33

2

Deidre Rose
Bon-Ton
12"
Issued: 1997
Value: $55

3

Photo Unavailable

Delanie
The San Francisco Music Box Company
♪ Are You Lonesome Tonight?
#41-72935
Issued: 2000
Value: N/E

4

Delilah & Twila Higgenthorpe
QVC
Issued: 1998
Value: N/E

5

Delmarva V. Crackenpot
QVC
Issued: 1997
Value: $43

6

Delta
QVC
16"
Issued: 2000
Value: $72

7

Dessa & Rochelle
QVC
Issued: 1998
Value: N/E

8

Diane D. Beansford & Toppsey F. Wuzzie
QVC
12" & 3"
Issued: 2000
Value: $45

9

Dion Bearberg
Select Retailers
Issued: 1998
Value: $35

10

Donna
Minneapolis Gift Show
Issued: 1999
Value: N/E

11

Doodle & Yankee McBear
QVC
6" & 6"
Issued: 1999
Value: $27

12

Doonuttin Buckshot
QVC
12"
Issued: 2000
Value: N/E

13

Dorinda
Minneapolis Gift Show
Issued: 1999
Value: N/E

14

Douglas
Select Retailers
Issued: 1996
Value: N/E

Bears

	Price Paid	Value
1.		
2.		
3.		
4.		
5.		
6.		
7.		
8.		
9.		
10.		
11.		
12.		
13.		
14.		
Totals		

1

Duncan
Select Retailers
info unavailable
Value: N/E

2

Eddie Bauer Diamond
Eddie Bauer
Issued: 1997
Value: $58

3

Eddie Bauer Hunter
Eddie Bauer
Issued: 1996
Value: $75

4

Edith & James Henry Maybeary
QVC
10" & 10"
Issued: 2000
Value: N/E

5

Edmund
Eddie Bauer
Issued: 1994
Value: N/E

6

Edward Q. Bearstone & Apopka
GCC
16" • #94874GCC
Issued: 1999
Value: N/E

7

Photo Unavailable

Edwin R. Elfstein
Lord & Taylor
Issued: 1996
Value: $30

8

Effie May
Bon-Ton
12"
Issued: 1998
Value: $54

9

Elisia P. Bearypoppin, Darrell & Ross
QVC
Issued: 1997
Value: $140

10

Ella
Dillard's
8" • #94724DL
Issued: 1997
Value: $40

11

Elliot
Select Retailers
info unavailable
Value: $50

12

Photo Unavailable

Elmore Elf Bear
QVC
Issued: 1996
Value: $36

13

Elsbeth
Dillard's
#94704DL
Issued: 1996
Value: N/E

14

Elton
QVC
Issued: 1996
Value: $70

Bears

	Price Paid	Value
1.		
2.		
3.		
4.		
5.		
6.		
7.		
8.		
9.		
10.		
11.		
12.		
13.		
14.		
Totals		

1

Emily Claire
Welcome Home
Issued: 1998
Value: $50

2

Emily E. Dobbs
Coach House Gifts
10"
Issued: 1999
Value: N/E

3

Emma
Elder-Beerman
Issued: 1998
Value: $48

4

Englebert Q. Elfberg
GCC
10" • #94857GCC
Issued: 1998
Value: $32

5

Erin
Lord & Taylor
Issued: 1997
Value: $33

6
Photo Unavailable
Eugenia
Dillard's
Issued: 1997
Value: $70

7

Eugenia
The San Francisco Music Box Company
♪ Can't Help Falling In Love
16" • #56-66601
Issued: 1997
Value: N/E

8

Evan & Sheldon Bearchild
QVC
5.5" & 5.5"
Issued: 1998
Value: N/E

9
Photo Unavailable
Eve
Select Retailers
info unavailable
Value: N/E

10

Ewell Manitoba Mooselman (LE-2,400)
Canadian
#BC94275
Issued: 1997
Value: $90

11

Father Kristmas Bear & Northwind P. Bear
QVC
16" & 8"
Issued: 1999
Value: $43

12

Fawn W. Fallsbeary
Dealer Show Exclusives
10" • #919806
Issued: 2000
Value: $35

13

Felicity
Lord & Taylor
Issued: 1997
Value: $20

14
Photo Unavailable
Fidelity
QVC
17"
Issued: 1999
Value: $23

Bears

	Price Paid	Value
1.		
2.		
3.		
4.		
5.		
6.		
7.		
8.		
9.		
10.		
11.		
12.		
13.		
14.		
Totals		

1

Fidelity
The San Francisco Music Box Company
♪ Love Will Keep Us Together
17" • #41-72638
Issued: 1998
Value: N/E

2

Fillmore
QVC
Issued: 1998
Value: $200

3

Photo Unavailable
Florence B. Bearhugs
QVC
12"
Issued: 1999
Value: $26

4

Photo Unavailable
Foodle, Bunky & Nat
QVC
10" & 10" & 10"
Issued: 1999
Value: N/E

5

Photo Unavailable
Forrest B. Bruin
QVC
11"
Issued: 1999
Value: $20

6

Francesca
Bon-Ton
14"
Issued: 1998
Value: $39

7

Frankie Bearberg
Select Retailers
Issued: 1998
Value: $40

8

Photo Unavailable
Franklin T. Rosenbearg
GCC
#227735GCC
Issued: 2000
Value: $35

9

Fredrica
Select Retailers
Issued: 1997
Value: $35

10

GP Gold Bear (LE-4,800)
Canadian
10" • #BC94283
Issued: 1999
Value: $45

11

Gabriella
Boscov's
Issued: 1999
Value: N/E

12

Gabriella
Parade Of Gifts
6" • #94579POG
Issued: 1998
Value: $26

13

Gabriella Angelfaith
QVC
12"
Issued: 1999
Value: $40

14

Gannon Bear
GCC
16" • #94883GCC
Issued: 2000
Value: N/E

Bears

	Price Paid	Value
1.		
2.		
3.		
4.		
5.		
6.		
7.		
8.		
9.		
10.		
11.		
12.		
13.		
14.		
Totals		

1

Photo Unavailable

Gareth & Glynnis
QVC
8" & 8"
Issued: 1998
Value: N/E

2

Gary B. Bean
QVC
10.5"
Issued: 2000
Value: $30

3

Gatsby
Bon-Ton
12"
Issued: 1998
Value: N/E

4

Geneva
Select Retailers
Issued: 1996
Value: $48

5

George
May Department Store Company
6"
Issued: 1998
Value: N/E

6

George
QVC
Issued: 1996
Value: $55

7

Photo Unavailable

George & Martha
QVC
5" & 5"
Issued: 2000
Value: N/E

8

George & Thomas Bearington
QVC
6" & 6"
Issued: 2000
Value: N/E

9

George Berriman
Spring 2000 Gift Show
10" • #919803
Issued: 2000
Value: $28

10

Georgie
Parade Of Gifts
6" • #94583POG
Issued: 1999
Value: $27

11

Geraldine & Sylvester
QVC
Issued: 1998
Value: $100

12

Getty Bearberg
Select Retailers
Issued: 1999
Value: N/E

13

Gideon
QVC
10"
Issued: 1998
Value: $28

14

Photo Unavailable

Girdwood & Juneau
QVC
6.5"
Issued: 2000
Value: $38

Bears

	Price Paid	Value
1.		
2.		
3.		
4.		
5.		
6.		
7.		
8.		
9.		
10.		
11.		
12.		
13.		
14.		
Totals		

1

Glenna
Dillard's
7" • #94721DL
Issued: 1997
Value: $60

2

Gloria
QVC
14"
Issued: 1999
Value: N/E

3

Gomez
Select Retailers
10"
Issued: 1999
Value: N/E

4

Photo Unavailable

Gourdie Frightmare
Select Retailers
8"
Issued: 1999
Value: N/E

5

Gracie
Dillard's
6"
Issued: 1999
Value: N/E

6

Gracie
May Department Store Company
6"
Issued: 1998
Value: N/E

7

Grandma Henrietta & Lizzie
QVC
Issued: 1997
Value: $130

8

Grant S. Bearington
Norm Thompson
Issued: 1997
Value: $72

9

Grovsnor S. Grizbear
QVC
18"
Issued: 2000
Value: N/E

10

Photo Unavailable

Guildford Q. Bearrister
QVC
12"
Issued: 2000
Value: N/E

11

Guilford
GCC
6" • #94852GCC
Issued: 1997
Value: $37

12

Guinella
Ideation
11"
Issued: 1999
Value: N/E

13

Guinevere
Lord & Taylor
Issued: 1996
Value: N/E

14

Guinevere
QVC
11"
Issued: 1997
Value: N/E

Bears

	Price Paid	Value
1.		
2.		
3.		
4.		
5.		
6.		
7.		
8.		
9.		
10.		
11.		
12.		
13.		
14.		
Totals		

1

Guinevere
The San Francisco Music Box Company
♪ La Vie En Rose
11" • #41-72139
Issued: 1998
Value: N/E

2

Photo Unavailable

Gunnar
Select Retailers
info unavailable
Value: $29

3

Gunter
Dillard's
10" • #94722DL
Issued: 1997
Value: $32

4

Guthrie P. Mussy
QVC
Issued: 1997
Value: N/E

5

Gwennora
QVC
11"
Issued: 1999
Value: $20

6

Hannah
Elder-Beerman
8" • #8242437EB
Issued: 1999
Value: N/E

7

Hannah, Ursula, Greta & Sarabeth
QVC
14" & 8" & 6" & 2.5"
Issued: 2000
Value: $100

8

Harry
Lord & Taylor
8"
Issued: 1997
Value: N/E

9

Hayes R. Bearrington (LE-2,000)
The San Francisco Music Box Company
♪ What A Feeling
15" • #41-72766
Issued: 1999
Value: $150

10

Heathcliff
QVC
Issued: 1997
Value: N/E

11

Hedda
QVC
Issued: 1996
Value: $108

12

Heidi & Bethany Thistebeary
QVC
9" & 6"
Issued: 1999
Value: N/E

13

Henry
Dillard's
14" • #94726DL
Issued: 1997
Value: $54

14

Henry Bearymore
May Department Store Company
14" • #94156MC
Issued: 1999
Value: N/E

Bears

	Price Paid	Value
1.		
2.		
3.		
4.		
5.		
6.		
7.		
8.		
9.		
10.		
11.		
12.		
13.		
14.		
Totals		

1

Henry Bearymore
May Department Store Company
14"
Issued: 2000
Value: N/E

2

Photo Unavailable

Heywood Barlinski
Bon-Ton
14"
Issued: 1999
Value: N/E

3

Holly
Lord & Taylor
8"
Issued: 1999
Value: $28

4

Holly Bearberry
QVC
Issued: 1996
Value: $56

5

Photo Unavailable

Honey B. Bear
Spiegel
Issued: 1994
Value: N/E

6

Honey B. Elfberg
Parade Of Gifts
14" • #94578POG
Issued: 1998
Value: $38

7

Honey B. Growin
Parade Of Gifts
14"
Issued: 1999
Value: $42

8

Honey B. Mine
Parade Of Gifts
14" • #94576POG
Issued: 1998
Value: $33

Bears

	Price Paid	Value
1.		
2.		
3.		
4.		
5.		
6.		
7.		
8.		
9.		
10.		
11.		
12.		
13.		
14.		
Totals		

9

Photo Unavailable

Honey Bee Bear
Faith Mountain Company
Issued: 1995
Value: N/E

10

Photo Unavailable

Honeybrain With Topaz F. Wuzzie
QVC
Issued: 2000
Value: N/E

11

Honeybunch & Uncle Gus (sold as set with "Uncle Gus & Gary . . . The Gift" resin piece)
QVC
13" & 6.5" & 4.75"
Issued: 1997
Value: $95

12

Photo Unavailable

Hoskins Q. Hugmeister
QVC
30"
Issued: 2000
Value: $95

13

Howard P. Potter
QVC
12"
Issued: 2000
Value: N/E

14

Hubbard
QVC
Issued: 1996
Value: $55

1

Huett
QVC
Issued: 1997
Value: $17

2

Huntley
QVC
Issued: 1997
Value: $17

3

Ike D. Bearington
QVC
14"
Issued: 1998
Value: N/E

4

Indigo Jones
QVC
Issued: 1997
Value: $105

5

Ingrid & Tasha Norbruin With Toggle F. Wuzzie (LE-2,400)
QVC
16" & 8" & 3"
Issued: 1999
Value: $80

6

Ingrid S. Witebred
GCC
8" • #94871GCC
Issued: 1999
Value: $35

7

Isabella
Bon-Ton
16" • #945608BT
Issued: 1999
Value: N/E

8

JC Penney Bear
JC Penney
info unavailable
Value: N/E

9

J.C. Von Fuzzner
JC Penney
14" • #773/6271/01
Issued: 1999
Value: N/E

10

J.T. Jordan
Welcome Home
Issued: 1997
Value: $50

11

Jackson
May Department Store Company
Issued: 1998
Value: N/E

12

Jacqueline K. Bearington
QVC
Issued: 1998
Value: $170

13

Jaime Lisa
Dillard's
Issued: 1998
Value: $68

14

Jake
Dillard's
8"
Issued: 1998
Value: N/E

Bears

	Price Paid	Value
1.		
2.		
3.		
4.		
5.		
6.		
7.		
8.		
9.		
10.		
11.		
12.		
13.		
14.		
Totals		

1

James & Malachi
QVC
Issued: 1998
Value: $62

2

Photo Unavailable

Jameson J., Deacon T. & Cameron G. Bearsford
QVC
6" & 6" & 6"
Issued: 1999
Value: $45

3

Jamie
Canadian
6" • #BC94286PO
Issued: 2000
Value: $35

4

Jan B. Bearberg
Select Retailers
Issued: 1998
Value: N/E

5

Jarvis Boydsenberry
QVC
16"
Issued: 1998
Value: $90

6

Jean
Canadian
14" • #BC100905
Issued: 1997
Value: $33

7

Jenny McBruin
QVC
16"
Issued: 2000
Value: N/E

8

Photo Unavailable

Jeremiah
Country Living
Issued: 1997
Value: N/E

Bears

	Price Paid	Value
1.		
2.		
3.		
4.		
5.		
6.		
7.		
8.		
9.		
10.		
11.		
12.		
13.		
14.		
Totals		

9

Jeremy
Dillard's
14" • #94712DL
Issued: 1997
Value: $45

10

Jesse
Lord & Taylor
8"
Issued: 1999
Value: N/E

11

Jillian
Dillard's
16"
Issued: 1998
Value: $45

12

Joanne Pearl
Bon-Ton
#94569BT
Issued: 2000
Value: N/E

13

Jobie & Kibby Bearington
QVC
Issued: 1998
Value: N/E

14

Photo Unavailable

Jocelyn Thistlebeary & Carson T. Bibbly
QVC
16" & 6"
Issued: 1999
Value: $42

1

Joe
Canadian
10" • #BC100508
Issued: 1997
Value: $38

2

John
Canadian
10" • #BC100505
Issued: 1997
Value: $45

3

John William
QVC
Issued: 1997
Value: N/E

4

Jolee
May Department Store Company
Issued: 1998
Value: N/E

5

Jonathan Macbear
QVC
16"
Issued: 2000
Value: N/E

6

Jordan T. Fallsbeary
Dealer Show Exclusive
8" • #919805
Issued: 2000
Value: $28

7

Joyelle
Ideation
Issued: 1998
Value: N/E

8

Julia
Dillard's
14" • #94719DL
Issued: 1997
Value: $68

9

Julian
Dillard's
info unavailable
Value: N/E

10

Jupiter
QVC
Issued: 1996
Value: $40

11
Photo Unavailable
Justin
Dillard's
11" • #5106-11DL
Issued: 1997
Value: $32

12

Justina & Matthew
QVC
Issued: 1997
Value: $160

13

Kaitlin Lovebear (LE-10,000)
Kirlin's
11"
Issued: 2000
Value: N/E

14

Karen B. Bearsdale
QVC
13"
Issued: 2000
Value: N/E

Bears

	Price Paid	Value
1.		
2.		
3.		
4.		
5.		
6.		
7.		
8.		
9.		
10.		
11.		
12.		
13.		
14.		
Totals		

1

Karl Von Fuzzner
QVC
10"
Issued: 1998
Value: N/E

2

Karly & Melanie Bearibug
QVC
6" & 6"
Issued: 2000
Value: N/E

3

Karmen
Frederick Atkins
10" • #94767FA
Issued: 2000
Value: N/E

4

Kassandra Berrywinkle
QVC
12"
Issued: 1997
Value: $75

5

Kaufmann Bear
Kaufmann's
info unavailable
Value: N/E

6

Kayla Mulbeary & Krista Blubeary
QVC
6" & 6"
Issued: 1999
Value: $23

7

Kelby
Frederick Atkins
14"
Issued: 1998
Value: N/E

8

Kelsey
Dillard's
12" • #94747DL
Issued: 1999
Value: $35

9

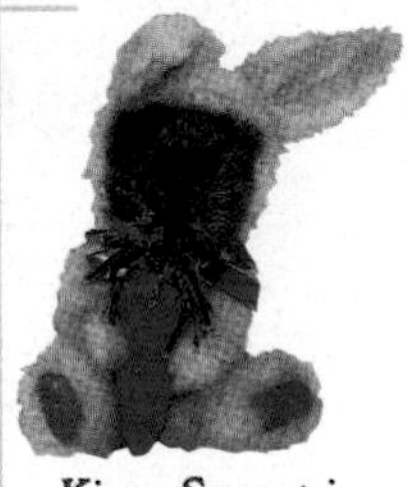

Kinsey Snoopstein
QVC
6" & 6"
Issued: 1999
Value: $17

10

Klaus Von Fuzzner
The San Francisco Music Box Company
♪ Let It Snow
13" • #41-72764
Issued: 1999
Value: $50

11

Photo Unavailable

Knut C. Berriman
QVC
8"
Issued: 1998
Value: N/E

12

Photo Unavailable

Kris
Lord & Taylor
5"
Issued: 1997
Value: N/E

13

Photo Unavailable

Kristen
Proffitt's
6"
Issued: 1999
Value: N/E

14

Kristoff
QVC
12"
Issued: 1998
Value: $30

Bears

	Price Paid	Value
1.		
2.		
3.		
4.		
5.		
6.		
7.		
8.		
9.		
10.		
11.		
12.		
13.		
14.		
Totals		

1

Kyle
Select Retailers
Issued: 1998
Value: $28

2

Labelle
Ideation
8.25"
Issued: 1997
Value: N/E

3

LaDonna & Darlene du Beary
QVC
10" & 6"
Issued: 2000
Value: N/E

4

Lady Flora Monarch
GCC
14" • 94891GCC
Issued: 2000
Value: N/E

5

Lara
QVC
Issued: 1997
Value: $140

6

Laura Ann
Dillard's
14"
Issued: 1998
Value: $47

7

Laura E. Bearburn (LE-5,000)
JT Webb
8"
Issued: 1997
Value: $47

8

Leigh Ann Beansford
QVC
10"
Issued: 2000
Value: $38

9

Photo Unavailable
Leo Bruinski
QVC
info unavailable
Value: N/E

10

Leon
Lord & Taylor
info unavailable
Value: N/E

11

Leonardo B. Hartbreak
QVC
12"
Issued: 1999
Value: N/E

12

Lester
Canadian
12" • #BC100705
Issued: 1997
Value: N/E

13

Letitia T. Bearington
GCC
10" • #94879GCC
Issued: 1999
Value: $60

14

Lewis
QVC
Issued: 1998
Value: N/E

Bears

	Price Paid	Value
1.		
2.		
3.		
4.		
5.		
6.		
7.		
8.		
9.		
10.		
11.		
12.		
13.		
14.		
Totals		

1

Libearty C. Star
Rocking Horse Classics
10"
Issued: 2000
Value: N/E

2

Lindsey
Belk
Issued: 1997
Value: N/E

3

Lindy & Nell Bradbeary
QVC
14" & 6"
Issued: 1999
Value: $75

4

Linsey McKenzie
QVC
Issued: 1997
Value: $50

5

Little Larson
Ideation
Issued: 1997
Value: N/E

6

Liza Mae & Alex
QVC
Issued: 1998
Value: $135

7

Lizzie McBee
QVC
Issued: 1998
Value: $38

8

Logan
QVC
Issued: 1997
Value: $58

9

Lone Star
Dillard's (Texas)
#94707DL
Issued: 1996
Value: $60

10

Lorraine P. Bearsley
QVC
15"
Issued: 2000
Value: N/E

11

Lucinda D. Bearsley
QVC
10"
Issued: 1998
Value: N/E

12

Lucy
Gottschalk's
12"
Issued: 1999
Value: N/E

13

Lucy Bea LeBruin
QVC
Issued: 1997
Value: $50

14

Ludmilla Berriman & Ludwig Von Fuzzner (LE-2,400)
QVC
14" & 8"
Issued: 1998
Value: $115

Bears

	Price Paid	Value
1.		
2.		
3.		
4.		
5.		
6.		
7.		
8.		
9.		
10.		
11.		
12.		
13.		
14.		
Totals		

1

Lula B. Lightfoot
QVC
12"
Issued: 2000
Value: N/E

2

Maci E. Kringlebeary
Macy's
12"
Issued: 2000
Value: $70

3

Madeline
Elder-Beerman
8"
Issued: 1998
Value: N/E

4

Madison
Select Retailers
Issued: 1996
Value: N/E

5

Magdalena
Frederick Atkins
6"
Issued: 1998
Value: N/E

6

Mallory Witebruin
GCC
14" • #94866GCC
Issued: 1999
Value: N/E

7

Mamie E. Bearington
QVC
Issued: 1998
Value: $220

8

Manchester S. Bearrister
QVC
21"
Issued: 1999
Value: $75

9

Maranda Hollybear
Parade Of Gifts
6" • #84588POG
Issued: 2000
Value: $30

10

Margaret Hollybear
Parade Of Gifts
14" • #94587POG
Issued: 2000
Value: N/E

11

Margarita & Vermooth
QVC
Issued: 1998
Value: N/E

12

Marian
Kirlin's
10"
Issued: 1998
Value: $50

13

Marilyn
Select Retailers
Issued: 1996
Value: $60

14

Marina
Lord & Taylor
10"
Issued: 1998
Value: N/E

Bears

	Price Paid	Value
1.		
2.		
3.		
4.		
5.		
6.		
7.		
8.		
9.		
10.		
11.		
12.		
13.		
14.		
Totals		

1

Marjorie Ellen Bearsley
GCC
14" • #94880GCC
Issued: 2000
Value: $48

2

Photo Unavailable

Marnie
Elder-Beerman
10"
Issued: 1999
Value: N/E

3

Photo Unavailable

Marvelle
Lord & Taylor
11"
Issued: 1997
Value: N/E

4

Mary Elizabeth, Becca & Ruth
QVC
14" & 8" & 6"
Issued: 2000
Value: N/E

5

Mary Louise Bearington
QVC
10"
Issued: 2000
Value: N/E

6

Photo Unavailable

Mary Lucinda & Marjorie Mayberry
QVC
10" & 6"
Issued: 1999
Value: $37

7

Mattie C. Bearsley
GCC
6"
Issued: 2000
Value: N/E

8

Photo Unavailable

Max
Select Retailers
info unavailable
Value: N/E

Bears

	Price Paid	Value
1.		
2.		
3.		
4.		
5.		
6.		
7.		
8.		
9.		
10.		
11.		
12.		
13.		
14.		
Totals		

9

Maximilian, Elford & Thornton
QVC
14" & 6" & 3.5"
Issued: 1998
Value: N/E

10

Maxine T. Bearsley
GCC
8" • #94881GCC
Issued: 2000
Value: N/E

11

Maxton P. Bean
QVC
Issued: 1998
Value: N/E

12

Photo Unavailable

Mayberry
QVC
Issued: 2000
Value: N/E

13

Meg
Dillard's
14" • #94770DL
Issued: 2000
Value: N/E

14

Megan
Kirlin's
Issued: 1999
Value: N/E

1

Melanie Lockley & Sam F. Wuzzie
QVC
13" & 3"
Issued: 1999
Value: $32

2

Melinda M. Milestone
QVC
10"
Issued: 2000
Value: $28

3

Michael
Dillard's
14" • #94717DL
Issued: 1997
Value: $40

4

Michaela
Dillard's
10" • #94718DL
Issued: 1997
Value: $40

5

Michelle B. Bearsley
QVC
9"
Issued: 2000
Value: N/E

6

Mindy Witebruin
GCC
6" • #94867GCC
Issued: 1999
Value: N/E

7

Miss Amirella & Ripley
QVC
8" & 3"
Issued: 2000
Value: N/E

8

Miss Isabelle Q. Bearworthy
QVC
10"
Issued: 1998
Value: N/E

9

Miss MacIntosh & Sarabeth With Topsey (LE-3,000)
QVC
16" & 8" & 2.5"
Issued: 1999
Value: $63

10

Miss Maggie & Theo
Welcome Home
10" & 6"
Issued: 1998
Value: N/E

11
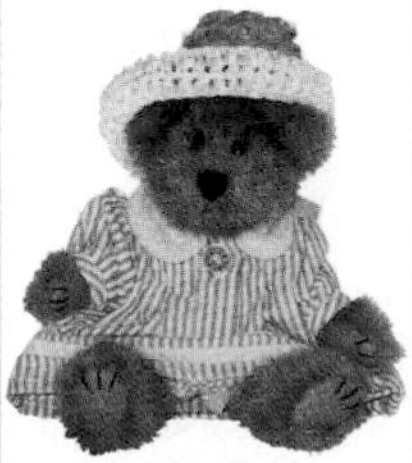
Miss Marla Mae
Welcome Home
6"
Issued: 2000
Value: N/E

12

Mohair Classic Pooh (LE-600)
Disney Gallery Stores
12"
Issued: 1999
Value: $190

13

Mohair Santa Pooh (LE-600)
Disney Gallery Stores
12"
Issued: 1999
Value: $79

14

Momma Bear, Allouetta & Victor (LE-1,800)
QVC
Issued: 1997
Value: $148

Bears

	Price Paid	Value
1.		
2.		
3.		
4.		
5.		
6.		
7.		
8.		
9.		
10.		
11.		
12.		
13.		
14.		
Totals		

1

Momma Berrywinkle & Woodrow (LE-2,400)
QVC
12"
Issued: 1998
Value: $130

2

Momma McBear & Cedric
QVC
Issued: 1997
Value: $60

3

Momma McBear & Delmar
The San Francisco Music Box Company
♪ You're Nobody 'til Somebody Loves You
10" & 6" • #41-72585
Issued: 1998
Value: N/E

4

Momma McGoldberg & Cissy
GCC
10" • #94856GCC
Issued: 1998
Value: $50

5

Monica
Frederick Atkins
10"
Issued: 1998
Value: N/E

6

Mother Bearston & Bluebell
QVC
Issued: 1998
Value: $60

7

Mr. Barnum
GCC
14" • #94872GCC
Issued: 1999
Value: $48

8

Mr. BoJingles
Select Retailers
Issued: 1997
Value: $48

9

Mr. Chucklebeary
QVC
12"
Issued: 2000
Value: $60

10

Photo Unavailable
Mr. Miles & Miss Mabel Bearister
QVC
8" & 8"
Issued: 1999
Value: $30

11

Mr. Peepers
QVC
10"
Issued: 1999
Value: N/E

12

Mrs. Beariwell
GCC
10" • #94877GCC
Issued: 1999
Value: $32

13

Mrs. Bradley
Linda Anderson's Collectibles
10" • #11-0320
Issued: 1998
Value: $30

14

Mrs. Northstar
The San Francisco Music Box Company
♪ Moonlight Serenade
13" • #41-40001
Issued: 2000
Value: N/E

Bears

	Price Paid	Value
1.		
2.		
3.		
4.		
5.		
6.		
7.		
8.		
9.		
10.		
11.		
12.		
13.		
14.		
Totals		

1

Mrs. Potter & Amadeus (LE-1,200)
QVC
Issued: 1997
Value: $145

2

Mrs. Trumbull
The San Francisco Music Box Company
♪ Puttin' on the Ritz
11" • #41-72769
Issued: 1999
Value: $44

3

Ms. Odetta & Neville
QVC
Issued: 1996
Value: $180

4

Nadia
Kirlin's
10"
Issued: 1998
Value: $55

5

Nadia Berriman
QVC
10"
Issued: 1998
Value: $26

6

Nancy D. Bearington
QVC
16"
Issued: 1999
Value: $140

7

Photo Unavailable

Nettie
QVC
Issued: 1994
Value: N/E

8

Niagra (LE-3,600)
Centre Gift Shoppe
Issued: 1999
Value: $40

9

Nichley
Dillard's
Issued: 1998
Value: $32

10

Nicholas, Ansel & Fitzgerald
QVC
Issued: 1996
Value: $152

11

Nicholas & Nikki II
Select Retailers
info unavailable
Value: N/E

12

Nicholas Bearington & Tinker F. Wuzzie
QVC
4.5" & 2"
Issued: 1999
Value: $28

13

Nickleby S. Claus
QVC
16"
Issued: 1999
Value: $40

Bears

	Price Paid	Value
1.		
2.		
3.		
4.		
5.		
6.		
7.		
8.		
9.		
10.		
11.		
12.		
13.		
Totals		

1

Photo Unavailable

Nicole
Dillard's
8"
Issued: 1998
Value: N/E

2

Nicole & Amy Berriman With Tassle F. Wuzzie (LE-3,000)
QVC
16" & 8" & 3"
Issued: 1999
Value: $85

3

Nicole de la El-bee
Elder-Beerman
14"
Issued: 1997
Value: $49

4

Niklas (LE-1,800)
QVC
Issued: 1997
Value: $150

5

Photo Unavailable

Noelle
Ethel M Chocolates
6"
Issued: 1998
Value: N/E

6

Olas & Omar
QVC
Issued: 1997
Value: $35

7

Oliver
Dillard's
#94701DL
Issued: 1996
Value: N/E

8

Oliver
GCC
#94850GCC
Issued: 1997
Value: $45

9

Olivia Q. Witebred
QVC
Issued: 1997
Value: N/E

10

Ophelia W. Witebred
QVC
Issued: 1997
Value: $63

11

Opie Paddypasture & T. Ferdinand Wuzzie
QVC
11.5" & 3"
Issued: 2000
Value: N/E

12

Photo Unavailable

Oppie
Select Retailers
info unavailable
Value: N/E

13

Orabella Fitzbruin
QVC
Issued: 1997
Value: N/E

14

Orella Berrywinkle
QVC
Issued: 1997
Value: N/E

Bears

	Price Paid	Value
1.		
2.		
3.		
4.		
5.		
6.		
7.		
8.		
9.		
10.		
11.		
12.		
13.		
14.		
Totals		

1

Orianna
Welcome Home
16"
Issued: 1997
Value: N/E

2

Ottilie Wilhemina
GCC
#94860GCC
Issued: 1998
Value: $45

3

PJ
Lord & Taylor
8"
Issued: 1998
Value: N/E

4

P.J. Bearsdale & Tink F. Wuzzie
QVC
7" & 2"
Issued: 1999
Value: $27

5

Pansy
QVC
Issued: 1995
Value: $290

6

Patches & Tatters B. Beariluved
QVC
10" & 8"
Issued: 2000
Value: N/E

7

Patricia L. Cooksbeary
Longaberger
11" • #94630LB
Issued: 2000
Value: $70

8

Pee Wee
QVC
Issued: 1997
Value: N/E

9

Photo Unavailable

Pendleton
The San Francisco Music Box Company
♪ *Whistle a Happy Tune*
16" • #41-72934
Issued: 2000
Value: N/E

10

Penney Bearsley
JC Penney
10" • #JP045-1010A
Issued: 2000
Value: $35

11

Petula P. Fallsbeary
Dealer Show Exclusive
6" • #919804
Issued: 2000
Value: $22

12

Peyton
Frederick Atkins
14"
Issued: 1999
Value: N/E

13

Pierre
Canadian
14" • #BC100908
Issued: 1997
Value: $40

14

Piper P. Plumbottom
QVC
14"
Issued: 2000
Value: $60

Bears

	Price Paid	Value
1.		
2.		
3.		
4.		
5.		
6.		
7.		
8.		
9.		
10.		
11.		
12.		
13.		
14.		
Totals		

1

Poof Pufflebeary
The San Francisco Music Box Company
♪ Rock-a-Bye Babe
15" • #41-72981
Issued: 2000
Value: $35

2

Prudence Bearimore
The San Francisco Music Box Company
♪ Oh, What A Beautiful Morning!
12" • #41-72765
Issued: 1999
Value: $45

3

Puff & Poof Fuzzibutt
QVC
10" & 8"
Issued: 1999
Value: $40

4

Putnam & Kent
QVC
Issued: 1997
Value: $58

5

Quinn
Frederick Atkins
16"
Issued: 1999
Value: N/E

6

Ragna
Select Retailers
Issued: 1998
Value: $38

7

Raylee
Dillard's
14"
Issued: 1998
Value: $34

8

Reba & Roxie DuBeary
QVC
6" & 6"
Issued: 1999
Value: N/E

Bears

	Price Paid	Value
1.		
2.		
3.		
4.		
5.		
6.		
7.		
8.		
9.		
10.		
11.		
12.		
13.		
14.		
Totals		

9

Regan
Dillard's
10" • #94772DL
Issued: 2000
Value: N/E

10

Reginald
Lord & Taylor
16"
Issued: 1996
Value: $90

11

Remington B. Bean
QVC
Issued: 1997
Value: $46

12

Rhoda
GCC
#94854GCC
Issued: 1997
Value: $35

13

Richard Tee Dobbsey
Coach House Gifts
14"
Issued: 2000
Value: N/E

14

Roberto
Ideation
14" • #900216IDE
Issued: 2000
Value: $55

1

Robyn
Canadian
7" • #BC94287PO
Issued: 2000
Value: $40

2

Photo Unavailable

Rocky Mountberg
Select Retailers
Issued: 1999
Value: $19

3

Rodney
Select Retailers
Issued: 1998
Value: $32

4

Roland
Dillard's
11" • #94725DL
Issued: 1997
Value: $45

5

Ronald
Select Retailers
8"
Issued: 1997
Value: N/E

6

Rosalind
The San Francisco Music Box Company
♪ Mr. Sandman
14" • #41-72125
Issued: 1997
Value: N/E

7

Rosalind II
The San Francisco Music Box Company
♪ Mr. Sandman
14" • #41-72583
Issued: 1998
Value: N/E

8

Rosie B. Goodbear
Country Clutter
10"
Issued: 2000
Value: N/E

9

Rudolph
Select Retailers
info unavailable
Value: $42

10

Rudy Z. Mooseburg
GCC
10" • #94875GCC
Issued: 1999
Value: N/E

11

Russett
Frederick Atkins
10" • #94762FA
Issued: 1999
Value: N/E

12

Rutledge
QVC
Issued: 1998
Value: N/E

13

Ryan
Dillard's
14" • #94771DL
Issued: 2000
Value: N/E

Bears

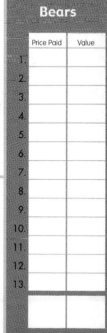

	Price Paid	Value
1.		
2.		
3.		
4.		
5.		
6.		
7.		
8.		
9.		
10.		
11.		
12.		
13.		
Totals		

1

Sadie
Kirlin's
10"
Issued: 1999
Value: N/E

2

Photo Unavailable

Sadie Bearymore
May Department Store Company
8" • #94157MC
Issued: 1999
Value: $40

3

Sakary Millenia
Select Retailers
Issued: 1999
Value: $40

4

Sally Quignapple & Annie
The San Francisco Music Box Company
♪ That's What Friends Are For
10" • #41-72978
Issued: 2000
Value: N/E

5

Samantha
Kirlin's
10"
Issued: 1997
Value: $50

6

Santa Pooh (sold as set with "Santa Pooh" resin ornament)
Disney Catalog & Stores
9.75" & N/A • #20212MM
Issued: 1999
Value: $85

7

Sara Beth
POG
14" • #94584POG
Issued: 2000
Value: $55

8

Sarah
Canadian
8" • #BC94288PO
Issued: 2000
Value: $43

Bears

	Price Paid	Value
1.		
2.		
3.		
4.		
5.		
6.		
7.		
8.		
9.		
10.		
11.		
12.		
13.		
14.		
Totals		

9

Sarah Anne Bearsly & T. Foster Wuzzie
QVC
10" & 5"
Issued: 1999
Value: N/E

10

Sarasota & Windsor
QVC
Issued: 1998
Value: N/E

11

Savannah Berrywinkle & Bentley
QVC
Issued: 1997
Value: $80

12

Scotch
Select Retailers
Issued: 1996
Value: N/E

13

Sedgewick T. Bruin
QVC
16"
Issued: 1998
Value: N/E

14

Sidney
Dillard's
10"
Issued: 1998
Value: N/E

1

Sissy
Lord & Taylor
8"
Issued: 1998
Value: N/E

2

Skylar & Starlynn
QVC
Issued: 1997
Value: N/E

3

Photo Unavailable

Skylar Thistlebeary
The San Francisco Music Box Company
♪ *A Dream is a Wish Your Heart Makes*
16" • #41-72940
Issued: 2000
Value: N/E

4

Smith Witter II
The San Francisco Music Box Company
♪ *You've Got A Friend*
Issued: 1997
Value: $42

5

Smokey Mountberg
Select Retailers
Issued: 1999
Value: $25

6

Photo Unavailable

Snicklefritz
QVC
Issued: 2000
Value: N/E

7

Snuggems B. Joy
GCC
10" • #94884GCC
Issued: 2000
Value: N/E

8

Sophie B. Goodbear
Country Clutter
10"
Issued: 2000
Value: $42

9

Spearmint & Peppermint Hollibeary
QVC
8" & 8"
Issued: 1999
Value: $48

10

Stafford & Devon
GCC
8" • #94859GCC
Issued: 1998
Value: $52

11

Starlight B. Bearsworth
QVC
17"
Issued: 2000
Value: N/E

12

Starry (LE-3,600)
Canadian
8"
Issued: 1999
Value: $40

13

Stella & Baby Mae
QVC
10" & 5"
Issued: 2000
Value: N/E

14

Sterner
Frederick Atkins
10"
Issued: 1998
Value: $40

Bears

	Price Paid	Value
1.		
2.		
3.		
4.		
5.		
6.		
7.		
8.		
9.		
10.		
11.		
12.		
13.		
14.		
Totals		

1

Strawbeary
Smuckers Catalog
12"
Issued: 1999
Value: N/E

2

Photo Unavailable

Sunny B. Hugsworth
QVC
14"
Issued: 1999
Value: $43

3

Sunny Buzzbee (LE-3,600)
J.T. Webb
10"
Issued: 1999
Value: $40

4

Susie
Lord & Taylor
8"
Issued: 1999
Value: N/E

5

Sven B. Frostman
QVC
14"
Issued: 1999
Value: $30

6

Sydney (LE-2,400)
Canadian
8" • #BC94276
Issued: 1997
Value: $50

7

T. Dean Newbearger
GCC
10" • #948656GCC
Issued: 1998
Value: N/E

8

T.G. Nichee
Gift Niche
Issued: 2000
Value: N/E

9

Tammy
QVC
Issued: 1996
Value: $110

10

Tara, Tia & Tilly F. Wuzzie
QVC
3" & 3.5" & 3.5"
Issued: 1999
Value: N/E

11

Photo Unavailable

Tartan Tess
Country Peddler
Issued: 1996
Value: N/E

12

Taylor
Dillard's
16" • #94705DL
Issued: 1996
Value: $82

13

Photo Unavailable

Ted & Teddy
QVC
Issued: 1994
Value: N/E

14

Teddy Bauer
QVC
Issued: 1995
Value: N/E

Bears

	Price Paid	Value
1.		
2.		
3.		
4.		
5.		
6.		
7.		
8.		
9.		
10.		
11.		
12.		
13.		
14.		
Totals		

1

Texanne
Dillard's (Texas)
14" • #94708DL
Issued: 1996
Value: $65

2

Thea St. Griz & Everett Elfston
QVC
17" & 7.5"
Issued: 1998
Value: $120

3

Theodora Maria
QVC
Issued: 1998
Value: $65

4

Thor & Katrinka Berriman
QVC
12" & 7"
Issued: 1998
Value: N/E

5

Tiana
Frederick Atkins
6" • #94765FA
Issued: 2000
Value: N/E

6

Tilden, Tessa & Tori F. Wuzzie
QVC
3.5" & 3.5" & 3.5"
Issued: 1999
Value: $40

7

Tillie
Select Retailers
Issued: 1998
Value: $40

8

Tristan
Frederick Atkins
16" • #94763FA
Issued: 1999
Value: N/E

9

Turner with Kris
GCC
10" • #94888GCC
Issued: 2000
Value: N/E

10

Tyler
Dillard's
11"
Issued: 1998
Value: $52

11

Uncle Edward O'Beary
GCC
14" • #94889GCC
Issued: 2000
Value: N/E

12

Uncle Zeb & Cousin Minnow
QVC
Issued: 1998
Value: N/E

13

Ursula Berriman
QVC
12"
Issued: 1998
Value: $78

14

Valentina, Caterina, Evalina, & Michelina
QVC
Issued: 1998
Value: $92

Bears

	Price Paid	Value
1.		
2.		
3.		
4.		
5.		
6.		
7.		
8.		
9.		
10.		
11.		
12.		
13.		
14.		
Totals		

1

Photo Unavailable

Valerie
Ideation
6"
Issued: 1999
Value: N/E

2

Venus
Elder-Beerman
Issued: 1998
Value: N/E

3

Verdeia
Frederick Atkins
16"
Issued: 1998
Value: N/E

4

Vernette
Frederick Atkins
8" • #94764FA
Issued: 1999
Value: N/E

5

Veronica Bearskov
Platinum Dealer Exclusive
16" • #9198078
Issued: 2000
Value: N/E

6

Veronica Laflame
QVC
16"
Issued: 2000
Value: N/E

7

Virginia Dobbsey
Coach House Gifts
12"
Issued: 1999
Value: N/E

8

Virginia Thistlebeary
Spring 2000 Gift Show
8" • #919802
Issued: 2000
Value: $32

Bears

	Price Paid	Value
1.		
2.		
3.		
4.		
5.		
6.		
7.		
8.		
9.		
10.		
11.		
12.		
13.		
14.		
Totals		

9

Waitsfield
GCC
11" • #94853GCC
Issued: 1997
Value: $55

10

Walton
Canadian
Issued: 1997
Value: $52

11

Wesley, Willoughby & Woodward
QVC
Issued: 1998
Value: $30

12

Whihley With Winkle & Pip (LE-3,000)
QVC
12" & 6" & 3"
Issued: 1999
Value: $53

13

Photo Unavailable

Whitley B. Beariluved
QVC
10"
Issued: 2000
Value: N/E

14

Will
Dillard's
6"
Issued: 1998
Value: N/E

1

Wilson (w/boat)
QVC
Issued: 1995
Value: $45

2

Photo Unavailable

Wilson (w/pie)
QVC
Issued: 1994
Value: N/E

3

Winifred
Valentine's Day
Issued: 1997
Value: $43

4

Winnie II
The San Francisco Music Box Company
♪ Love Is Blue
14"
Issued: 1999
Value: $35

5

Photo Unavailable

Winnie Wuzzwhite
The San Francisco Music Box Company
♪ You are the Sunshine of My Life
14" • #41-72939
Issued: 2000
Value: N/E

6

Winstead & Pensacola
QVC
15" & 6"
Issued: 1998
Value: N/E

7

Winter Holiday Mohair Pooh
Disney
13"
Issued: 2000
Value: N/E

8

Winter Holiday Pooh & Resin Ornament
Disney
Issued: 2000
Value: N/E

9

Younker Bear
Younkers
info unavailable
Value: N/E

10

Yu'Kon B. Bear (LE-10,000)
Canadian
10" • #BC94278
Issued: 1998
Value: $45

11

Yvonne & Yvette
QVC
Issued: 1998
Value: N/E

12

Zwick
Dillard's
#94748DL
Issued: 1999
Value: N/E

Bears

	Price Paid	Value
1.		
2.		
3.		
4.		
5.		
6.		
7.		
8.		
9.		
10.		
11.		
12.		
Totals		

Exclusive Camels

1

Abdul Duneworthy
QVC
9"
Issued: 2000
Value: N/E

Exclusive Cats

2
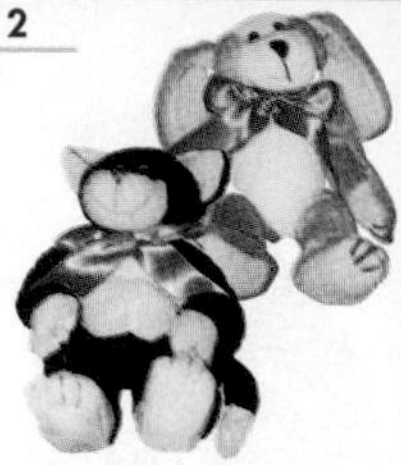
Allie Fuzzbucket & Mugsy Tirebiter
QVC
9" & 9"
Issued: 1998
Value: N/E

3

Aspen P. Ninelives
GCC
12" • #94870GCC
Issued: 1999
Value: $50

4

Blake, Dickens & Ogden Wordsworth
QVC
6" & 6" & 6"
Issued: 2000
Value: N/E

5

Caleigh
Dillard's
11"
Issued: 1998
Value: N/E

6

Casper Cat O'Lantern
Select Retailers
11"
Issued: 1999
Value: N/E

7

Cassandra Purrsley
QVC
14"
Issued: 2000
Value: N/E

8

Cher S. Fussberg
Select Retailers
Issued: 1998
Value: N/E

9

Claudia & Rowena Pussytoes
QVC
Issued: 1997
Value: $50

10

Cleo P. Pussytoes
QVC
Issued: 1997
Value: $75

11

Cleo P. Pussytoes
The San Francisco Music Box Company
♪ *What's New Pussycat?*
16" • #41-72140
Issued: 1998
Value: N/E

12

Crackers & Roquefort
QVC
Issued: 1998
Value: $42

Camels

	Price Paid	Value
1.		

Cats

	Price Paid	Value
2.		
3.		
4.		
5.		
6.		
7.		
8.		
9.		
10.		
11.		
12.		
Totals		

1

Fuzzy Jake Cattington
QVC
10"
Issued: 1999
Value: N/E

2

Grosvenor Catberg
QVC
Issued: 1997
Value: $88

3

Heranamous
The San Francisco Music Box Company
♪ *Ebony And Ivory*
17" • #41-72639
Issued: 1998
Value: N/E

4

Holly
Elder-Beerman
8"
Issued: 1999
Value: N/E

5

Ivana Purrkins
QVC
11"
Value: $40

6

Jenna
Dillard's
11"
Issued: 1999
Value: N/E

7

Katie Kat
Lord & Taylor
16"
Issued: 1998
Value: $70

8

Leslie G. Catberg
Select Retailers
Issued: 1998
Value: N/E

9

Lindsey II & Tucker F. Wuzzie
QVC
Issued: 1998
Value: N/E

10

Lyndon B. & Mondale W. Cattington
QVC
Issued: 1998
Value: $50

11

Margaux P. Pussyfoot
QVC
14"
Issued: 1999
Value: $32

12

Marissa P. Pussytoes
The San Francisco Music Box Company
♪ *Mr. Sandman*
14" • #41-72979
Issued: 2000
Value: $32

13

Photo Unavailable

Miss Annie Fuzzybuns
QVC
14"
Issued: 1999
Value: $22

Cats

	Price Paid	Value
1.		
2.		
3.		
4.		
5.		
6.		
7.		
8.		
9.		
10.		
11.		
12.		
13.		
Totals		

1

Momma McFuzz & Missy
The San Francisco Music Box Company
♪ You and Me Against the World
12" • #41-72977
Issued: 2000
Value: N/E

2

Mrs. Petrie
QVC
13"
Value: N/E

3

Muffles T. Toastytoes
QVC
11.5"
Issued: 1999
Value: $25

4

Nana Purrington & Gouda
Select Retailers
Issued: 1999
Value: N/E

5

Pepper
Dillard's
11" • #94746DL
Issued: 1999
Value: $30

6

Pookie W. Penworthy & Midnight Sneakypuss
QVC
8" & 6"
Issued: 2000
Value: N/E

7

Purrcilla Pusskins
QVC
14"
Issued: 2000
Value: N/E

8

Pussy Broomski
Select Retailers
5.5"
Issued: 1999
Value: N/E

Cats

	Price Paid	Value
1.		
2.		
3.		
4.		
5.		
6.		
7.		
8.		
9.		
10.		
11.		
12.		
13.		
14.		
Totals		

9

Salem Thumpkin
Select Retailers
16"
Issued: 1999
Value: N/E

10

Snooker T. Sootyfoot
QVC
14"
Issued: 2000
Value: N/E

11

Terence, Thad & Thristan
QVC
info unavailable
Value: $42

12

Thomasina Purrkins
QVC
info unavailable
Value: N/E

13

Whitefurd Felinsky
QVC
12"
Value: N/E

14

Zoe R. Grimilkin
QVC
11"
Issued: 1997
Value: $50

Exclusive Cows

1

Adelaide & Aggie
QVC
Issued: 1998
Value: $53

2

Clovis Hoofheifer & Ferdinand Bullsworth
QVC
8" & 8"
Issued: 2000
Value: N/E

3
Photo Unavailable
Myrtle MacMoo
QVC
11"
Issued: 1999
Value: $21

Exclusive Dogs

4

Ambrose P. Hydrant III
QVC
Issued: 1997
Value: N/E

5
Photo Unavailable
Ambrose Q. Hydrant
Lord & Taylor
Issued: 1998
Value: N/E

6

Bartley & Wilbur
QVC
10" & 10"
Issued: 2000
Value: N/E

7

Bath & Body Works Dog
Bath & Body Works
Issued: 1996
Value: $42

8

Buzz
Lord & Taylor
10"
Issued: 1997
Value: N/E

9

Caesar Q. & Cosmo G. Hydrant
QVC
10" & 10"
Issued: 1998
Value: N/E

10

Corky
QVC
Issued: 1998
Value: N/E

11

Fred Farfle
QVC
10"
Issued: 2000
Value: N/E

Cows	Price Paid	Value
1.		
2.		
3.		
Dogs		
4.		
5.		
6.		
7.		
8.		
9.		
10.		
11.		
Totals		

Exclusive Dogs

1

Petey Von Pup
GCC
6" • #94887GCC
Issued: 2000
Value: N/E

2

Salty
Casual Living
Issued: 1995
Value: $50

Exclusive Donkeys

3

Winter Holiday Eeyore & Resin Ornament
Disney
Issued: 2000
Value: N/E

4

Elf Eeyore (sold as set with "Elf Eeyore" resin ornament)
Disney
8" • #20214MM
Issued: 1999
Value: N/E

Exclusive Frogs

5

Nikali Q. Ribbit
QVC
Issued: 1997
Value: N/E

6

Ribbit Sisters . . . Lilly, Tilly & Toots
QVC
4" & 4" & 4"
Issued: 2000
Value: N/E

Exclusive Gorillas

7

Jake, Jay & Jette Magilla
QVC
Issued: 1998
Value: N/E

Exclusive Hares

8

Alice Hopplebeary
Boscov's
9"
Issued: 2000
Value: N/E

9

Allison Babbit
The San Francisco Music Box Company
♪ I Only Have Eyes For You
14" • #41-72141
Issued: 1998
Value: N/E

10

Alpine
Select Retailers
info unavailable
Value: N/E

	Price Paid	Value
Dogs		
1.		
2.		
Donkeys		
3.		
4.		
Frogs		
5.		
6.		
Gorillas		
7.		
Hares		
8.		
9.		
10.		
Totals		

1

Anissa
Select Retailers
Issued: 1998
Value: $40

2

Ashley
The San Francisco Music Box Company
♪ Love Me Tender
14" • #41-66847
Issued: 1997
Value: N/E

3

Bath & Body Works Snowbunny
Bath & Body Works
Issued: 1997
Value: $22

4

Belle
Harry & David
8"
Issued: 1998
Value: N/E

5

Brittany
Dillard's
8" • #94711DL
Issued: 1997
Value: $35

6

Photo Unavailable

Caitlin
Dillard's
8"
Issued: 1997
Value: N/E

7

Chantanay
Select Retailers
info unavailable
Value: N/E

8

Chloe
Elder-Beerman
11"
Issued: 2000
Value: N/E

9

Demi
QVC
Issued: 1996
Value: $48

10

Dutch
Select Retailers
Issued: 1998
Value: N/E

11

Ellie
Select Retailers
Issued: 1998
Value: N/E

12

Emily Babbit
QVC
Issued: 1998
Value: N/E

13

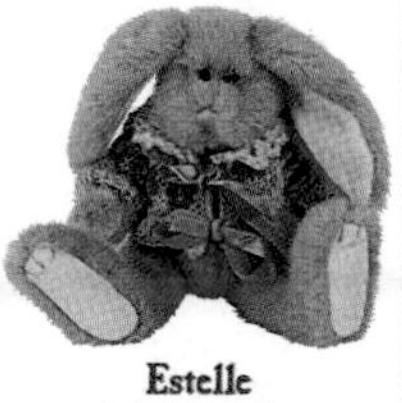

Estelle
Select Retailers
Issued: 1998
Value: N/E

14

Flopsie, Mopsie & Moxie Angelbuns
QVC
5.5"
Issued: 2000
Value: N/E

Hares

	Price Paid	Value
1.		
2.		
3.		
4.		
5.		
6.		
7.		
8.		
9.		
10.		
11.		
12.		
13.		
14.		
Totals		

1

Floradora
Select Retailers
Issued: 1998
Value: N/E

2

Giselle & Monique de la Fleur
QVC
Issued: 1998
Value: $35

3

Grandma Babbit & Elsinore
QVC
Issued: 1996
Value: $185

4

Grayling
Select Retailers
Issued: 1998
Value: $30

5

Gretchen
Bon-Ton
info unavailable
Value: N/E

6

Gretchen
Frederick Atkins
8.5"
Issued: 1998
Value: N/E

7

Harvey
QVC
Issued: 1995
Value: $58

8

Heather
Dillard's
8" • #94709DL
Issued: 1997
Value: $30

9

Iris & Petunia de la Hoppsack
QVC
Issued: 1998
Value: $35

10

Photo Unavailable

Jenna Kathlean
Dillard's
11" • #94740DL
Issued: 1999
Value: $20

11

Photo Unavailable

Jennifer & Annie Hopkins
QVC
8" & 6"
Issued: 1999
Value: $38

12

Lacey V. Hare
QVC
Issued: 1998
Value: $28

13

Lady Harington
QVC
Issued: 1997
Value: $45

14

Lady Harriwell
QVC
Issued: 1998
Value: $23

Hares

	Price Paid	Value
1.		
2.		
3.		
4.		
5.		
6.		
7.		
8.		
9.		
10.		
11.		
12.		
13.		
14.		
Totals		

1

Lady Pembrooke
The San Francisco Music Box Company
♪ *Music Box Dancer*
12" • #41-72647
Issued: 1998
Value: N/E

2

Lavinia V. Hariweather
The San Francisco Music Box Company
♪ *You Are My Sunshine*
10" • #41-72644
Issued: 1998
Value: N/E

3

Lindsey
Dillard's
8" • #94710DL
Issued: 1997
Value: $30

4

Lindy
Elder-Beerman
13"
Issued: 1999
Value: N/E

5

Mandy, Melissa & Michael
QVC
Issued: 1998
Value: $43

6

Meredith
Frederick Atkins
10"
Issued: 1999
Value: N/E

7

Miss Abby & Lexie Dowbunny
QVC
8" & 8"
Issued: 2000
Value: N/E

8

Ms. Magnolia, Lauren & Elizabeth
QVC
Issued: 1997
Value: $110

9

Mitzie Mae (LE-7,000)
Kirlin's
12"
Issued: 2000
Value: $22

10

Nanna O'Harea & Audrey
QVC
11" & 6"
Issued: 1998
Value: $64

11

Natalie
Dillard's
14" • #94716DL
Issued: 1997
Value: N/E

12

Parker
Select Retailers
Issued: 1998
Value: $30

13

Pauline
Kirlin's
10"
Issued: 1997
Value: $52

14

Penelope
Select Retailers
10"
Issued: 1998
Value: N/E

Hares

	Price Paid	Value
1.		
2.		
3.		
4.		
5.		
6.		
7.		
8.		
9.		
10.		
11.		
12.		
13.		
14.		
Totals		

1

Reno
Select Retailers
info unavailable
Value: N/E

2

Sarina
Frederick Atkins
9" • #94766FA
Issued: 2000
Value: $25

3

Stamford
QVC
Issued: 1997
Value: $45

4

Stanford
QVC
info unavailable
Value: N/E

5

Virginia Bluebell Bunny
The San Francisco Music Box Company
♪ *April Love*
10" • #41-72938
Issued: 2000
Value: N/E

6

Zelda Fitzhare
The San Francisco Music Box Company
♪ *Feelin' Groovy*
17" • #41-72643
Issued: 1998
Value: N/E

Exclusive Ladybugs

7

Teedle, Tinger & Tiffany F. Wuzzie (set/3)
QVC
2" & 2" & 2"
Issued: 2000
Value: N/E

Exclusive Lambs

8

Abbey Ewe
The San Francisco Music Box Company
♪ *Mairzy Doats*
14" • #41-72648
Issued: 1998
Value: N/E

9

Brianne
Select Retailers
Issued: 1997
Value: $27

10

Ivy M. Fuzzyfleece
QVC
10"
Issued: 1999
Value: $35

11

Photo Unavailable

Lucy Belle Lambston
QVC
14"
Issued: 1999
Value: N/E

12

Olivia
Dillard's
#94749DL
Issued: 2000
Value: $20

Hares

	Price Paid	Value
1.		
2.		
3.		
4.		
5.		
6.		
Ladybugs		
7.		
Lambs		
8.		
9.		
10.		
11.		
12.		
Totals		

1

Photo Unavailable

Oliver
Dillard's
Issued: 2000
Value: N/E

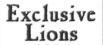

Exclusive Lions

2

Braden
Select Retailers
Issued: 1997
Value: $35

3

Leo, Topper & Tumble
QVC
3" & 3" & 3"
Issued: 2000
Value: N/E

4

Photo Unavailable

Leonard S. Uproarious
QVC
14"
Issued: 2000
Value: N/E

5

Marley Dredlion & Maybelle B. Bahoodle
QVC
9" & 9"
Issued: 1999
Value: $20

6

Zack
QVC
Issued: 1997
Value: $36

Exclusive Mice

7

Photo Unavailable

Colby & Port S. Mouski
QVC
6" & 6"
Value: N/E

8

Dick, Harry & Tom
QVC
Issued: 1997
Value: $36

9

Gouda & Edam
QVC
Issued: 1998
Value: $53

10

Havarti Chrismouse
GCC
#94864GCC
Issued: 1998
Value: $35

Exclusive Monkeys

11

Giseppi Renaldi
QVC
8"
Issued: 2000
Value: N/E

	Price Paid	Value
Lambs		
1.		
Lions		
2.		
3.		
4.		
5.		
6.		
Mice		
7.		
8.		
9.		
10.		
Monkeys		
11.		
Totals		

Exclusive Moose

1

Eddie Bauer
Eddie Bauer
Issued: 1994
Value: $90

2

Emily Ann
Lord & Taylor
17"
Issued: 1997
Value: $88

3

Izzy
Dillard's
#94745DL
Issued: 1999
Value: N/E

4

Magnus P. Mossfield
QVC
17"
Value: $75

5

Manfred Von Merrymoose
GCC
#94581GCC
Issued: 1997
Value: $50

6

Maxine Von Hindenmoose
QVC
Issued: 1997
Value: $75

7

McCormic T. Moosleton
GCC
10" • #94873GCC
Issued: 1999
Value: $30

8

McKinley (LE-1,800)
QVC
10"
Issued: 1999
Value: $55

9
Photo Unavailable
Meeka
Select Retailers
info unavailable
Value: $72

10

Mookie
Select Retailers
info unavailable
Value: $60

11

Mortimer
Lord & Taylor
Issued: 1996
Value: N/E

12

Mukluk
Select Retailers
Issued: 1995
Value: $75

13

T. Fargo, T. Foster & T. Fuzzball Wuzzie
QVC
5" & 5" & 5"
Issued: 1999
Value: N/E

Moose

	Price Paid	Value
1.		
2.		
3.		
4.		
5.		
6.		
7.		
8.		
9.		
10.		
11.		
12.		
13.		
Totals		

Exclusive Pandas

1

Shi Wong Panda
QVC
12"
Issued: 1999
Value: $49

2

Xin Fu Wongbruin
QVC
12"
Issued: 2000
Value: N/E

3

Photo Unavailable

Yolanda Panda
QVC
Issued: 1998
Value: $20

Exclusive Penguins

4

Tuxie, Tweedle & Opie Waddlewalk
QVC
8" & 6" & 3.5"
Issued: 1999
Value: N/E

Exclusive Pigs

5

Baby Rosebud
Harry & David
Issued: 1996
Value: N/E

6

Big Pig, Little Pig
Canadian
12" & 9" • #BC94279
Issued: 1998
Value: $60

7

Photo Unavailable

Big Pig, Little Pig
Select Retailers
10" & 8"
Issued: 1998
Value: N/E

8

Photo Unavailable

Erin
Dillard's
8"
Issued: 1998
Value: N/E

9

G. Wilbur McSwine
QVC
8"
Issued: 1997
Value: $50

10

Hamilton
Cracker Barrel
11"
Issued: 1999
Value: $46

	Price Paid	Value
Pandas		
1.		
2.		
3.		
Penguins		
4.		
Pigs		
5.		
6.		
7.		
8.		
9.		
10.		
Totals		

1

Kaitlin & Kendall McSwine
QVC
8" & 5"
Issued: 1998
Value: N/E

2

Katie
Select Retailers
info unavailable
Value: N/E

3

Katie O'Pigg
Dillard's
Issued: 1997
Value: $27

4

Lena O'Pigg
Dillard's
12" • #94706DL
Issued: 1997
Value: $40

5

Merentha
Dillard's
11" • #94727DL
Issued: 1997
Value: $50

6

Olympia
QVC
Issued: 1997
Value: N/E

7

Photo Unavailable

Primrose
QVC
11"
Issued: 1999
Value: $20

8

Rosebud
Harry & David
8"
Issued: 1998
Value: N/E

9

Rosie O'Pigg
The San Francisco Music Box Company
♪ *Second Hand Rose*
11" • #41-72641
Issued: 1998
Value: N/E

10

Santa's Helper Piglet (sold as set with "Santa's Helper Piglet" resin ornament)
Disney
6" • #20215MM
Issued: 1999
Value: N/E

11

Truffleina & Twila
QVC
6" & 6"
Issued: 2000
Value: N/E

12

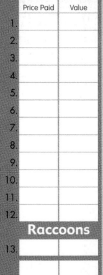

Winter Holiday Piglet & Resin Ornament
Disney
Issued: 2000
Value: N/E

Exclusive Raccoons

13

Photo Unavailable

Burwell Busheytail & Bud
QVC
10" & 3"
Issued: 2000
Value: N/E

Pigs

	Price Paid	Value
1.		
2.		
3.		
4.		
5.		
6.		
7.		
8.		
9.		
10.		
11.		
12.		
Raccoons		
13.		
Totals		

Exclusive Tigers

1

Elf Tigger (sold as set with "Elf Tigger" resin ornament)
Disney
11" • #20213MM
Issued: 1999
Value: $50

2

Winter Holiday Tigger & Resin Ornament
Disney
Issued: 2000
Value: N/E

Exclusive Ornaments

3

Angelina
The San Francisco Music Box Company
♪ Love Me Tender
6" • #41-72768
Issued: 1999
Value: $10

4

Annette Bearburg
Select Retailers
Issued: 1998
Value: $19

5

Arcturus & Aurora
QVC
5.5" & 5.5"
Issued: 1998
Value: N/E

6

Ardyth
GCC
#94861GCC
Issued: 1998
Value: $25

7

Ariel
QVC
Issued: 1996
Value: $52

8

Ariel
The San Francisco Music Box Company
♪ Jingle Bells
2" • #41-66894
Issued: 1997
Value: $45

9

Athena
Lord & Taylor
Issued: 1994
Value: $42

10

Baby Bailey (set/2)
QVC
6" & 6"
Issued: 1999
Value: $40

11

Barret, Belinda & Berg Blizzard
QVC
4.5" & 4.5" & 4.5"
Issued: 1999
Value: N/E

12

Photo Unavailable

Bud Buzzby
The San Francisco Music Box Company
♪ My Favorite Things
#41-72937
Issued: 2000
Value: N/E

Tigers

	Price Paid	Value
1.		
2.		

Ornaments

	Price Paid	Value
3.		
4.		
5.		
6.		
7.		
8.		
9.		
10.		
11.		
12.		
Totals		

1

Comet
Lord & Taylor
Issued: 1996
Value: N/E

2

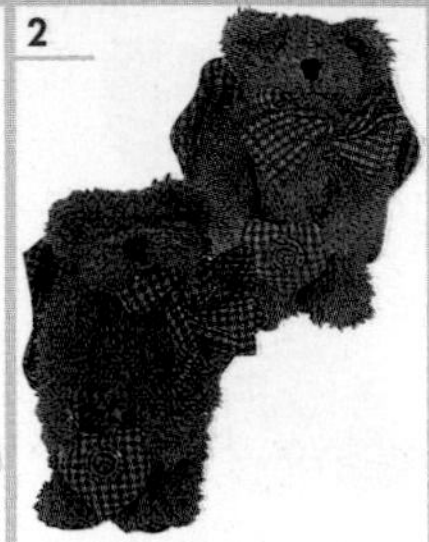

Dolly & Jed
QVC
Issued: 1997
Value: N/E

3

Eeyore
Disney
6"
Issued: 2000
Value: $35

4

Eeyore
Disney
Issued: 1998
Value: N/E

5

Evergreen Elfston
GCC
#94876GCC
Issued: 1999
Value: N/E

6

Fannie, Farrah & Flora
QVC
Issued: 2000
Value: N/E

7

Fenton & Forest Silverton
QVC
Issued: 1998
Value: N/E

8

Galaxy
The San Francisco Music Box Company
♪ *Twinkle, Twinkle, Little Star*
7" • #41-72767
Issued: 1999
Value: $15

Ornaments

	Price Paid	Value
1.		
2.		
3.		
4.		
5.		
6.		
7.		
8.		
9.		
10.		
11.		
12.		
13.		
14.		
Totals		

9

Josanna, Katalina & Latte
QVC
5.5" & 5.5" & 5.5"
Issued: 2000
Value: N/E

10

Juliette
The San Francisco Music Box Company
♪ *Love Me Tender*
4" • #41-72646
Issued: 1998
Value: N/E

11

Lapis
QVC
Issued: 1996
Value: $40

12

Matilda
Lord & Taylor
Issued: 1994
Value: N/E

13

Max
Lord & Taylor
8"
Issued: 1999
Value: N/E

14

Photo Unavailable

Mimsie, Myrtle & Melba Bahsworth
QVC
5" & 5" & 5"
Issued: 1999
Value: N/E

1

Morley (set/3)
QVC
Issued: 1998
Value: N/E

2

Morty
Elder-Beerman
5"
Issued: 1999
Value: N/E

3

Photo Unavailable

Mrs. Bear In-The-Moon
Lord & Taylor
Issued: 1996
Value: N/E

4

Piglet
Disney
Issued: 1998
Value: $35

5

Piglet
DIsney
6"
Issued: 2000
Value: N/E

6

Photo Unavailable

Pooh
Disney
6"
Issued: 1999
Value: N/E

7

Pooh
Disney
6"
Issued: 2000
Value: N/E

8

Pooh 1999
Disney
Issued: 1999
Value: N/E

9

Pooh 2000
Disney
Issued: 1999
Value: N/E

10

Pooh, Tigger, Eeyore & Piglet
Disney
8.5" & 8.5" & 8.5" & 8.5"
#19725MM
Issued: 1999
Value: N/E

11

Priscilla
Lord & Taylor
10"
Issued: 1997
Value: N/E

12

Sheila
Lord & Taylor
5"
Issued: 1999
Value: N/E

13

Snowbeary (set/3)
QVC
Issued: 1998
Value: N/E

14

Tabble, Tricky & T.F. Wuzzie
QVC
3" & 3" & 3"
Issued: 2000
Value: N/E

Ornaments

	Price Paid	Value
1.		
2.		
3.		
4.		
5.		
6.		
7.		
8.		
9.		
10.		
11.		
12.		
13.		
14.		
Totals		

1

Tessa
Lord & Taylor
8"
Issued: 1999
Value: N/E

2

Tigger
Disney
Issued: 1998
Value: $40

3

Tigger
Disney
6"
Issued: 2000
Value: N/E

4

Timmy
Lord & Taylor
5"
Issued: 1999
Value: N/E

5

Winnie The Pooh
Disney
Issued: 1998
Value: $35

6

Yukon & Homer
QVC
7"
Issued: 2000
Value: $45

Exclusive Puppets

7

Photo Unavailable

Maxwell Mittbruin
QVC
16"
Issued: 1999
Value: $35

Ornaments

	Price Paid	Value
1.		
2.		
3.		
4.		
5.		
6.		
Puppets		
7.		
Tree Toppers		
8.		
9.		
Totals		

Exclusive Tree Toppers

8

Auriela Angelfrost
QVC
10"
Issued: 1999
Value: N/E

9

Joy N. Goodcheer
QVC
12"
Issued: 2000
Value: N/E

Future Releases

Check our web site, ***CollectorsQuest.com***, for new product releases and record the information here.

Boyds Plush Animals	Original Price	Price Paid	Value

Total:	Price Paid	Value

Future Releases

Check our web site, ***CollectorsQuest.com***, for new product releases and record the information here.

Boyds Plush Animals	Original Price	Price Paid	Value

	Price Paid	Value
Total:		

Future Releases

Check our web site, ***CollectorsQuest.com***, for new product releases and record the information here.

Boyds Plush Animals	Original Price	Price Paid	Value

	Price Paid	Value
Total:		

Total Value Of My Collection

Record your collection here by adding the totals from the bottom of each Value Guide page.

Boyds Plush Animals			Boyds Plush Animals		
Page Number	Price Paid	Value	Page Number	Price Paid	Value
Page 32			Page 57		
Page 33			Page 58		
Page 34			Page 59		
Page 35			Page 60		
Page 36			Page 61		
Page 37			Page 62		
Page 38			Page 63		
Page 39			Page 64		
Page 40			Page 65		
Page 41			Page 66		
Page 42			Page 67		
Page 43			Page 68		
Page 44			Page 69		
Page 45			Page 70		
Page 46			Page 71		
Page 47			Page 72		
Page 48			Page 73		
Page 49			Page 74		
Page 50			Page 75		
Page 51			Page 76		
Page 52			Page 77		
Page 53			Page 78		
Page 54			Page 79		
Page 55			Page 80		
Page 56			Page 81		
Subtotal:			**Subtotal:**		

	Price Paid	Value
Total:		

Total Value Of My Collection

Record your collection here by adding the totals from the bottom of each Value Guide page.

Boyds Plush Animals		
Page Number	Price Paid	Value
Page 82		
Page 83		
Page 84		
Page 85		
Page 86		
Page 87		
Page 88		
Page 89		
Page 90		
Page 91		
Page 92		
Page 93		
Page 94		
Page 95		
Page 96		
Page 97		
Page 98		
Page 99		
Page 100		
Page 101		
Page 102		
Page 103		
Page 104		
Page 105		
Page 106		
Subtotal:		

Boyds Plush Animals		
Page Number	Price Paid	Value
Page 107		
Page 108		
Page 109		
Page 110		
Page 111		
Page 112		
Page 113		
Page 114		
Page 115		
Page 116		
Page 117		
Page 118		
Page 119		
Page 120		
Page 121		
Page 122		
Page 123		
Page 124		
Page 125		
Page 126		
Page 127		
Page 128		
Page 129		
Page 130		
Page 131		
Subtotal:		

	Price Paid	Value
Total:		

Total Value Of My Collection

Record your collection here by adding the totals from the bottom of each Value Guide page.

Boyds Plush Animals			Boyds Plush Animals		
Page Number	Price Paid	Value	Page Number	Price Paid	Value
Page 132			Page 157		
Page 133			Page 158		
Page 134			Page 159		
Page 135			Page 160		
Page 136			Page 161		
Page 137			Page 162		
Page 138			Page 163		
Page 139			Page 164		
Page 140			Page 165		
Page 141			Page 166		
Page 142			Page 167		
Page 143			Page 168		
Page 144			Page 169		
Page 145			Page 170		
Page 146			Page 171		
Page 147			Page 172		
Page 148			Page 173		
Page 149			Page 174		
Page 150			Page 175		
Page 151			Page 176		
Page 152			Page 177		
Page 153			Page 178		
Page 154			Page 179		
Page 155			Page 180		
Page 156			Page 181		
Subtotal:			**Subtotal:**		

	Price Paid	Value
Total:		

Total Value Of My Collection

Record your collection here by adding the totals from the bottom of each Value Guide page.

Boyds Plush Animals			Boyds Plush Animals		
Page Number	Price Paid	Value	Page Number	Price Paid	Value
Page 182			Page 206		
Page 183			Page 207		
Page 184			Page 208		
Page 185			Page 209		
Page 186			Page 210		
Page 187			Page 211		
Page 188			Page 212		
Page 189			Page 213		
Page 190			Page 214		
Page 191			Page 215		
Page 192			Page 216		
Page 193			Page 217		
Page 194			Page 218		
Page 195			Page 219		
Page 196			Page 220		
Page 197			Page 221		
Page 198			Page 222		
Page 199			Page 223		
Page 200			Page 224		
Page 201			Page 225		
Page 202			Page 226		
Page 203			Page 227		
Page 204			Page 228		
Page 205			Page 229		
Subtotal:			**Subtotal:**		

	Price Paid	Value
Total:		

Secondary Market Overview

No one who has ever seen a Boyds bear can deny their extreme cuteness. Collectors fall in love with them on sight and strive to fill their display shelves (or their dressers, office desks, etc.) with an extended family of Gary Lowenthal's adorable creations. After all, they do thrive on company and love to be surrounded by friends!

However, the chase for new Boyds pieces can be a challenging endeavor. Each year, the face of the collection changes when new pieces are introduced and older ones retire to the ol' plush resting home. Usually a piece's retirement will be announced in advance, but sometimes a piece will be subject to "sudden death" retirement and its stint on the store shelf abruptly ends. So carefully building your family of Boyds beasts can be harder than it looks.

But it doesn't have to be. If you know where (and how) to look, assembling a complete collection of Boyds critters can be as simple as clicking a mouse or dialing a phone – just don't get too carried away with the joy of "bear-hunting."

They don't call the Internet an "information super-highway" for nothing. Once you get on, you'll see all kinds of exits for Boyds plush critters. Message boards, retailers, fan sites and collectors' clubs will be within your reach and ready to link you with collectors from all over the country who share your fascination with Boyds plush. With so many sources available, you just might meet someone who happens to have that piece you've been searching high and low for.

Fellow collectors aren't the only kinds of people you'll find in cyberspace. You can also find special retailers who deal in retired pieces, and there are a number of auction sites where you can search for that special piece!

There are things to "bear" in mind when you're surfing the net on a Boyds quest, however. You can't see what you're buying, so be sure to ask as many questions as possible about the piece you want, and make sure you ask for a picture of it before you buy it. And remember that the quality of a piece will affect its value. The most valuable Boyds plush items are the ones in "mint" condition or in perfect, "like-new" condition.

If you prefer a more personal, face-to-face approach, there is no shortage of ways to find that elusive piece. It may be no further away than your favorite collectibles store, because many such shops will stock retired items after the pieces are no longer in production. Even if the store don't have it, the retailer may be able to put you in touch with other collectors who might. Swap and sell events and flea markets can also bring you into contact with other collectors looking to buy and sell. As helpful as the Internet may be, it's no substitute for the personal contact among fellow collectors. So don't be afraid to seek out others who share your love of Boyds.

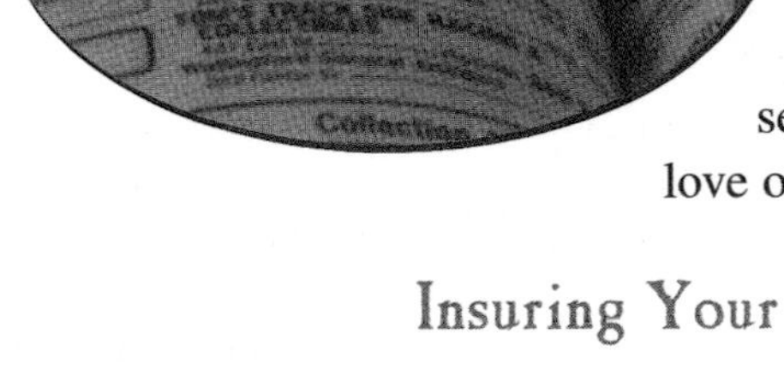

Insuring Your Collection

Now that you've made the effort to put together your prized collection, it's time to protect and insure it. While that may sound very complicated, it's really as easy as 1, 2, 3.

1. EDUCATE: Homeowners or renters insurance policies often cover collectibles. Ask your agent if your policy will cover any kind of unexpected damage to your collection. Your policy may also cover claims at "current replacement value," or the amount it would cost to replace any damaged items.

2. EVALUATE: You need to calculate how much it would take to replace your collection if anything happened to it. Then compare it to how much your insurer would pay for it. Some policies can include a Personal Articles Floater or Fine Arts Floater to cover your collection for a specific dollar amount.

3. SAVE & DATE: To properly make a claim for damaged pieces, you'll need a record of your collection's contents. Your insurance agent can tell you what kind of documentation the company will accept. Keeping receipts and an inventory in a safe place can help, as long as it includes the purchase date, price paid, size, issue year and secondary market value of each item. Photographs or video footage may be acceptable too.

So that said, it's time to enjoy building your collection. While this process is almost like a lottery – you never know what the outcome will be – the quest itself is always an experience. And an enjoyable one at that!

The Life Of A Plush Bear: From Conception To Store Shelves

As with any other art form, Boyds plush animals don't just spring from thin air. From the moment inspiration strikes Gary Lowenthal, to the final finishing touches, it is a long and complicated process. These adorable critters make a long journey before coming to rest in your home!

When The Head Bean's eyes get that special gleam, it usually signals that he has a new idea for a plush critter. Gary sketches the critter on paper before doing anything else, but the first drawing is never perfect. He'll go through a great many drafts before eventually settling on one that's just right.

After the drawing is refined to perfection, the dedicated crew at Boyds creates a prototype – the master pattern upon which to base all the other patterns used for making that piece. They try all sorts of designs, colors and fabrics until Gary is satisfied with the look and approves the prototype. The Head Bean would never attach the Boyds name to a product which he didn't feel meets his tough standards!

Once the prototype is approved, it's time for more copies of it to be made and sent to the factory. This is where the process gets even more difficult because most of the work for Boyds plush is done meticulously by hand. The patterns are hand cut and the stitching is done by hand as well. However, the factory sometimes uses a sewing machine for the more complex pieces. After all, it's not easy to hand-stitch antler patterns!

Most important of all is the stuffing that gives Boyds plush their snuggly quality. Most critters get a filling of plastic pellets (or "beans") and fiber fill, although there are some plush that just get one or the other instead of both. Either way, all that stuffing gives Boyds plush their plump shape – perfect for hugging.

But it's still not over! After being stuffed, it's time to add the details that give a Boyds critter its personality. Eyebrows, footpads and eyes are skillfully stitched before the piece gets a final hand brushing to make sure it's the best-looking bear (or hare, cat, pig, etc.) it can possibly be. Finally, it's time to give our little buddy a name tag. Boyds plush have a tendency to forget things (except the elephants, of course!), so Boyds always makes sure to affix the little tag right where he or she can get a look at it.

When all that final detailing is done, a Boyds plush character is ready to meet the world. Boyds plush are shipped to retailers all over the country in plastic bags, ready to be displayed at the store as they wait for someone to take them home. The Mohair Bears, however, arrive differently. You'll find them in special gift boxes, every bit as attractive as the bears they contain.

So the next time you look at your Boyds plush, remember that it took a lot of work, many skilled people and The Head Bean himself to bring them into the world.

Separated At Birth

Boyds plush fans have known for years that Gary Lowenthal often names his critters after politicians, literary figures, pop stars and other famous folk. CheckerBee Publishing speculates that some of these plush animals and famous people were actually separated at birth. Just take a look!

Aphrodite

When the Greek goddess of love and Boyds' own seductive swine walk into a room, heads will turn! These two beauties may as well be twin sisters. Just look at those "come hither" eyes, those long, elegant snouts – er, noses . . . Of course, Boyds' "Aphrodite" might be a more expensive dinner date, but at least she can hold a fork!

A statue of Aphrodite and the Boyds' "Aphrodite."

©AP/WWP

Buffy The Vampire Slayer and "Buffy" the bear.

Buffy

Don't be fooled by these two adorable Buffys – they each have the heart of a huntress! While Buffy The Vampire Slayer hunts down the undead with a variety of weapons, "Buffy" the bear prefers to "slay" her victims with her big, loving bear hugs.

"Chedda" the mouse and a block of cheese.

Chedda

Okay, so this might be the "cheesiest" entry in this section. But the important thing to remember is, if that block of cheese *does* start to resemble Boyds' "Chedda," check the expiration date!

©AP/WWP

Prime Minister Churchill and Boyds' "Churchill."

Churchill

Talk about twins! Put a top hat on Boyds' "Churchill" the bear and he's the spitting image of the British prime minister of the 1940s and 1950s. Now if only we knew for sure if the PM's spiffy tie was red . . .

Lincoln

It's true that President Lincoln might be a little taller than "Lincoln B. Bearington," but the stately postures and dashing black bow ties are dead give-aways. No need to check the president's feet!

"Lincoln" the bear and President Lincoln.

Marley Dredlion

©AP/WWP

Bob Marley and "Marley Dredlion."

When the soulful father of reggae music gets together with his "dreaded" Boyds look-alike, the fun never stops! "Marley Dredlion" looks like he could be grooving at a Bob Marley and the Wailers show. Good thing he's fully jointed!

Samuel Adams

Sam Adams – brewer, patriot and . . . cuddly bear? It's doubtful that the real Samuel Adams ever wore a sweater with a heart on it. But then, Boyds' "Samuel Adams" is more skilled in fashion than rabble-rousing – or brewing, for that matter!

"Samuel Adams" the bear and Samuel Adams the beer.

Waldo Bearsworth

Where's Waldo? Over there, and over there! "Waldo Bearsworth" would be a little more anonymous if he took off that red-and-white striped sweater. But then, he wouldn't look much like the elusive cartoon character he resembles!

Boyds' "Waldo Bearsworth" and *The Where's Waldo* books.

Only On QVC . . .

When Gary Lowenthal shared the QVC stage with Mary Beth Roe on December 2, 2000, it was definitely a most amusing show. In between the exclusive offers, Gary pranced around the stage in a tartan kilt, making the audience laugh themselves silly with his attempt at a Scottish accent. But it was still a sad day for Boyds fans everywhere. According to an announcement made by Gary that day, it would be his final QVC appearance.

For the past seven years, fans had looked forward to seeing The Head Bean co-host "The Mary Beth and Gary Show" with Mary Beth Roe. Where else could your average collector watch the head of an award-winning collectibles line clown around the stage and enjoy every second of it? Gary had thrilled the crowds at the studio and the fans at home with his zany antics, down-to-earth manner and enough costumes to stock a Broadway musical.

Beary Amusing

Ever since it first went on the air, "The Mary Beth and Gary Show" proved itself to be far more than you average run-of-the-mill shopping program. The chemistry between the hosts was enough to carry the show. But when Mary Beth first met her co-host, he seemed anything but outrageous. "He was very nervous, and he was very quiet. I thought, oh boy, this is going to be a tough guest, because he isn't going to have much to say . . . little did I know that when the red light came on, suddenly he would have plenty to say."

And in seven years, Gary never did run out of material. He was always ready with a joke, a story or a creative pun to make the audience laugh right along with him. Like any good artist, Gary knew and loved everything he created and wouldn't hesitate to joke about his pieces' names, expressions or just any old thing that came to mind. While on the show, he showed collectors one of his greatest assets – the ability to laugh at himself.

Clothes Make The Man

In one of his more memorable appearances, Gary referred to himself as "Joan Rivers in drag." In his time on the show, there was little he would not do or wear on camera. Being far from a suit-and-tie man, Gary would always show up in costumes so surprising that not even his co-host knew what to expect.

Gary often planned his costumes to go with the seasons. His Santa Claus outfits got many a laugh out of the crowd, and a Thanksgiving episode saw him pay homage to the founders of Plymouth in comical pilgrim garb. But Gary never limited his costumes to human ones! He showed up on camera dressed as a deer, a penguin, a turkey and even a pumpkin, just to name a few.

The End . . .

After a successful run, Gary decided it was time to hang up the costumes. He wanted to spend more time with his family, and hosting a television show can take up lots of time. On the final show, Gary read a touching poem to the audience and made a point of thanking all of his collectors for beings the ones who make Boyds what it is – and always will be. Fans may miss The Head Bean on the popular show, but they can bet he'll never be far away from the fans for long.

Variations

A big part of the appeal of Boyds plush is the fact that each character has its own, er, character! Because every bear, hare and moose in the collection is handmade, small differences in fur color, posture or facial details are the norm. These variations can also be a deliberate design change on the part of The Boyds Collection Ltd. The list below isn't comprehensive, but are examples of the most common variations you'll see among your plush critters.

What To Wear, What To Wear?

You'd think that a plush critter wouldn't have fashion issues, but some Boyds characters have been spotted in various outfits. The spring 1994 "Edmund" bear has worn blue coveralls as well as his usual black pair. Then there's "Helmut" the moose, who traded in his green hooded sweater for a red one. Meanwhile, "Alastair & Camilla" (bear and hare) can now both be found wearing matching sweaters instead of their original coordinated fashionable sweater (Alastair) and dress (Camilla) ensemble. Also, as if those exclusive pieces don't prove challenging enough, it seems as if many of the same critters may make appearances at multiple outlets with a change of attire.

"Alastair & Camilla" in their matching sweaters.

Both Deweys thought it was due time for a change in eye color.

Don't It Make My . . . Green Eyes Yellow?

Maybe it has to do with feline finickiness, but it seems like most of the Boyds plush who've had changes in their eye color have been cats. "Dewey R. Cat," "Dewey Q. Grimilkin," "Ophilia Q.

Grimilkin" and "Millicent P. Pussytoes" have all had at least two different eye colors over the years.

The light and dark sides of "Newton."

Fur To Dye For

It's not unusual to find a Boyds plush character with slightly different tones in his or her fur. The elephant, "Newton" wasn't sure whether he wanted to make light or dark of things, neither was "Corinna," whose fur ranges from dark to light brown. "Callaghan" and "Leon," two other bears, also have slightly different fur tones. This is one of the most common variations you'll find among the Boyds plush.

A new look for "Avery B. Bean."

About Face (And Arms, Legs And Ears)

Sometimes a plush character's design pattern will be tweaked by The Head Bean. The result may be longer ears, smaller antlers or a different facial texture. For example, "Avery B. Bean" the bear completely changed expressions, from a gape-mouthed to a tight-lipped look. "Bessie Moostein" and "Elmo Beefcake," two cows, underwent similar "cosmetic surgery" that smoothed their chubby cheeks. Meanwhile, "Abercrombie B. Beanster" the bear hit a growth spurt, as his ears, arms and feet seemed to grow overnight!

Mistaken Identities And Other Changes

"Alex," "Alec" . . .a bear of many names.

For some reason, a few Boyds plush critters have felt the need to change their identities (actually, they probably had nothing to do with it!). "Alec" the bear has also been known as "Alex," while "Diana" the hare has been referred to as "Elizabeth." "Father Krismoose" dropped the formal appellation to be known only as "Kris Moose," while "Eddie Beanbauer" changed his name to the less recognizable "Eddie Beanberger." Other common "identity" variations involve changes in item numbers and heights of the characters, although these are often the result of deliberate style or measuring changes and not production errors.

Just call this critter "Kris Moose."

A Word To The Wise

Boyds plush variations are a little different from those of other collectibles. Because every plush critter is handmade, there can be all sorts of small design changes, but that doesn't mean they're all going to result in a valuable and coveted version of the character. In fact, they rarely do! So the rule of thumb is, collect variations for the fun or the challenge of finding different versions of your favorite critter – not for the money.

Starlight, Starbright: A Generous Donation

If you haven't already noticed, the Boyds Collection Ltd. is in business for the fun of it — and also to give a little something back to the folks who need it most. Boyds has an honorable history of charitable donations and, in the first year of the new century, they've found a most worthy cause with which to ally themselves – the Starlight Children's Foundation.

Although serious illness is always a tragedy, a bit of generosity can bring a smile of hope and happiness to everyone's face. Actress Emma Samms and film producer Peter Samuelson learned that in 1983, when they granted the wish of a young London cancer patient who wanted more than anything to see Disneyland. Since then, Samms' Starlight Foundation has bloomed into an organization that provides seriously ill children with entertainment to make their lives a little brighter. Beginning in 2000, Boyds joined the foundation in bringing joy to over 74,000 children a month!

The resin piece "Charity Angelhug And Everychild . . . Cherish The Children" and its companion pin was such a big hit with collectors that over $225,000 was raised for the foundation and the pieces were retired. The monies raised provide funding to purchase VCRs, television sets and Nintendo 64 sets to ease the pain and isolation that children experience when they are hospitalized. Boyds will also sponsor a Starlight Room – a place where kids can gather to play, read or watch movies.

If you missed your chance to buy the resin piece in 2000, don't worry! A plush bear will be introduced and sold early in 2001 with 100% of the profits from its sales donated to the foundation. Bear hugs to all who have helped Boyds and the Starlight Foundation bring smiles to these children!

Accessories

So you just got your new Boyds bear home and you've got a place all picked out for it. Plunk. That's it? Don't tell me you're just going to leave it perched up on a book case or propped up on a guest bed! Why, Boyds plush critters aren't just *any* critters – they're critters of action and fashion, critters who demand a little more than just a comfy place to sit! That's where Boyds plush accessories come into the picture!

It's a Bear's Life!

Give your house-bound bears and other critters a change of scenery by arranging them with some of the great garden accessories from Boyds. You can choose from gardening tools, baskets and pails in a wide variety of styles, watering cans, harvest hauling wagons, and even a set of three lip-smacking, juicy watermelons! Your bears will love going back to "nature" with these special bear-sized spades and shovels!

But bears cannot live by outdoor work alone. Your plush animals might want to spend a more relaxed day reading. If your critters are a little near or far sighted, a fine assortment of eye glasses is available to keep them from squinting. Fashionable as well as functional, these eyeglasses will give your bears a distinctive look, whether it's "Hendrix Sunglasses" or "Niles Preppy Glasses."

Places To Eat, Places For Feet

Of course, your plush critters can't read standing up! That's why Boyds has created a selection of chairs and beds for your critters to lounge on. You can choose from wood benches, suede lounge chairs, director's chairs or wicker chairs, while beds come with solid wood or iron frames. There are foot stools and ottomans for your critters to prop up their tired feet (er . . . paws!) after a long day. You can accent their "quiet places" with a selection of dressers, cabinets, wardrobes and window frames to complete a tranquil scene.

Like many of us, Boyds plush animals love to spend time in the kitchen (especially when something really yummy is on the stove!). Several Boyds accessories are designed for you to create a warm kitchen scene, including cabinets, tables and chairs of all styles. Once the tables and chairs are in place, your plush critters can serve their furry friends with a variety of cups, bowls and afternoon tea sets.

Cold Noses And Cozy Quilts

Once lunch is eaten and the dishes are cleared away, a little physical activity might be in order. Luckily, there are Boyds accessories to help with that, too. For a great winter display scene, you can set your critters up with crosscountry skis or sitting in a sled.

And when play time is done and it's time to settle into bed for the night, your critters can curl up under a variety of colorful quilts or lay their weary (and furry) heads down on "Potter's Patchwork Pillows." That way, they'll be good and rested to do it all again tomorrow!

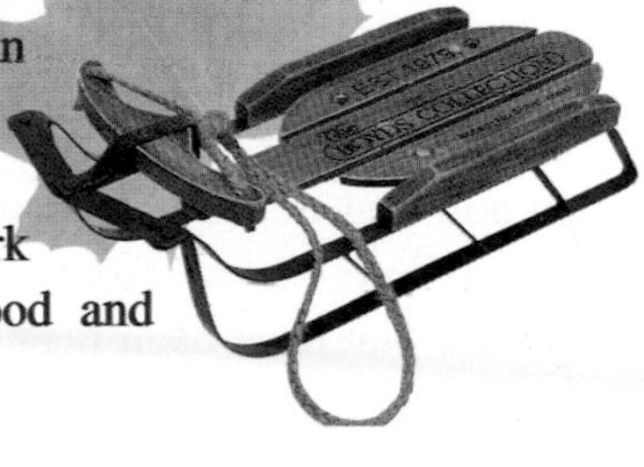

Fun For Momma & Poppa Bear, Too

OK! There are lots of goodies for your plush critters – how about some for you? Don't worry, there are all sorts of beary wonderful accessory items that will brighten any room in your home.

For the kitchen, Boyds provides everything from resin magnets to give your fridge a Boyds Bears touch, to mugs with original "Head Bean" art on the outside and inside! Also available are resin utensil and recipe holders, as well as *Bearware Potteryworks™* – glazed platters, creamers, tea pots and other kitchen and desk accessories. In an attempt to keep up with the technologically inclined, Boyds now offers a clever paper clip holder (that looks like a computer!).

But the home decorating options don't stop here! *The Beatrice Collection™* of miniature ceramic boxes gives you a stylish and charming place to put your valuables, while the *La Bearmoge™ Collection* of hinged boxes come in a variety of designs, including some matching your favorite resin figurines.

The new *Noah's Nursery* decor series offers all sorts of resin accent items for the baby room, like light switch covers, a ceiling fan pull chain, picture frames and even a treasure jar that features Zeke & Zenobia – characters from the *Pageant Series*. . Want to add a bit of Boyds to your bath? "Stretch & Skye . . . Soap Dish" is ready to hold your favorite bar of scented soap.

Licensed Products

In addition to the wide range of accessories offered by Boyds, collectors can choose from all sorts of other goodies made by companies that have been licensed to make products with the image of your favorite Boyds Bears characters.

If you're a "person of letters," keep your eyes peeled for longtime greeting card manufacturer Sunrise's line of Boyds-themed cards, journals, note cards and scrapbooks. Sunrise also offers gift bags, party invitations and tissue wrap for life's festive occasions. For you rubber stamp enthusiasts (you know who you are!), Uptown Rubber Stamps offers several different Boyds stamp kits that will brighten up everything from envelopes to school book covers, while Concept Direct produces Boyds-themed address labels for your personalized envelopes.

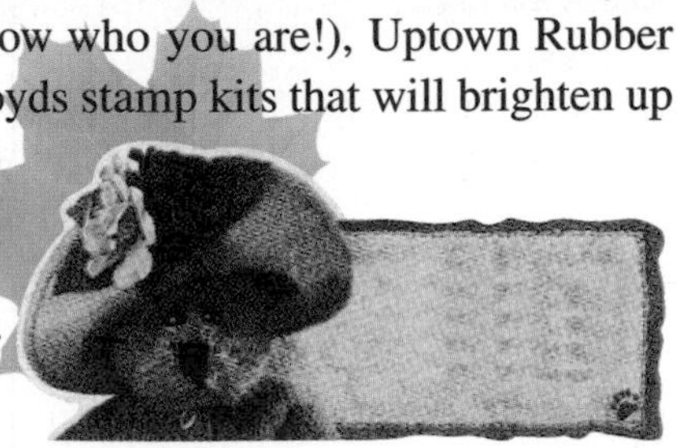

If you like staying cozy on cold nights (and who doesn't?), Manual Woodworkers and Weavers can warm you up with a line of soft chenille afghans, pillows and throws, as well as wall hangings and tapestry calendars. And when you leave the house, you can shout out your love of Boyds Bears with several different styles of T-shirts, sweatshirts, denim shirts and polo shirts by High Wind Productions.

Whether you're decorating your home, your plush bears or even yourself (!), there's a Boyds Bears accessory out there for you. But the accessories tend to come and go quickly, so you'll want to check with your retailer, the Boyds Bears official web site *(www.boydsstuff.com)* or The Boyds Bear Retail *Inquirer* newsletter to keep track of what's new and not-so-new!

– Key –

All Boyds plush animals are listed below in alphabetical order. The first number refers to the piece's location within the Value Guide section and the second to the box in which it is pictured on that page.

Acknowledgements

CheckerBee Publishing would like to extend a very special thanks to Suzie Hocker. We would also like to thank Julie Christensen, Harry and Millie Croft, Harole Ann Harper, Alan Koper, Melody Mayfield, Dave and Linda Reinhart, and the many collectors and retailers who contributed their valuable time to assist us with this book. Also many thanks to the great people at The Boyds Collection Ltd.

Boyds Bears & Friends™

presents the

The Loyal Order of Friends of Boyds
2001
COLLECTORS'
CLUB
A Slightly Off-Center Collectors' Club
for people who still believe in...
...Bears and Hares...
You can Trust™
R.S.V.P. to become the
Greatest F.o.B. on Earth!

And have we got a story for you,
turn the page ☛

Here's how to join the Boyds Circus.
Don't wanna fill out paperwork?
Apply online at www.BoydsStuff.com!

PLEASE PRINT

CHECK ONE: ❑ Current / Former Member ID# ________
❑ New Member

NAME ______________________________

ADDRESS ______________________________

CITY ______________________________

STATE ________ ZIP CODE ______________________________

DAYTIME PHONE (____) ______________________________

E-MAIL ADDRESS ______________________________

DATE OF BIRTH ______________________________ (YEAR OPTIONAL)

You don't have to wait until your anniversary date (the date you joined the Club) to renew!

❑ I want to be one of the Greatest F.o.B.s on Earth for the Year 2001 for an admission price of **$34.50**
(NY & TX Residents add 8 1/4% sales tax = total $37.35)

❑ I want to join for Two Years for just $67.00 (a $2.00 discount!) (NY & TX Residents add 8 1/4% sales tax = total $72.52) ________

❑ And throw in the Circus Tent Treasure Box, too, for **$13.00**
(NY & TX Residents add 8-1/4% sales tax = total $14.07)

My Grand Total is ________

Form of Payment:

❑ Check ❑ Money Order ❑ Master Card ❑ Visa

Credit Card Number: (Exp. Date ___/___)

Make payable to: The Boyds Collection Ltd.®
P.O. Box 4386, Attn. F.o.B. Dept., Gettysburg, PA 17325-4386

Authorized Signature:

____

(Authorized signature must accompany charge request. Card will be processed at time of shipment.)

I understand my membership kit will be shipped two to four weeks following receipt of this application at The Boyds Collection Ltd.

Offer Expires December 31, 2001

WHO IS YOUR RETAILER?
(You know, the place where you purchase your Boyds stuff.)

Name ______________________________ ID# ________

City ______________________________ State ________ Zip ____

JOIN THE CIRCUS!

Our 2001 club kit is all about circus memories…the circus train pullin' into town, that big striped canvas tent bein' hoisted high in the sky, the brightly colored balloons, the smell of the popcorn and roasted peanuts. Come join The Head Bean and the Folks at Boyds as we recreate those childhood memories with our 2001 Collectors' Club Kit.

EXCLUSIVE PIECES

★ Send in the clowns, baby! Our white plush clown bear "Gadget," measures 6" and is ready to take center ring!

★ The 2001 club kit will also include our Bearstone Masterpiece, "Gizmoe…Life's A Juggle," 5", who's performin' the ultimate jugglin' act.

★ Our "Greatest F.o.B. 2001 Bearwear Pin" features our Bearstone Clown Bear showin' off his jugglin' skills.

★ It's a circus out there, folks, so we're addin' yet another surprise—a window cling! No matter where ya go, people will know… yer an F.o.B. and proud of it! The cling measures 7 1/2" by 6" and is certain ta stop traffic!

OTHER CLUB GOODIES:

★ A year's subscription (four big issues) of the F.o.B. Inquirer…all the Boyds Newz that's fit to print, and then some!

★ Free copies of our wunnerful Spring and Fall Plush and Resin catalogs (over 250 pages of full-color photos!).

★ The Kit Box, which features Boyds circus scenes and transforms into a Big Top—the perfect display piece for your club goodies!

★ Exclusive web Privileges! Your membership number entitles you to enter the "VIP" part of our web site. There, you'll find late-breakin' product newz; special offers; and the Boyds Bulletin Board, for soundin' off on Boyds-related topics!

Ya get all of these "Greatest F.o.B. on Earth" goodies for a mere $34.50.

THE LOYAL ORDER OF FRIENDS OF BOYDS